THE LEARNING COMPANY

Second Edition

THE LEARNING COMPANY

Second edition

A strategy for sustainable development

Mike Pedler
John Burgoyne
Tom Boydell

The McGraw-Hill Companies

London · New York · St Louis · San Francisco · Auckland
Bogotá · Caracas · Lisbon · Madrid · Mexico · Milan
Montreal · New Delhi · Panama · Paris · San Juan
São Paulo · Singapore · Sydney · Tokyo · Toronto

Published by McGraw-Hill Publishing Company
Shoppenhangers Road, Maidenhead, Berkshire SL6 2QL, England
Telephone 01628 502500
Fax 01628 770224

British Library Cataloguing in Publication Data
Pedler, Mike
   The learning company : a strategy for sustainable
development. – 2nd ed.
   1. Executives – Training of 2. Organizational behavior
   I. Title   II. Burgoyne, John,   III. Boydell, Tom,
   658.4'07'124

   ISBN 0-07-709300-3

Library of Congress Cataloging-in-Publication Data

Pedler, Mike.
   The learning company: a strategy for sustainable development/
Mike Pedler, John Burgoyne, Tom Boydell. – 2nd ed.
      p.   cm.
   Includes index.
   ISBN 0-07-709300-3 (paperback: alk. paper)
   1. Organizational change.   2. Organizational learning.
I. Burgoyne, John (John G.)   II. Boydell, Tom.   III. Title.
HD58.8.P43   1996
658.4'063–dc21   96–46425
                                                                              CIP

McGraw-Hill
A Division of The McGraw·Hill Companies

2345 CUP 998

Typeset by BookEns Ltd., Royston, Herts.
and printed and bound at the University Press, Cambridge

Printed on permanent paper in compliance with ISO Standard 9706.

Contents

Table of Glimpses

Chapter 17 A Learning Climate

Chapter 18 Self-development Opportunities for All

The Authors

Mike Pedler is a writer, researcher and consultant, known for his work on self-development, action learning and the learning organization. He is currently a visiting professor at York University and his most recent book with McGraw-Hill is *Perfect plc?: the purpose and practice of organizational learning* co-authored with Kath Aspinwall.

John Burgoyne has spent 22 years at the University of Lancaster, as research director and then professor and head of department of Management Learning. Over this time he has established a high reputation for his work in management thinking. His initial training was in psychology and he has a PhD from the Manchester Business School, where he was also lecturer.

Tom Boydell is director of his two companies, The Learning Company Project and Transform, where he researches, writes, consults and runs development programmes. His current 'frontier' research involves the use of IT for organizational learning. He has written over 30 books on management and organizational learning, including a number of management self-development manuals and resource packages.

We began working together in 1976 and developed our relationship through collaborating on research, conferences, books and now in the Learning Company Project. The partnership owes some of its longevity to self-development, a fringe idea of the 1960s and 1970s that has since been absorbed into mainstream thought.

By the mid-1980s, while continuing to work out of self-development, we were becoming aware that it was not enough and were looking for something new. Empowering individuals within hierarchical, restrictive organizations was insufficient, even hazardous, for those individuals. There was a need to go further, to embrace both the individual and the organization.

A speech made in early 1986 by Geoffrey Holland, then Director of the Manpower Services Commission, calling for a new management development initiative in the UK, proved a turning point:

> If we are to survive – individually or as companies, or as a country – we must create a tradition of 'learning companies'. Every company must be a 'learning company'.

Here was new language – Learning Company – not the Learning Organization or Learning System of the organization development literature, nor the Learning Community used by adult educationalists. *Learning Company* had a good ring to it. Geoffrey Holland didn't know where he'd got it from and encouraged us to do some research. The Learning Company became an idea into which we began to put our individual and collective energies.

This book is an outcome of that work. The idea of the Learning Company has not diminished in its brilliance in the years that have passed since the first edition in 1991. Our work has developed further, particularly due to the founding of the Learning Company Project and with it the arrival of several new colleagues, especially Gloria Welshman and Chris Blantern – the latter figuring prominently in Part 4 of this book.

Although the Learning Company idea sometimes seems no nearer in terms of realization, it continues to excite our imaginations and encourage our ambitions. Perhaps the biggest shift in the last five years has been away from the search for the Learning Organization as a 'Holy Grail', towards a more pragmatic but also healthier focus upon the *process* of organizational learning. Why search for the Learning Organization, perfect and complete in all its parts, when we can improve the processes of learning in *all* companies? If we can do this then we can do much, not only for those who live and work in them, but also for the survival and development of those organizations who contribute to our social well-being.

In this book you will find ideas, methods and useful tools to improve the organizational learning in your company. Individual learning is not the same thing as organizational learning. The company may be full of bright, creative, self-developing individuals, but that does not mean that it can learn and change as a whole living organism. Understanding and improving how we learn together, as a collective, is the new frontier. How can we transform ourselves as a whole when we need to? By what means do we change in order to better achieve our collective purposes? What is our distinctive contribution to all those who have an interest in our work? These are the consuming questions for the Learning Company.

This book is in four parts, forming a learning cycle of *Idea, Diagnosis, Action* and *Reflections* which you are invited to follow as you work through the book. Part 1 deals with the question: 'What is the Learning Company?'

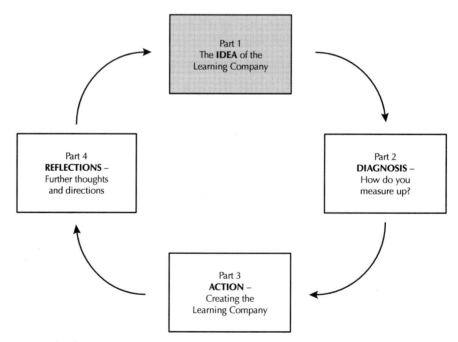

Figure P.1 The learning cycle

REFERENCE

Holland, G. (1986) *Excellence in Industry: Developing Managers – A New Approach*, Dorchester Hotel, London, 11 February 1986, Manpower Services Commission, Sheffield.

PART 1 THE IDEA
– OF THE LEARNING COMPANY

1. The idea of the Learning Company

This book is for people who believe that there is massive underdeveloped potential in our organizations – and who want to set about releasing it. The resulting energy can transform us as individuals and change the way we do things together – if we dare and if we have the skills to manage this daring process.

The Learning Company is a vision of what might be possible. It is not brought about simply by training individuals; it can only happen as a result of *learning at the whole organization level*. In the first edition of this book we defined it in this way:

> A Learning Company is an organization that facilitates the learning of all its members and continuously transforms itself.

Since then, and as a result of our experience, further reflection and drawing on an ever expanding literature, we have changed that to:

> A Learning Company is an organization that facilitates the learning of all its members and **consciously** transforms itself **and its context**.

The reason for the first change – from *continuously* to *consciously* – is partly on the grounds of realism. Any organization continuously changing itself as a whole would hardly ever be able to function, and in many organizations the evidence seems to point to transformation being a more episodic process, taking place every so often. Secondly, however, the word 'consciously' adds awareness and intentionality; the Learning Company transforms itself as a result of self-awareness and will.

We have added *and its context* as a result of becoming more aware of the full implication of our sub-title – 'A strategy for sustainable development'. For many organizations, the vision of organizational learning is of the efficient adaptive unit – always in the right place at the right time to take advantage of environmental change. This is a powerful image, and an appropriate one in some situations, but our view is that it is just the mid-point of a three-stage process (see Figure 1.1):

Stage 3 **Sustaining** Companies that create their contexts as much as they are created by them, who achieve a sustainable, though adaptive, position in a symbiotic relationship with their environments

Stage 2 **Adapting** Companies that continuously adapt their habits in the light of accurate readings and forecasts of environmental changes

Stage 1 **Surviving** Companies that develop basic habits and processes and deal with problems as they arise on a 'fire fighting' basis

---

Figure 1.1 A three-stage evolution of the Learning Company

Stage 3 explains a number of mysteries such as the apparent conservatism of some of the oldest organizations in society – universities for example – and the highly regular behaviour of some global brand companies. At this level, learning companies not only adapt to their environments and learn from their people, *they also contribute to the learning of the wider community or context of which they are a part.* Stage 3 organizational learning is not just individual *or* organizational *or* contextual – it is simultaneously all three.*

This is the dream – that we can create organizations that are capable of changing, developing and transforming themselves in response to the needs and aspirations of people inside and outside the company *and* that enrich and sustain the wider world of which they are a part. The Learning Company maintains its viability by adapting to its context, and in doing so maintains meaningful work and development for its members, but also develops that context to achieve a sustainable relationship with it. This means that the people in such companies can, through their work, make contributions not just to their organizations but *through* them to the wider society. In return they receive an enhanced sense of personal contribution and meaning.

We believe that this breaking through to stage 3 is part of the emergent evolution of work organizations where the principal concern for all stakeholders – owners, customers, users, staff and so on – becomes the production of meaning. Burgoyne (1995) has suggested that this is the culmination of a long-term progression in frontier work from *agriculture* (culturing nature) through the industrial revolution to *manufacture* (making artifacts with hands and tools); through the knowledge revolution to *mentofacture* (made by the mind); and through the quality and learning revolutions to *spiroculture* (the creation of meaning and identity).

---

* Stage 3 functioning should not be confused with the environmental domination and degradation practised by some global companies – which may even be held up as examples of learning organizations because of their survival and adaptability at whatever cost. This is the 'shadow' or distorted side of stage 3. In fact all three stages have light and shadow sides. For example, stage 1 functioning offers basic stability, preserving the learning and wisdom of the past in valuable procedures that work; but it can also represent rigidity, automatic, habitual behaviour and an inability to innovate. These ideas are developed further in various chapters in Part 4.

Learning *Company*

In the light of this, the old usage of the 'company' is worth recovering. The original idea of eating bread together and of creating meaning through relationships, captures the conviviality of working together better than the more mechanical and lifeless 'organization'. As one of our oldest words for a group of people engaged in a joint enterprise, we continue to 'accompany' others and do things 'in company'. So, in this book, we use 'Learning Company' rather than 'Learning Organization' for any collective endeavour and not for any particular legal form or ownership pattern.

An old dream?

Although the terms 'Learning Company' or 'Learning Organization' are relatively recent, the idea has been around for a long time and the relevant literature is voluminous. The struggle for compatibility between personal growth and organized human relationships goes back at least to Moses. Since the 1950s, the development of systems thinking, and particularly the socio-technical systems view of organizations, are probably most responsible for allowing us to imagine organizations as organisms – as living things – that can therefore, among other things, learn.

The writings of Gregory Bateson (1973) on types of learning have been influential, especially his theory of 'deutero-learning', or learning to learn. John Gardner (1963) used the term 'self-renewal' and Gordon Lippitt (1969) 'organization renewal', to capture this living, learning quality. The term 'learning system' was used by Revans (1982) in 1969 and brought into the mainstream by Donald Schon in his 1971 Reith Lectures. Much of the literature is focused on the 'organization development' movement which makes change its central concern, though this is often expressed rather too systematically for our taste as 'planned organizational change'.

The recent interest in the Learning Company perhaps begins with Argyris and Schon's *Organizational Learning* (1978). The idea was picked up but not developed by Peters and Waterman (1982) when they said, 'The excellent companies are learning organizations'. Revans (1982) and Garratt (1987) have made it the prime responsibility of company directors and senior managers, Attwood and Beer (1988) have applied it to the Health Service, Holly and Southworth (1989) to schools and, with his bestseller, Senge (1990) has described it as the idea most likely to preoccupy managers in the coming years.

So, although the Learning Company is not a new dream, it has never been more relevant. The aim of this book is to help you to take courage and make a start. To act and to learn from acting, for action alone is not enough. Action in the Learning Company always has two purposes:

● to resolve the immediate problem
● to learn from that process.

The emphasis in this book is upon managerial action as experiment rather than as the 'right answer'. The history of managing is littered with the remains of yesterday's 'right answers' – scientific management, theories X and Y, Blake's Grid, MbO, Quality Circles, the search for excellence and so on. So, where are they now and what did we learn from these experiments?

We are all sometimes tempted by the promise of the 'quick fix'. Each of the methods listed above contain good ideas, but ideas bought and sold as right answers quickly become empty techniques and the life goes out of them. We know in our hearts that there are no easy answers to the complex problems of organizing work, so how can we get beyond the quick fix mentality?

Only by learning, which increases our confidence and empowers us to enquiry, action and further learning. If ideas, such as briefing groups or profit centres, can be seen as experiments rather than solutions then we can learn from them. The company that can learn from experience of trying out new ways of operating will have a massive advantage over one that does not.

Learning is the key to survival and development for the companies of today. In the last 20 years we have learned a lot about helping individuals to learn; now the challenge is to understand and master the art of corporate learning. This book is written as part of that quest.

How do companies come to be the way they are?

When we think about what companies are like, why they are the way they are and what is involved in their change and evolution, we come up with a number of different perspectives. We find three of these particularly helpful.

- **Ideas**   Companies are first a product of the visions and images that their founders sought to create, which are passed on through history and mythology and which succeeding generations try to recreate. These are the idea of building the world's best mousetrap, to be 'excellent', to realize a concept of a holding company portfolio of autonomous operating units, a clever matrix structure or, indeed, our own working list of the characteristics of a Learning Company. In the beginning is the idea – nothing starts without it – and a company can be anything its members design and plan it to be, provided that they can put this into practice.

- **Life stage**   Are they new, infant, pioneering, established, mature, trying to change long-established customs and ways of doing things, winding up (or down), passing on resources, assets and expertise to new ventures and partnerships? Although companies can be given new life, rather like George Washington's axe in the American museum that has had three new heads and six new handles since he used it, perhaps a company needs to be of a form and behaviour appropriate to its age or stage. In these terms it will be a poor learner if it tries to hold back from, or run ahead of, its 'natural' stage of development.

- **Era** Companies are shaped by, and fit in with, the economic and cultural contexts in which they exist. As a general point this is easy to accept, but to be specific in terms of how this works is very difficult. The notion of era is partly to do with the broad macroeconomic phases of pre-industrial, industrial, post-industrial and also the locally predominant type of economic activity, e.g. primary, secondary, tertiary. These macropatterns progress in different forms and on different time-scales depending on location. For example, a hi-tech company in California operates in a different era from an agricultural business in a poor country. However, they are increasingly part of the same 'global village' and a computer-controlled irrigation project could be a good and feasible joint venture. This perspective is even further complicated by the post-modern thesis that we are entering the era that marks the end of era-style development. 'Progress' as such does not exist and development is multi-directional and paradoxical. Despite these difficulties, the notion of era and how we fit in with it, is a factor that makes our company what it is today.

Each of these three perspectives offers something to the way we think about how companies come to be the way they are and what form their development may take. In this book we try to work with all three, although our concern with the *idea* of the Learning Company shows a special allegiance to the force of ideas in shaping practice. We believe that it is possible to choose ideas, apply them and thereby shape the company, but we think that it is wise to do this with an awareness of, and a sensitivity to, the wider forces of life-stage and era.

Making a start

Who, then, are our companions – the members of the Learning Company? We take a wide view of who these people might be – staff, users and customers, owners and policy makers, suppliers and business partners, even competitors, neighbours, communities and the environment. Creating a Learning Company from these people is easier said than done. We can't bring out a blueprint or take you to visit somewhere where it has already been done – it is not like that. The magic of the Learning Company has to be realized from within. A key word is 'transformation' – a radical change in the form and character of what is already there.

There is plenty to do and to try out in this book. In Chapter 2 we develop the argument that the Learning Company is an idea for the present times; that its era has come. Chapter 3 offers a working framework of the idea so that any given company can be viewed from this perspective as the beginnings of the process of becoming a Learning Company. This framework includes two key models: The 11 Characteristics of the Learning Company and the E-Flow or Energy Flow model.

The next four chapters form Part 2 and follow the trilogy of Idea, Phase and Era offering diagnostic activities for each to help you compare and contrast your company with our models of the Learning Company. Chapters 4 and 5 focus on the idea with methods for looking at your company using the 11 Characteristics of the Learning Company and the E-Flow models. In Chapter 6 we look at a Biography approach to your company to interpret its current stage of development – what are the choices in this phase of life? Finally Chapter 7 considers the era we are in – what is the wider context in which your company operates and how might a Learning Company strategy fit with this?

You can also compare your company with the wide variety of organizations that feature in the 80 Glimpses of the Learning Company in action in Part 3. Chapters 8 to 18 focus in turn on each of the 11 Characteristics of the Learning Company culminating in the BICC story (Chapter 19) – a case study of a major organization development effort. Glimpses come from a wide variety of organizations and show some of the possibilities for action. We chose the word 'glimpse' to capture these partial visions and also to make it clear that, while no one has got it right, many companies are generating interesting and valuable experiences. We hope these help you to create your own vision.

In the introduction to Part 3, we suggest various starting points for developing a Learning Company strategy in your company. Of course, there is no one right point to start from among the many different possibilities that present themselves, but that is not too much of a problem – like the string bag, wherever you start, all aspects of the company eventually connect. Just take courage and start somewhere.

Part 4 reflects on the many new directions which mark this still emerging field of study and practice. We survey some of the important writers who have contributed to the ideas of learning organization and organizational learning before focusing on various exciting developments whose great promise has yet to be fulfilled. Dialogue, whole system development and the contribution of IT and computer networks to organizational learning feature here, as do the ideas of organizational ecology and the modes of development. No neat conclusion here, but a rich array of possibilities for experiment and further learning.

REFERENCES

Argyris, C. and Schon, D.A. (1978) *Organizational Learning: A Theory in Action Perspective*, Addison-Wesley, Reading MA.

Attwood, M. and Beer, N. (1988) 'Development of a learning organization', *Management Education and Development*, **19**(3), 201–214.

Bateson, G. (1973) *Steps to an Ecology of Mind*, Paladin, London.

Burgoyne, J.G. (1995) 'Learning from experience: From individual discovery to metadialogue via the evolution of transitional myths', *Personnel Review*, **24**(6), 62–73.

Gardner, J.W. (1963) *Self-renewal: The Individual and the Innovative Society*, Harper & Row, New York.

Garratt, R. (1987) *The Learning Organization*, Fontana, London.

Holly, P. and Southworth, G. (1989) *The Developing School*, Falmer Press, Brighton.

Lippitt, G.L. (1969) *Organization Renewal*, Appleton-Century-Crofts, New York.

Peters, T.J. and Waterman, R.H. (1982) *In Search of Excellence*, Harper & Row, New York.

Revans, R.W. (1982) 'The enterprise as a learning system' in *The Origins and Growth of Action Learning*, Chartwell-Bratt, Bromley.

Schon, D.A. (1971) *Beyond the Stable State*, Random House, New York.

Senge, P. (1990) *The Fifth Discipline: The Art and Practice of the Learning Organization*, Doubleday, New York.

2. Why is the Learning Company relevant today?

Today's organizational leaders are experiencing a consciousness shift. Where they sought excellence, they now seek *learning* – not only to achieve excellence but to stay that way through being flexible, intelligent and responsive. This does not just apply to commercial organizations. Schools, hospitals and cities find themselves competing for scarce resources and coping with turbulent and rapidly changing times, while trying to maintain and improve the quality of their services.

In our earlier research we identified some major drivers of interest in the idea of learning companies (Pedler, Burgoyne and Boydell, 1988, p.7) as shown in Figure 2.1.

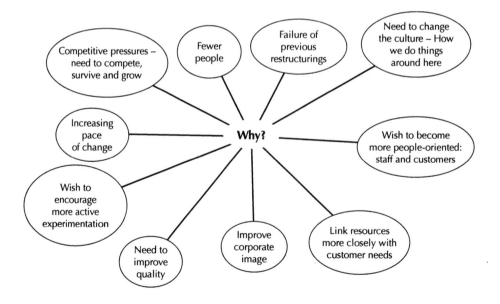

Figure 2.1 Pressures for change and development in organizations

Learning as the means of survival?

Theories of organization development tend to look on the bright side, but it is increasingly clear that 'organizational death' – through failure, acquisition and merger – is common and indeed, sooner or later, the likely fate of all companies:

> Of the corporations in the Fortune 500 rankings five years ago, 143 are missing today. (By comparison, in the twenty five years, 1955 to 1980, only 238 dropped out.) (Pascale, 1991, pp.11–17)

Although 'infant mortality' in new companies can be as much as 40 per cent in the first year, those that survive are often busy, active places, full of learning. Yet as organizations grow and age they can lose this 'natural' capacity to learn – and this includes the best of them. Commenting on Peters and Waterman's (1982) 'excellent' companies, Pascale again notes:

> Only five years after the book's publication, two thirds of the companies studied had slipped from the pinnacle. (1991, p.11)

Reg Revans is an architect of this new consciousness. His ecological formula; $L \geqslant C$, holds that learning in an organization must be equal to or greater than the rate of change in the environment. If learning within the organization is *less* than the rate of change outside, then the organization is by definition declining. Those not busy being born are busy dying. While this has always been true, it is especially obvious and important now because of the increasingly rapid and unpredictable rate of change. Because of the change pressures, the ability of the company to learn is paramount.

In his enquiry into the longevity of companies, de Geus (1995, pp.26–28) found that corporate survivors were:

- financially conservative
- sensitive to the environment
- had a sense of cohesion and company identity among employees
- were tolerant of 'activities in the margin'

Cash in hand gives flexibility, being outward-looking helps you to act earlier; you might survive better if a commitment to values rather than forms makes it clear what is important and what does not need to be preserved; and, finally, tolerance of experiments in the organization suggests that the centre has less need to control and that the margins might be full of ideas. It is also noted by de Geus that the 27 companies in his sample, ranging in age from 100 to 700 years old, had all undergone fundamental transformations or 'historic organizational learning'.

It seems clear that we need a new model of organization:

> The old bureaucratic command-and-control model, even in its current decen-tralised, supposedly lean and mean version, won't be up to the challenges ahead: it won't be fast enough … keen enough … smart and sensitive enough … (we)

> need a new kind of organization that accommodates radical change, indeed that builds in the capacity to thrive on change. (Kiechel, 1990)

This picture of organizations that can change and learn fits with the biological metaphor of organizations as organisms. In this view companies are in a dynamic process of becoming; and of *being* only in transition. We explore this idea further in Chapter 5 inviting you to think about the *biography* of your company with its birth, growth, its different ages and stages and finally, perhaps, its death.

The evolution of the Learning Company

These 'natural' processes of development in the company illustrate an essential aspect of evolution. The organization is born from a good idea, but over time this fades or becomes distorted or, if successful, perhaps over-the-top, too much of a good thing. 'Excellence' can degenerate into 'complacency', 'order' and 'structure' can become 'rigidity' and 'compartmentalization'. These 'doubles' – distorted forms of what was originally good – mirror the forces to disorder and decay found in the physical world. Although this is sad, it also has a creative, revitalizing aspect, for it is when the double gets the upper hand that we arrive at the threshold for the next developmental step, when we need a new idea.

This is why we never actually 'get there', for as we solve one problem or issue, another emerges, the seeds of which were sown by our previous solution. We can depict the evolution of the Learning Company in this manner – as a stage in the development of approaches to learning in organizations (Figure 2.2).

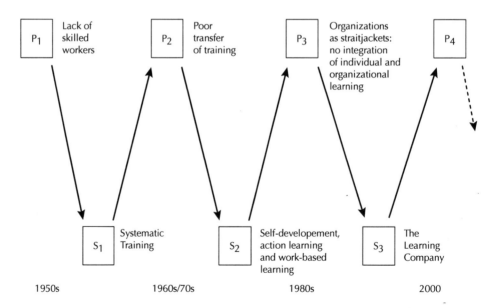

Figure 2.2 Learning problems in the UK and their solutions 1950–2000

After the Second World War, there was a great demand for goods and a need for greater productivity. Various studies concluded that the UK lacked skilled workers such as fitters, machinists, mechanics and while some companies were good at training, others didn't bother and relied on 'poaching'. The solution that emerged was *systematic training* and the 1964 Industrial Training Act set up Training Boards in all the main industries. Systematic training is based on very rational ideas and led, by way of best practice, to job descriptions, job specifications, the careful and expert identification of training needs, job analysis, measurable behavioural objectives, programme planning and systematic evaluation (Boydell, 1970).

Yet, as indicated by Figure 2.2, the solution (S_1) eventually led to a new problem (P_2) that arose out of the assumptions of S_1. Although systematic training was undoubtedly very effective in solving parts of the original problem, the outcomes turned out not to be as consistent and predictable as planned. Many jobs cannot be split into micro-skills and then put together again. Most jobs, especially those requiring social skills and anything involving managing other people, need discretionary and creative abilities.* Some people attended well-run courses, enjoyed them, felt they had learned, and then were unable to use much of the new learning in their actual jobs. Others disliked the process of systematic training. People were alienated by being treated as measurable, mouldable, purposeless units and having their essential differences of sex, race, class (and the many more that make up our real being) ignored and devalued. This became known as the 'transfer of training' problem (P_2).

The response to P_2 was to develop methods of learning and development (rather than training) that put the learner (rather than the trainer) at centre stage and that used work as the vehicle for learning. In the late 1970s and 1980s self-development and action learning came to the fore, encouraging people to learn from their daily experience and the problems they encountered at work. S_2 methodologies quickly moved from being rather on the fringe (why should any company want to encourage self-development as opposed to narrow job training?) to becoming more mainstream as the 'excellence' movement (Peters and Waterman, 1982) urged 'bureaucracy busting' and the shake-up of the old order.

As this happened P_3 began to emerge. Newly empowered self-developers – questioning anything, trying to improve everything – were not always welcomed back. Despite Revans's stirring aphorism, 'Doubt ascending speeds wisdom from above', pioneers often found their questions led not to wisdom but to retribution from on high. We had powerful new methods for individual learning but the collective was largely unchanged. Our rigid, centralized companies were not fit to house these proactive learners imbued with the spirit of self-development.

---

* Even now in the late 1990s, the Management Competencies movement appears to be making these same S_1 assumptions.

There was also a tendency in companies to use top-down organization development and change programmes to try to change or to 'bust the bureaucracy', which ran out of energy and resources long before they achieved their targets (in one major UK utility at this time there were 13 different company-wide change programmes, each championed by a director, each competing for resources, each getting in the way of the other 12).

Emerging in the late 1980s and early 1990s, S_3 seeks a learning collective staffed by a company of individual learners – the Learning Company. The ideas of Total Quality Management (Deming, 1988), Organizational Transformation (Owen, 1987), Whole Systems Thinking (Senge, 1990) and Future Search (Weisbord and Janoff, 1995) are part of this. The task of the times is to create organizations that can learn as whole systems or organisms. Yet this too will soon lead us to P_4.

Conclusion

The Learning Company has emerged as an idea in the time–space era of the 1990s as the ideas of organization, quality management and of training and development have evolved to this point and provided a way forward for organizations faced by the bureaucratic crisis. The evolution of ideas continues and P_4 will be a consequence of how the Learning Company idea is interpreted. Currently many organizations seem to be aiming at becoming Stage 2 learning organizations (Chapter 1) with an emphasis on survival, adaptability and responsiveness at all costs. If the Learning Company idea is seen as being about the 'survival of the fittest' whatever the cost to staff, business partners, or localities and environments, then it is not sustainable. Successful but selfish organisms impoverish and destroy rather than enrich their contexts and environments.

REFERENCES

Boydell T.H. (1970) *A Guide to Job Analysis*, Bacie, London.
de Geus, A. (1995) 'Companies: what are they?' *Royal Society of Arts Journal*, CXLIII, (5460) June, pp.26–35.
Deming, W.E. (1988) *Out of the Crisis*, Cambridge University Press, Cambridge.
Kiechel, W. (1990) 'The organization that learns', *Fortune*, 12 March.
Owen, H. (1987) *Spirit: Transformation and Development in Organizations*, Abbott, New York.
Pascale, R.T. (1991) *Managing on the Edge*, Penguin, Harmondsworth.
Pedler, M.J., Burgoyne, J.G. and Boydell, T.H. (1988) *The Learning Company Project Report*, Training Agency, Sheffield, p.7.
Peters, T. and Waterman, R. (1982) *In Search of Excellence*, Harper & Row, New York.
Senge, P. (1990) *The Fifth Discipline: The Art and Practice of the Learning Organization*, Doubleday Currency, New York.
Weisbord, M.R. and Janoff, S. (1995) *Future Search: An Action Guide to Finding Common Ground in Organizations and Communities*, Berrett-Koehler, San Francisco.

3. What does a Learning Company look like?

So far we have looked at the evolution of the idea of the Learning Company, as flowing from various contemporary pressures and streams of thought. Now we can ask: What does a Learning Company look like? How would we recognize it? How does it differ from a *non*-learning company?

In trying to answer these questions we have drawn on three sources: our speculations about what the Learning Company ought to be, based on the apparent evolutionary flow; on the ideas of other workers in this field including Revans, Argyris and Schon, Senge and the others quoted in the earlier chapters; and on our own research and subsequent experience in a variety of organizations. From our research in particular came a list of common characteristics from all the organizations who are trying this idea out, which creates an 'identikit' Learning Company.

The 11 Characteristics of the Learning Company

1. A Learning Approach to Strategy
2. Participative Policy Making
3. Informating
4. Formative Accounting and Control
5. Internal Exchange
6. Reward Flexibility
7. Enabling Structures
8. Boundary Workers as Environmental Scanners
9. Inter-company Learning
10. A Learning Climate
11. Self-development Opportunities for All

As the Glimpses in Part 3 demonstrate, the way in which each company interprets these characteristics and puts them together will be unique to that organization. With this in mind, the ideal Learning Company exhibits the following:

A Learning Approach to Strategy

Where policy and strategy formation are consciously structured for learning, for example, deliberate pilots and small-scale experiments are used to create feedback loops for learning about direction and the formulation of 'emergent strategy'.

Participative Policy Making

Where all members of the organization together with key stakeholders have a chance to contribute and participate in policy making.

Informating

In the Learning Company information technology is used not just to automate, but to make information widely available to front-line staff in order to empower them to act on their own initiative.

Formative Accounting and Control

This is a particular aspect of *Informating*, where systems of budgeting, reporting and accounting are structured to assist learning for all members about how money works in the business.

Internal Exchange

Where there is a high degree of *Internal Exchange*, all internal units and departments see themselves as customers and suppliers in a supply chain to the end user or client; contracting with and learning from other departments is normal.

Reward Flexibility

With greater participation comes a need for more flexible and creative rewards. High *Reward Flexibility* means that there are alternatives in both monetary and non-monetary rewards to cater for individual needs and performance.

Enabling Structures

Roles, departments, organization charts and even procedures and processes are seen as temporary structures that can easily be changed to meet job, user or innovation requirements.

Boundary Workers as Environmental Scanners

Environmental scanning is carried out by all people who have contacts with external users, customers, suppliers, clients, business partners, neighbours, and so on. Processes are in place for bringing back and welcoming the information into the company.

Inter-company Learning

Through joint ventures and other learning alliances, the organization learns from other companies and meets with them for mutual exchange.

A Learning Climate

In the Learning Company all managers see their primary task as facilitating company members' experimentation and learning from experience, through questioning, feedback and support. The company seeks to export this *Learning Climate* to its context and business partners.

Self-development Opportunities for All

Resources and facilities for self-development are made available to all members, especially those in the front line with users or clients. People are encouraged to take responsibility for their own learning and development.

These 11 Characteristics are the basis for our jigsaw questionnaire (Figure 4.1, in the next chapter) where you are invited to see how your company measures up against this model. The 11 Characteristics of the Learning Company also provides the structure for Part 3 (Chapters 8–19) where they are developed in much more detail and illustrated with Glimpses of organizations putting them into practice.

Modelling the Learning Company

Developmental theories suggest that as any organism changes over its life cycle, it also seeks to preserve and maintain important aspects of itself. Change and conservation go hand in hand as successive phases emerge partially as a transformation of what already exists. As the wilful child may metamorphose into a self-disciplined adult, so the Learning Company may change to adapt to new circumstances while seeking to preserve its purpose, values and core identity.

Our own thinking about the Learning Company has followed a developmental path. In this section that progression of ideas is depicted, an attempt is made at an 'honest account of the voyage of invention', beginning with the 11 Characteristics and leading, via various turns, to the E-Flow or Energy Flow model of the Learning Company.

The 'blueprint'

The 11 Characteristics of the Learning Company first emerged as a list of features either from the literature or as referred to by the managers in our sample. At that time there was no necessary relationship implied between one characteristic and another, although it seemed probable that various linkages were likely to exist. The question was: Is there enough of a relationship between these 11 Characteristics or features to justify calling it a model – that is a simplified representation of how the various parts of the organization interact and fit together – of the Learning Company?

The first step in the modelling process was to attempt to order and cluster the characteristics (which were originally in a different order from that given above).

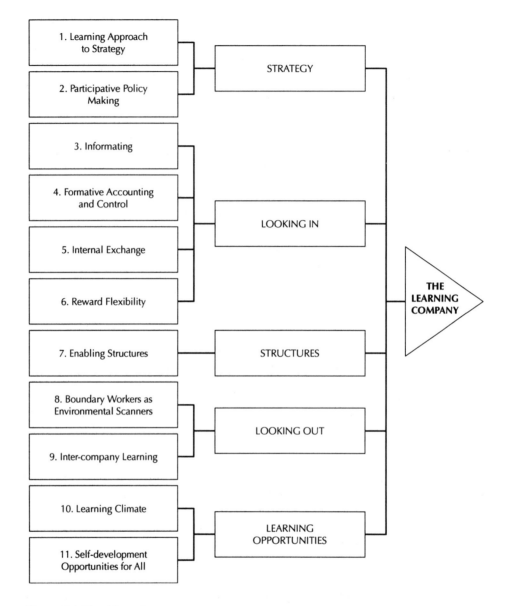

Figure 3.1 The blueprint

Figure 3.1 shows a blueprint of the first representation of this, in which the characteristics are clustered around a central pivot of *Structures*. Above this we have *Looking in* and, mirrored below, *Looking out*. *Strategy* tops the clusters, while *Learning opportunities* form the ground on which all else is built.

The blueprint was better than the earlier list and provided a 'commonsense' relationship between clusters.* On the other hand, this representation is rather mechanical and rigid; it implies completeness with no room for extra characteristics as yet unrecognized. For us, too, it lacked aesthetic appeal, and represents the rational/mechanical stage of our thinking – as yet lacking life. Finally and ironically, although we were saying that there was no grand plan for the Learning Company and that each must develop its own vision, transforming what already exists – here we were offering a *blueprint*.

The fish bone

We therefore began to experiment with different forms, the fishbone shown in Figure 3.2, for example:

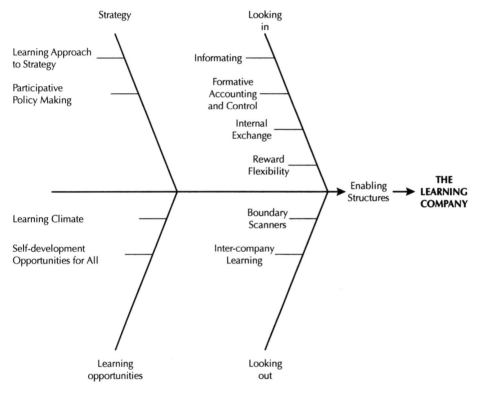

Figure 3.2 The fishbone

The fountain tree

This also had its own appeal, but was still rather static. So we continued playing, first rotating the fishbone to produce a fir tree with branches and roots, which at

---

* And in fact, these clusters have been empirically confirmed by our further research. See Figure 4.7 in the next chapter.

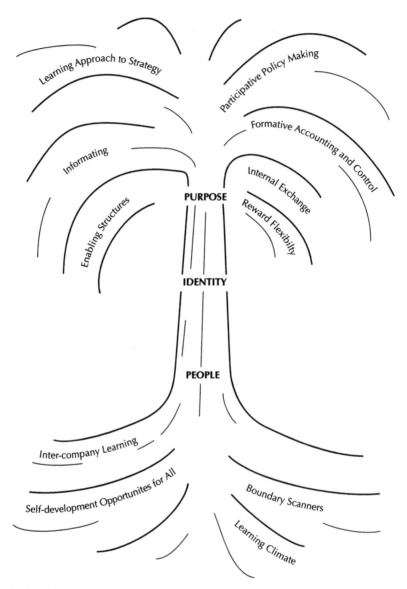

Figure 3.3 The fountain tree

least was living and growing. The final outcome of this line of thinking was the more symbolic fountain tree (Figure 3.3).

The fir tree and the fountain tree represent the organic or living phase of our modelling process. Here the Learning Company is living and changing, full of energy. Water, sap, life forces flow up from the ground, through the middle, outwards, downwards, back to the ground. There is a dynamic, ecological balance that seems characteristic of what a Learning Company should seek.

People are the ground of the company and it is their energy that rises to form the collective purpose of the organization, creating a shared identity, which is not fixed, but is a continuously produced quality of interactions and relationships.

The Learning Company as Energy Flow

The element of *flow* provides a link to the third, symbolic phase of our modelling process. The *E-Flow* or *Energy Flow* model of the Learning Company (see Figure 3.6 on page 23) is built up from a series of double-loop flows of energy – where energy might be information, resources, consciousness, attention and so on. Recognizing both the merits and limits of the 11 Characteristics of the Learning Company as descriptive and grounded in *practices*, we wondered if we could take a further inductive step to imagine what might integrate all these practices. What underlying *processes* might be present, to which all these practices contributed?

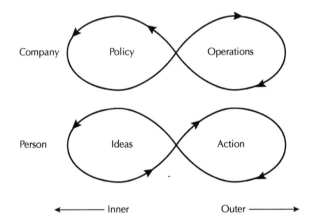

Figure 3.4 Energy Flow in the Learning Company (1)

Extended reflection led us to consider whether there was a parallel between individual and collective learning processes. The individual learning cycle of action, experience, observation, reflection and theorizing (Kolb, Rubin and McIntyre, 1971, p27) was the process underlying Characteristics 10 and 11 – *A Learning Climate* and *Self-development Opportunities for All*. This individual process was mirrored at a collective level in Characteristic 1 – *A Learning Approach to Strategy*. Putting these two together gave us two double-loop flows of energy or consciousness (Figure 3.4).

These double-loop flows show how feedback from action and operations is the source of our individual and collective learning, and also how the creativity and innovation of our ideas and policies enriches the productivity of people and of companies. Yet how are these individual and collective levels of learning connected in the Learning Company?

We noticed that Characteristic 2 – *Participative Policy Making* – involved a debate or exchange linking collective policy with the ideas and values of all the people in the company. We also noticed that some of the *Looking in* Characteristics – numbers 4, 5 and 7: *Formative Accounting and Control, Internal Exchange* and *Enabling Structures* – were about carrying out operations, management plans and with getting feedback from individual members as they implemented these plans. This gave us two vertical double-loop flows of energy to add to our previous pair of horizontals (Figure 3.5).

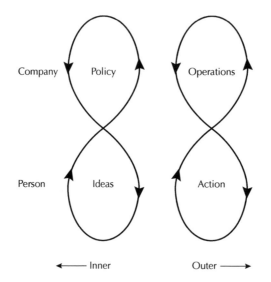

Figure 3.5 Energy Flow in the Learning Company (2)

Here the flows from individual to collective and vice-versa bring the Learning Company to life. The energy of individual action infuses collective operations that in turn ensure that we work well together, which feeds individual motivation and propensity to act. Another vertical energy flow links collective purpose and individual motivation. Here personal identity feeds company identity and in return a collective purpose gives personal meaning and a sense of one's place in the company.

From here it was a simple step to put the two pairs of double-loops together giving four figures of eight with the horizontal flows of *ideas* and *action* at the individual level joined with the collective flow of *policy* and *operations* by an 'inner' focused flow between *ideas* and *policy* and the flow between *action* and *operations*, which is more 'outer' facing (see Figure 3.6).

In the E-Flow model of the Learning Company, the solid lines of the earlier double-loops become flows – as depicted by the arrows. Characteristics 3, 5 and 6 – *Informating, Internal Exchange* and *Reward Flexibility* – are part of making these flows work. To include the world outside the company, with

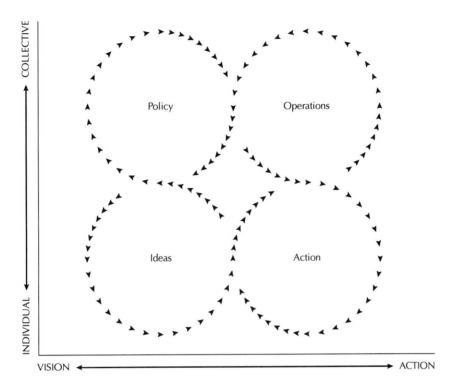

Figure 3.6 The E-Flow model of the Learning Company

Characteristics 8 and 9 – *Boundary Workers as Environmental Scanners* and *Inter-company Learning* – we must extend the definition of the 'members' of the company, to all those 'business partners' – suppliers, users, other agencies or even competitors – who are working with us in the organizing process to provide the service or product.

Four fundamental processes

The E-Flow model encompasses four fundamental processes that have emerged over time with the development of managerial and organizational thinking. These are given in Figure 3.7.

1.	*Operations (O)* ⟺ *Action (A)*	= **Managing**
2.	*Policy (P)* ⟺ *Operations (O)*	= **Directing**
3.	*Action (A)* ⟺ *Ideas (I)*	= **Learning**
4.	*Ideas (I)* ⟺ *Policy (P)*	= **Participating**

Figure 3.7 Four fundamental processes in the Learning Company

The outer, vertical double-loop of *Operations* ⟺ *Action* is the **Managing** process, historically the first to emerge as owners engaged the new professional managers to ensure the smooth and productive workings of their factories and businesses (Burnham, 1945).

It was not until the middle years of the twentieth century that the second process of **Directing** – the *Policy* ⟺ *Operations* double-loop – was differentiated from operations management. In particular, Barnard (1956) pointed out that the function of directors was different from that of managers, and Chandler (1962) built upon this emphasizing the importance of strategy.

Today, we are seeing the emergence of the the third double-loop of *Action* ⟺ *Ideas* or **Learning**. Learning is only now becoming recognized as a key strategic and operational process with the coming of the Learning Company: 'learning has become the key developable and tradable commodity of an organization' (Garratt, 1987, p.10).

The fourth key process **Participating** – *Ideas* ⟺ *Policy* – is underdeveloped in most organizations. Although this idea has old roots, for example in industrial democracy and workers participation (Coates and Topham, 1968), the Learning Company seeks dialogue or 'collective meaning making' (Drath and Palus, 1994) with all members of the company and not just the few who make up the current leadership. On similar lines McLagan and Nel claim: 'participation is the emerging dominant form of institutional governance' (1995, p.3), and as essential to whole systems development and organizational transformation.

These four fundamental processes can be seen at work in any organization. For example, in the new, small company growing from owner-operator to larger corporation, it is often possible to trace the development of managing, directing, learning and participating as sequentially important foci of attention and energy (Pedler and Aspinwall, 1996, pp.59–79)

Using the E-Flow model

One of the ways to use the E-Flow model is to check the status of each of these processes in your company. How healthy are your processes of managing, directing, learning and participating?

Learning disabilities can occur in companies because of *biases*, where one or more of Policy, Operations, Action or Ideas is emphasized at the expense of the others. For example, where a company is strong on operations management but has little interest in the ideas of its members.

Learning may also be obstructed by *blocks*, where instead of information and feedback flowing freely around the double-loops, it is blocked and interrupted. For example, policy may flow into the operations plan, but for some reason the directors are never given feedback on how possible it is to implement these policies.

In Part 2, Diagnosis, you will be invited to try some of these ideas on your company.

REFERENCES

Barnard, C.I. (1956) *The Functions of the Executive*, Harvard University Press, Cambridge, MA.

Burnham, J. (1945) *The Managerial Revolution*, Penguin, Harmondsworth.

Chandler, A.D. (1962) *Strategy and Structure*, MIT, Cambridge, MA.

Coates, K. and Topham, T. (eds) (1968) *Industrial Democracy in Great Britain*, McGibbon and McKee, London.

Drath, W.H. and Palus, C.J. (1994) *Making Common Sense: Leadership as Meaning Making in a Community of Practice*, Center for Creative Leadership, Greensboro, NC.

Garratt, R. (1987) *The Learning Organization*, Fontana, London.

Kolb, D.A., Rubin, I.M. and McIntyre, J.M. (1971) *Organizational Psychology: An Experiential Approach*, Prentice-Hall, New York.

McLagan, P. and Nel, C. (1995) *The Age of Participation: New Governance for the Workplace and the World*, Berrett Koehler, San Francisco.

Pedler, M.J. and Aspinwall, K.A. (1996) *"Perfect plc?": The Purpose and Practice of Organizational Learning*, McGraw-Hill, Maidenhead.

PART 2 DIAGNOSIS
– HOW DO YOU MEASURE UP AS A LEARNING COMPANY?

In Part 1, we introduced the *Idea* of the Learning Company with a brief history of its origins and some models of what it might look like. Part 2 offers some methods for *Diagnosis* – for assessing your organization as a Learning Company – before moving on to Part 3 – *Action* – which gives examples and 'Glimpses' of the Learning Company in practice.

Doing some diagnostic work – testing your company against these ideas – is important for at least two reasons. As a vision or metaphor for what might be

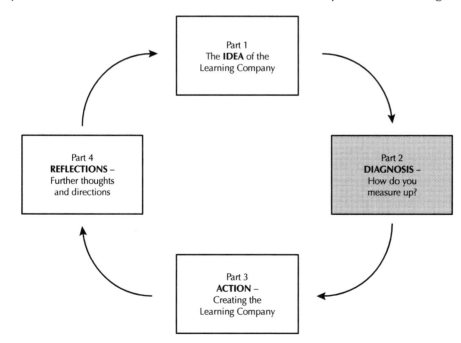

Figure P2.1 The learning cycle

possible, the Learning Company can only be realized in the specific context of a particular organization. The sooner we begin the application of the ideas the better.

The second reason concerns the learning process embedded in this book.

Bringing about the Learning Company requires an action learning process and no book can provide more than a starting place.

In Chapter 1 we suggested that companies are formed from three forces – *Ideas*, *Life stage* and *Era* – that companies are a product of the visions of their founders, that they pass through various ages and stages in a life cycle, and that they are also shaped by the economic and cultural contexts in which they exist.

The diagnostic activities in Part 2 are based on these three forces. We have most choice over *Idea* and for this reason we give it most space, but that choice is always in the context of the more determined *Life stage* and *Era*. Chapters 4 and 5 focus on the *Idea* and offer diagnostic methods based on the 11 Characteristics of the Learning Company and the E-Flow. Chapter 6 – The biography of your company – provides a means of thinking about the *Life stage* of your organization, and Chapter 7 considers the context of the *Era* we are in.

4. A Learning Company Questionnaire

You can create a profile of your company based on the 11 Characteristics of the Learning Company.

Alone, with a colleague or perhaps with a small working group, try the jigsaw questionnaire (Figure 4.1) for your organization – unit, department or whole company.

You can start the jigsaw anywhere, at any of the 11 pieces. In each piece there are five short descriptions of that characteristic in practice. Ask yourself, taking these five together: to what extent is my company like this? Each piece also has a small empty square which can be used to score the company on that characteristic. If you think your unit or company is very much like the picture created by the five descriptions combined together, then you might award it 8, 9 or even 10 points for that piece of the jigsaw. Continue until you have completed it.

Scores can then be plotted for the 11 Characteristics as a graph or histogram. Figure 4.2 shows the profile for one company which, for example, scores very well on Characteristics 1 and 11 – *A Learning Approach to Strategy* and *Self-development Opportunities for All*; but rather poorly on Characteristics 2 and 6 – *Participative Policy Making* and *Reward Flexibility*. This suggests that although the company appears to you to be well directed and providing plenty of learning for its staff, it is not very interested in their ideas and is unimaginative about how it rewards them.

How would you like it to be?

You could do the jigsaw a second time asking yourself, if this is how my company is at the moment, how would I like it to be in future? This second set of scores will provide a 'gap analysis' that, in effect, prioritizes the 11 Characteristics of the Learning Company as far as your company is concerned. In the example given in Figure 4.2, let us suppose that the biggest gap between 'what is' and 'what is desirable' turns out to be on Characteristic 2 – *Participative Policy Making*. This is useful information – especially if it is based on responses from more rather than less members of the company – perhaps it

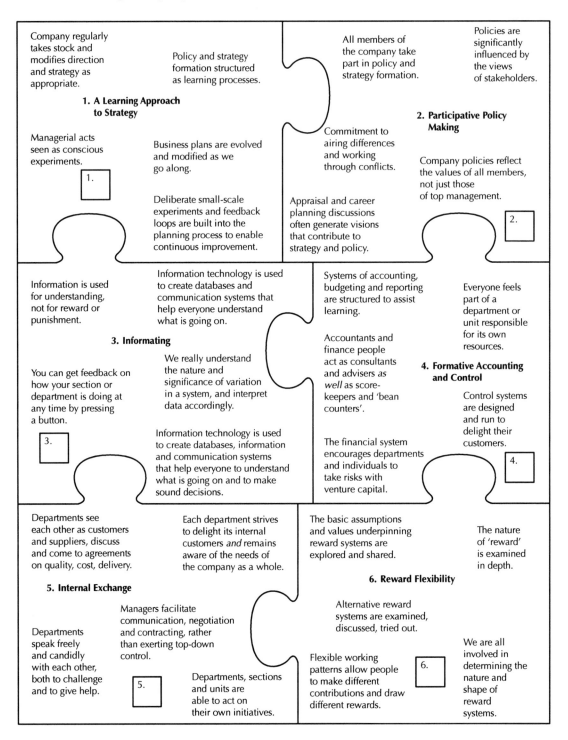

Company regularly takes stock and modifies direction and strategy as appropriate.

Policy and strategy formation structured as learning processes.

1. A Learning Approach to Strategy

Managerial acts seen as conscious experiments.

1.

Business plans are evolved and modified as we go along.

Deliberate small-scale experiments and feedback loops are built into the planning process to enable continuous improvement.

All members of the company take part in policy and strategy formation.

Policies are significantly influenced by the views of stakeholders.

2. Participative Policy Making

Commitment to airing differences and working through conflicts.

Company policies reflect the values of all members, not just those of top management.

2.

Appraisal and career planning discussions often generate visions that contribute to strategy and policy.

Information is used for understanding, not for reward or punishment.

Information technology is used to create databases and communication systems that help everyone understand what is going on.

3. Informating

You can get feedback on how your section or department is doing at any time by pressing a button.

3.

We really understand the nature and significance of variation in a system, and interpret data accordingly.

Information technology is used to create databases, information and communication systems that help everyone to understand what is going on and to make sound decisions.

Systems of accounting, budgeting and reporting are structured to assist learning.

Accountants and finance people act as consultants and advisers *as well* as score-keepers and 'bean counters'.

The financial system encourages departments and individuals to take risks with venture capital.

Everyone feels part of a department or unit responsible for its own resources.

4. Formative Accounting and Control

Control systems are designed and run to delight their customers.

4.

Departments see each other as customers and suppliers, discuss and come to agreements on quality, cost, delivery.

Each department strives to delight its internal customers *and* remains aware of the needs of the company as a whole.

5. Internal Exchange

Departments speak freely and candidly with each other, both to challenge and to give help.

Managers facilitate communication, negotiation and contracting, rather than exerting top-down control.

5.

Departments, sections and units are able to act on their own initiatives.

The basic assumptions and values underpinning reward systems are explored and shared.

The nature of 'reward' is examined in depth.

6. Reward Flexibility

Alternative reward systems are examined, discussed, tried out.

Flexible working patterns allow people to make different contributions and draw different rewards.

6.

We are all involved in determining the nature and shape of reward systems.

Figure 4.1 Jigsaw: a Learning Company questionnaire

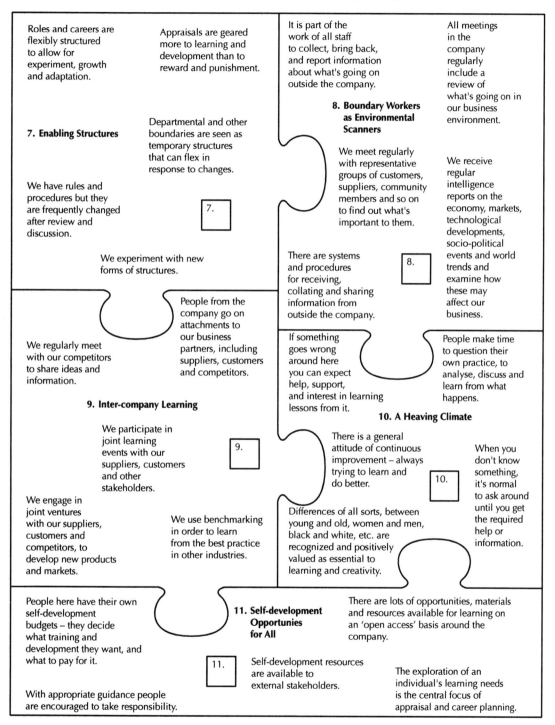

Roles and careers are flexibly structured to allow for experiment, growth and adaptation.

Appraisals are geared more to learning and development than to reward and punishment.

It is part of the work of all staff to collect, bring back, and report information about what's going on outside the company.

All meetings in the company regularly include a review of what's going on in our business environment.

7. Enabling Structures

Departmental and other boundaries are seen as temporary structures that can flex in response to changes.

8. Boundary Workers as Environmental Scanners

We have rules and procedures but they are frequently changed after review and discussion.

7.

We meet regularly with representative groups of customers, suppliers, community members and so on to find out what's important to them.

We receive regular intelligence reports on the economy, markets, technological developments, socio-political events and world trends and examine how these may affect our business.

We experiment with new forms of structures.

There are systems and procedures for receiving, collating and sharing information from outside the company.

8.

People from the company go on attachments to our business partners, including suppliers, customers and competitors.

If something goes wrong around here you can expect help, support, and interest in learning lessons from it.

People make time to question their own practice, to analyse, discuss and learn from what happens.

We regularly meet with our competitors to share ideas and information.

9. Inter-company Learning

10. A Heaving Climate

We participate in joint learning events with our suppliers, customers and other stakeholders.

9.

There is a general attitude of continuous improvement – always trying to learn and do better.

When you don't know something, it's normal to ask around until you get the required help or information.

10.

We engage in joint ventures with our suppliers, customers and competitors, to develop new products and markets.

We use benchmarking in order to learn from the best practice in other industries.

Differences of all sorts, between young and old, women and men, black and white, etc. are recognized and positively valued as essential to learning and creativity.

People here have their own self-development budgets – they decide what training and development they want, and what to pay for it.

11. Self-development Opportunies for All

There are lots of opportunities, materials and resources available for learning on an 'open access' basis around the company.

11.

Self-development resources are available to external stakeholders.

With appropriate guidance people are encouraged to take responsibility.

The exploration of an individual's learning needs is the central focus of appraisal and career planning.

Figure 4.1 cont'd

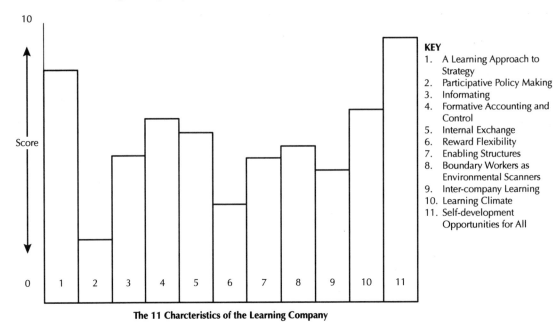

The 11 Charcteristics of the Learning Company

KEY
1. A Learning Approach to Strategy
2. Participative Policy Making
3. Informating
4. Formative Accounting and Control
5. Internal Exchange
6. Reward Flexibility
7. Enabling Structures
8. Boundary Workers as Environmental Scanners
9. Inter-company Learning
10. Learning Climate
11. Self-development Opportunities for All

Figure 4.2 A Learning Company profile

indicates that there would be widespread support for efforts to improve the *Participation* double-loop.

Alternatively you can rank each item perhaps just focusing on the top five priorities, giving 5 points to the most urgent, then 4 for the second, down to 1 for the fifth. These scores can be flipcharted on a grid like that of Figure 4.3, which shows not only the overall group priority but also significant diverse subsets. For example, in this case the two overall priority areas are clearly Characteristics 2 *Participative Policy Making* and 6 *Reward Flexibility*. However, for two people, Claire and Martin, Characteristic 10 *Learning Climate* is the most urgent.

Once a diagnosis has been done you will need to decide what action seems appropriate for your particular circumstances. In terms of your priority characteristics a typical approach might involve:

● imagining what the organization will look like once those characteristics are in place
● working 'back from the future' – imagining you *are* in the future with the characteristics in place – now, describe how you achieved it
● carrying out a force-field analysis* identifying the factors that are helping and hindering you from achieving the characteristics.

*This is a useful methodology for planning change. If you are not familiar with it, there is a worked example of how to analyse a problem and develop a strategy for action in Pedler, M.J., Burgoyne, J.G. and Boydell, T.H. (1994) *A Manager's Guide to Self-development*, 3rd edn, McGraw-Hill, pp. 122–127.

Individual priority scores

	Fred	Claire	Sheila	Martin	Andrew	Barbro	Kathleen	Total	Rank
1. Learning Approach to Strategy	2		1				1	4	8
2. Participative Policy Making	5		4		5	4	5	23	2
3. Informating								0	=10
4. Formative Accounting and Control	1	3		1		3	3	11	4
5. Internal Exchange								0	=10
6. Reward Flexibility	4	4	5		4	5	4	26	1
7. Enabling Structures		1	3	4	3	1	2	14	3
8. Boundary Workers as Environmental Scanners			2	2	1	2		7	7
9. Inter-company Learning	3			3	2			8	6
10. A Learning Climate		5		5				10	5
11. Self-development Opportunities for All		2						2	9

Figure 4.3 Priority rankings of the 11 Characteristics of the Learning Company

In the long run a holistic strategy, which addresses all 11 Characteristics, is essential. This was one of the main reasons for the transformation of BICC, when each one was tackled over a two-year period (see Chapter 19).

Diagnosing the whole company

While the jigsaw is a useful and creative way of presenting the 11 Characteristics questionnaire, it is difficult to do with large numbers of people. To do a large-scale diagnosis you would need to carry out a survey, preferably with a wide cross-section of various departments, and groups, for example by age, gender, length of service and so on. For these purposes, a more conventional questionnaire format is better, and both paper-based and software versions of the *11 Characteristics of the Learning Company Questionnaire* are available from the Learning Company Project (address on p.239).

This instrument also provides a measure of urgency or priorities for action by asking respondents to indicate:

- to what extent each characteristic is currently being achieved – 'how it is';
- how important they think it is for the organization to try to achieve that characteristic – 'how it should be'.

From these two scores a dissatisfaction index is calculated, given by:

$$Dissatisfaction\ index = 100 \times \frac{how\ it\ should\ be - how\ it\ is}{how\ it\ should\ be}$$

If people are totally dissatisfied, this index will be 100. If they are exactly satisfied, that is things are exactly as they would like them to be, it is zero.

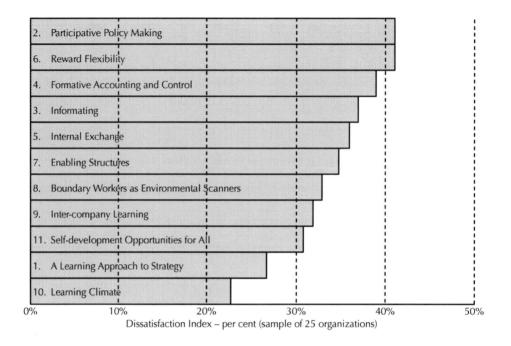

Figure 4.4 The 11 Characteristics of the Learning Company: dissatisfaction indices for 25 companies

Figure 4.4 shows data from 25 companies, presented in the rank-order of dissatisfaction. Thus, from this sample, the area seen as most in need of strengthening is *Participative Policy Making*, followed by *Reward Flexibility* and then *Formative Accounting and Control*.

From this particular sample, those characteristics most commonly associated with learning – *Self-development Opportunities for All* and *Learning Climate* – rank ninth and eleventh in terms of dissatisfaction. This suggests that what we might call the 'training' areas have been well addressed compared with the others; in fact this is quite a common phenomenon, either because this is the easiest place to start or because some companies think that doing a lot of training makes you a Learning Company.

Although this broad level of analysis is interesting, suggesting various possible conjectures, such data should be taken with caution. For example, in virtually all our surveys using this instrument, there are significant differences between various subgroups within the organization.

Figure 4.5 illustrates this. In this case the plotted points represent the rank-order of dissatisfaction; the greater the number of points (maximum 11, minimum 1), the greater the dissatisfaction.

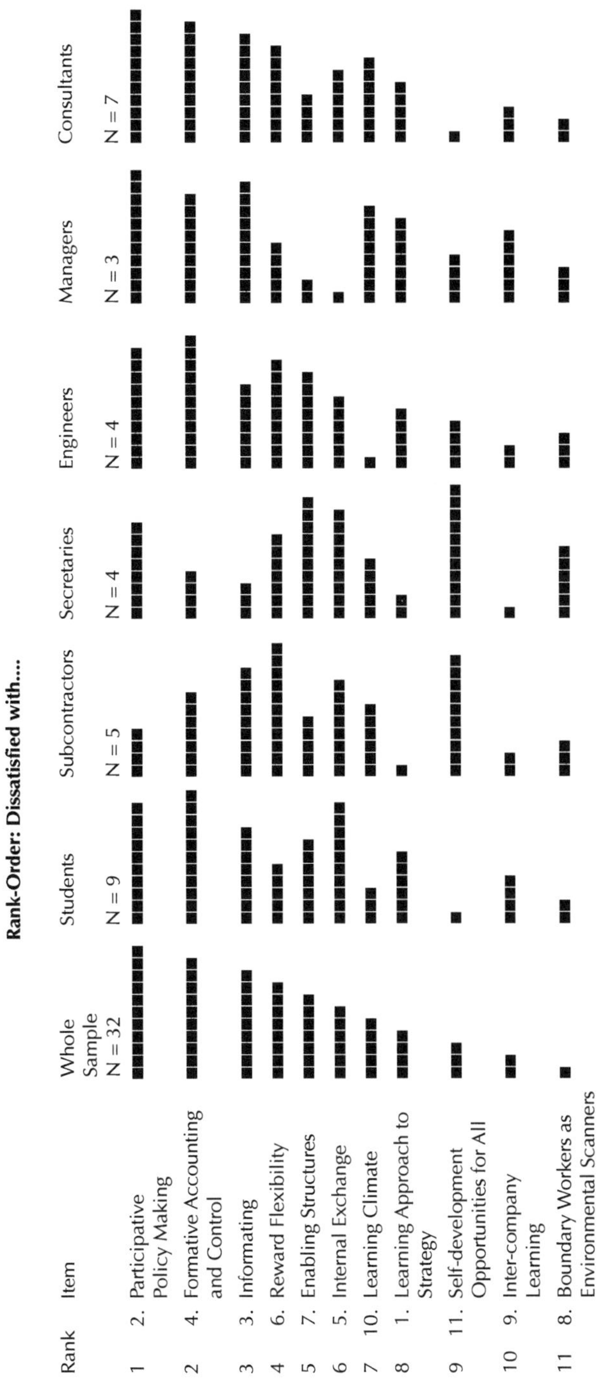

Rank-Order: Dissatisfied with....

Figure 4.5 Rank-order dissatisfaction for internal groups

The 11 Characteristics are presented here in order of dissatisfaction by the whole sample and it now becomes clear that this does not reflect some of the important internal differences. For example: for secretaries, their greatest dissatisfaction is *Self-development Opportunities for All* – which is lowest for students and ninth overall. This probably reflects secretaries' relative lack of development opportunities.

Still with secretaries, it is interesting to note that they are much more dissatisfied with *Boundary Workers as Environmental Scanners* than is the sample as a whole. What might this mean? Is it, for example, a reflection of their view that the information they receive by talking on the phone with customers and suppliers is largely ignored?

Again, although *Internal Exchange* is the area of least dissatisfaction for managers, it is second for students, third for secretaries, fourth for subcontractors and sixth overall. On *Inter-company Learning*, although everyone else seems satisfied, it is the managers who are not – is this because they are the ones who see the importance of this sort of learning for the company?

These examples show that when carrying out such a survey it is important not only to look at overall or 'average' responses, but also at differences of opinion. These can then be explored in depth, by interviews, dialogue meetings, and so on, for it is from these differences in perception that organizational learning is most likely to occur. The Learning Company actively seeks out diversity, exploring differences and meanings from as many subgroups and stakeholders as possible to create something new, rather than minimizing differences by working with majority views and lowest common denominators (see especially Glimpses 10, 11, 12 and 14 in Chapter 9).

Cluster analysis: the 11 Characteristics of the Learning Company

The data from our sample has been analysed to see how the 11 Characteristics link together in the minds of respondents. The result is shown in Figure 4.6.

We can compare this with our original blueprint model (Figure 3.1) by adding the five cluster labels of *Strategy, Looking out, Structures, Looking in* and *Learning opportunities*. This gives support to the original framework as in Figure 4.7.

Figure 4.6 Cluster analysis of the 11 Characteristics of the Learning Company

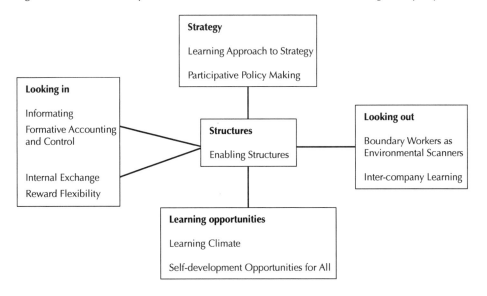

Figure 4.7 Cluster analysis and the blueprint categories of the 11 Characteristics of the Learning Company

5. E-Flow: mapping the Energy Flow of your company

- Are there any learning disabilities in your company caused by *biases* towards one or more of *Policy, Operations, Action* or *Ideas*?
- Is learning obstructed by *blocks* in the information and feedback flows between these four processes?
- How healthy are the activities of *managing, directing, learning* and *participating* in your company?

In Chapter 4, the 11 Characteristics of the Learning Company are used to create a profile of the organization based on the *practices* we might expect to see in place in a such a company. In this chapter, the *idea* of the Learning Company is taken further by working with the E-Flow model to look at the underlying learning *processes* in the organization. It includes diagnostic activities to encourage you to try these ideas in attempting to enhance learning company performance.

The company as flow

The E-Flow model is our central idea – its derivation, justification and how it works were introduced in Chapter 3. It is a proposition about the fundamental processes by which companies learn, in which the Learning Company is marked by vigorous flows of energy linking collective ideas (policy) with the collective action activities of *managing, directing, learning* and *participating*. The notion of 'energy' is a wide one, embracing flows of information, communication and learning, and also flows of consciousness, motivation and power.

The E-Flow model is based on a view of the company as a pattern of continuous interactions, exchanges and dialogues. The image of the organization as flux and transformation (Morgan, 1986) in turn rests on a systemic view of the world as a flowing and unbroken whole, composed of a mutuality of interconnected parts (Bohm, 1980). In this world:

- Companies are not just formed by their environments, but also take part in forming them.
- The old notion of causality – that A causes B – breaks down here, because the mutual causality of A and B interacting and changing each other makes more sense.

- You can't fix parts in isolation; organizational and social problems are not resolved by 'quick fix', piecemeal, solutions, but rather by mutual adjustments in the whole system.
- Relationships between parts are circular feedback loops rather than straight lines.

The flow of the organizational learning cycle thus becomes crucial to companies (Dixon, 1994). Deficiencies and blockages in the flow of learning become positively dangerous for the organization and its stakeholders. The most critical task for managers is that of *integration* – bringing wholeness and balance to parts that might otherwise be isolated, confused, fragmented. The idea of the learning organization allows us to think about and develop the organization of learning in the company. How good are the learning relationships in the company? How do the learning opportunities, activities and processes support each other to benefit the company and its stakeholders?

The E-Flow model is concerned with what we do with our energy – how we use it to learn, to dialogue and make new meaning together in the company as a 'community of practice' (Drath and Palus, 1994). The E-Flow can be used to diagnose a company in respect of its learning performance, and its ability to benefit from this. In a process closely allied with action research and action learning, this diagnosis can identify whether or not a company is fully functional in learning terms. The action learning/research process queries the consequences of the current patterns of learning in the company, asks what specific actions might be taken to increase learning, and seeks ways in which the consequences of any interventions may be observed and continuously modified.

Biases and blocks

The E-Flow model is used to identify the problems that can occur in flows of energy that make up the basic learning processes of the company (see Figure 5.1).

Basically these problems are of two kinds – *biases* or imbalances of energy, awareness or consciousness, and *blocks* or constrictions of information, dialogue or feedback. Before moving on to discuss these in detail, try this simple diagnostic activity for checking your company's 'sense of balance'.

Diagnostic activity 1: Mapping energy balance

Step 1
You can do this alone or in groups of any size. Each person (or pair or small group) needs a fresh copy of the E-Flow model as in Figure 5.1. (This should be of at least A4 size; A3 is better in a group if you want to make a visual display in the room.)

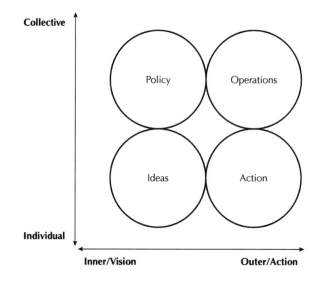

Figure 5.1 The E-Flow model of the Learning Company

Each person (or pair or small group) also needs a supply of 20 coloured sticky dots. (These are obtainable from most stationers, but you could use a coloured pen as a substitute.)

Step 2
Now allocate the 20 sticky dots to the four areas of Policy, Operations, Action or Ideas according to how you see the current balance of the company's energy, resources, attention.

Obviously there is no right answer to this, it depends on how a person or a group sees the situation from their perspective. If you see the company as perfectly balanced, you could put five dots in each; if you see the company as heavily biased towards operations management, then you might put ten or more dots there, and so on.

In the example of company X (Figure 5.2), the company is heavily biased towards *Operations*, and next towards *Action*, with a comparative neglect of *Policy* and especially of people's *Ideas*. This suggests a company that is strongly managed, very outer-oriented, but that doesn't value the ideas of its people much or see much use for thinking, planning and 'inner work' in general. Such an organization might be very efficient and successful, especially in the short term, or it might be over-managed, busy but not especially effective.

Step 3
- What sense can you make of your pattern?
- What does it tell you about the current balance of the company's energy flow?
- What does it tell you about learning relationships and dialogue in the company?

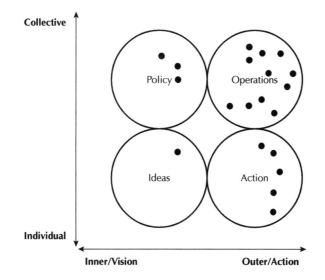

Figure 5.2 Company X: a sense of balance

If you are working in a group, you could ask each person (or pair or small group) to display their picture of how they see the company. You can also test your analysis of your company against the general list and description of *biases* which follow this activity.

Step 4
As a final step, ask yourself: if this is how it is now, *how would I like it to be?*

If you are working with a group of people, this step can be done alone, in pairs or small groups. Each person, pair or small group will need a new supply of five sticky dots of different colours (or different coloured pens).

Now, you have five new units of energy to use as you think best for the company. Allocate the 5 new sticky dots to the four areas of Policy, Operations, Action or Ideas *according to how you would like to see the company direct this new supply of energy, resources, attention.*

Again there is no right answer to this, but if you are working with a group, you can use this new picture to start a discussion about how you would like to see things change in the company. Is there a consensus about what needs to be done? What could be done to shift the energy balance in the direction you would like to see?

In our fictional example, company X, let's imagine that the people concerned want to balance the strong management of the company with more creativity and encouragement of ideas. So, in allocating their five new units of energy,

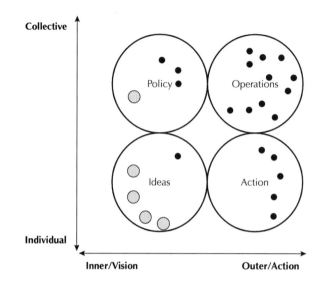

Figure 5.3 Company X: a better balance

they could put four into *Ideas* and one into *Policy* to create a better balance (Figure 5.3).

All they have to do now is to agree how to do it.

Biases

Biases occur when any one, two or three of the basic processes predominate to the exclusion or diminution of the others. In the 'Mapping energy balance' activity you can get a quick and surprisingly consensual diagnosis of the current bias of your company. From this, it becomes clear that any imbalance has an effect on the way the company works. For example, a company biased towards *Policy* may have a strong and impressive set of policies that are not translated into *Operations*, that is collective actions, or are not owned in terms of a working set of *Ideas* by members of the company, and are therefore not realized through people's *Actions*.

This is not just a failure of implementation – which is how it might first strike you from a conventional management perspective – but a major loss of learning. Here there is little or no feedback from the successes or failures of putting the policy into practice, and little influence from individuals in touch with the day-to-day activities of the company. The policy may achieve a certain stability, but it is cut off from operational reality.

There are 14 possible biases:

- 4 'singles' – towards any of the processes of *Policy, Operations, Action* or *Ideas*

- 4 'doubles' – towards any of the double-loops of *managing, directing, learning* and *participating*
- 4 'trebles' – towards a collective emphasis on any three of the single processes and conversely a neglect of any one (for example a company emphasizing *policy, operations* and *action* but not *ideas* – a common bias for organizations that major on strong top-down management and who do not develop their people)
- 2 'diagonals' – towards the two diagonal loops of *policy* and *action, operations* and *ideas.*

All 14 biases are listed below (Table 5.1), each illustrated with a name and a brief description. These illustrations are only indicative of what may be produced by particular patterns of bias – other descriptions might fit the pattern created in particular companies. If you haven't already identified your company pattern from the 'Mapping energy balance' activity, you might find it in this list:

Table 5.1   14 possible biases in the E-Flow of the company

Single biases

1.	P o i a	STRONG POLICY, not shared or applied	Clearly stated policy, but without implementation or ownership
2.	p O i a	ROUTINE DRIVEN, no planning or commitment	The stereotypical 'bureaucratic' organization: dominated by procedures followed for their own sake, irrespective of purpose or efficiency
3.	p o i a	BRIGHT IDEAS, no agreement or action	A community of people with bright ideas who cannot agree or act on them
4.	p o i A	BUSY ACTION, no coordination or thought	The dynamic, action driven, fire- fighting organization, little planning, much muddle and self defeating effort

Double biases

5.	P O i a	STRONG DIRECTION, lack of commitment and initiative	Decisive and authoritative leadership, with coercive and partial implementation in detail and little voice for grass roots ideas
6.	p O i A	STRONG MANAGEMENT driving out thinking and planning	A neat and smoothly running organization with clear and owned procedures, but unable to see the needs for change and unable to act on them
7.	p o I A	INDIVIDUAL LEARNING and initiative at cost of coordination	An organization centred around members' interests and developing ideas, but which fails to coordinate and exploit these

| 8. | P o
l a | HIGH PARTICIPATION
displacing action | An organization 'hooked' on consultation and participation for its own sake, with little agreed or implemented |

Treble biases

9.	P o l A	PSYCHIC CONTROL mission, culture, 'hearts and minds' control, groupthink	The brainwashed company, 'overdosed' on mission, vision and empowerment, with dedicated, cult-like behaviour and people unable to question beliefs and practices
10.	P O l a	ADDICTION to PLANNING, avoidance of action	All the 'right' plans, policies, ideas but the will and ability to actually do it are missing
11.	P O i A	COMMAND AND CONTROL at the cost of local initiative	The classic, formal structure-driven organization with little space for ideas and local initiatives
12.	p O l A	CONTINUOUS IMPROVER no bold moves	A company with bottom-up continuous improvement in a clear operational system but with a lack of overall direction

Diagonal biases

| 13. | P o
i A | LOOSELY COUPLED
independent actors under
a loose policy umbrella | An organization made up of people doing their own thing, sheltered by a 'policy' story giving the space for this |
| 14. | p O
l a | CREATIVES IN A
ROUTINE SPACE | A routinized organization which is unaffected by the individually creative ideas of its people |

Blocks

Having established some ideas about your company's *biases* or imbalances of energy, what *blocks* or constrictions of information, dialogue or feedback are currently impairing organizational learning? Blocks occur when one or more of the flows of energy implied by the arrowed lines in the E-Flow model are broken. Blocks are not always complete, and are often partial.

Blocks may contribute to biases or indeed may result from them. Although it is useful for diagnostic purposes to consider blocks and biases separately, it is in other ways unhelpful to divide them. Both are aspects of the 'mutually arising' patterns of dialogue and interaction in the company and, in terms of any actions you might decide to take, the distinction probably does not matter. For diagnostic purposes, however, an analysis of blocks can add a great deal in terms of thinking of how to improve the learning processes in your company.

For example, consider a block on the upflow from *Ideas* to *Policy* – a company with just this one blockage would be communicating policy clearly to its people but would not be hearing any suggestions from them in return. Here the policy is being made by a very few people, or passed down from on high, perhaps from government or from an owner, and does not take into account the ideas of the people who are responsible for putting it into action. Some of the 'learning loss' here is in possibly missing good ideas for future direction, of relying on the few to think for the many, and in not engaging most people in the policy-making process.

As another example, consider the alternative block on this double-loop – a block on the downflow from *Policy* to *Ideas*. This would mean that policy making was actually widely open to influence, yet the company is not communicating policy to its members in order to make it easy for them to make their contributions. Perhaps people find out about policy when a new operational plan is launched rather than through being involved in discussing it first. In such a company people would be able to raise matters of policy and make suggestions arising from their operational experience, and this would be genuinely taken into account, but no one would ever get much feedback from this. Thus people would find their ideas either disappear out of sight in the policy debate, or emerge as a change to operational procedures some time later. The overall effect of this lack of feedback may be to discourage individuals from participation.

A company that has only this one block might be in pretty good shape as a Learning Company, but it would miss a few tricks by not making policy as accessible to debate as it might be. As such blocks can lead to biases, if participation in general is weakened, leading, for example, to a bias towards *managing* (*operations/action*), then the company could have neat and effective day-to-day operations, but be weak on renewing purpose and direction through policy debate and formation.

There are many possible blockages in the E-Flow model. The most important are the eight found in the four double-loops of *managing*, *directing*, *learning* and *participating* – in each of these double-loops there are two single blocks of the sort exampled above for the *Policy/Ideas* or *participation* double-loop – and the four double blocks which, if found, sever the double loops entirely. A consideration of these blocks provides the second diagnostic activity in this chapter.

Diagnostic activity 2: Unblocking company learning

Step 1
This activity is best done with a group, although you could work through it alone or with a colleague (from now on it is described as if it is being done in a group).

Divide into four subgroups, each taking one of the four double-loops of *managing, directing, learning* and *participating*. (Each subgroup needs a copy of its double-loop, preferably in A3 size for visual display.)

Each subgroup then explores its own particular double loop dealing with the following questions:

- Is the flow through both parts of the loop working well?
- Are there any restrictions or blockages in the flow in either direction?
- What are the effects of these restrictions?
- Are there any facts, figures, stories or anecdotes that illustrate these effects?

Step 2
Each group then marks the blockages or restrictions on their sheet as in Figure 5.4.

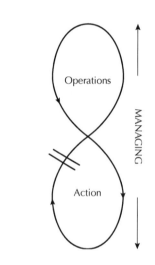

Figure 5.4 Unblocking company learning – The 'managing' double-loop

In this particular case, there is a flow of energy from *Operations* down to *Action*, showing that the 'chain of command' is working well and that instructions and communications from management are getting through, but that there is no flow back up from *Action* to *Operations*. This means that management are not getting feedback about the usefulness or effectiveness of their planning, allocation and work procedures that might enable them to improve. At the same time, it looks as if the people taking the action are not encouraged to look for continuous improvement in their work organization.

Of course, the effects of this blockage can only be gauged in the particular company by those on the spot. In the case of the subgroups in your company, they may find that the blockages are partial, or apply in some parts and not in others, and so on. They should be encouraged to map these as fully as possible, illustrating them with stories or anecdotes wherever they can.

Step 3

When sufficient time has been given for each group to finish its work, have them assemble their sheets and display them together. Each group should introduce its picture illustrating it with stories and examples. This will create a picture of the whole company in terms of blocks and restrictions on the flow of energy and learning.

- What collective picture emerges of the learning blocks in the company?
- Are there any patterns of restrictions that are repeated in different parts of the company?
- What do the stories and anecdotes tell us about our learning culture?

Step 4

Each group now takes time to consider what proposals it could make to unblock its double-loop. What could be done to improve matters?

Step 5

Finally, each group presents its proposals to the others, who question and critique them, looking in particular for unforeseen 'knock-on' effects. Depending on the status of the whole group, it could then agree some collective actions or further work to improve organizational learning processes and to unblock the company.

As a follow-up to this diagnostic activity 'Unblocking company learning', 12 possible blocks are detailed below (Table 5.2), with names and brief descriptions. Again, these descriptions are only illustrations and it needs careful thought to determine the effects of a given blockage in any particular company. Blockage patterns can become very complicated and you have to use your own judgement about how far to take this sort of analysis.

With this caution in mind, do any of these blocks apply to your company? If so, how would you describe their effects on your organizational learning?

Table 5.2   12 possible blocks in the E-Flow of the company

Single Blocks

1.	P to I block: DISAPPEARING PROPOSALS	Ideas taken but not acknowledged
2.	I to P block: MISSIONARY LEADERSHIP	Policy making based on leading without listening
3.	P to O block: NON-IMPLEMENTATION	Policy is done when it is agreed – no will/action to implement
4.	O to P block: GUNG-HO POLICY	The 'carry on regardless' approach to policy implementation
5.	O to A block: RESISTANCE TO MANAGEMENT	Failure or rejection of day to day management

6.	A to O block: UNCORRECTED ACTION	An operations management style that tells but does not listen
7.	A to I block: BLIND ACTION	An organization of people who do not observe or think about the results of their actions
8.	I to A block: INHIBITED INITIATIVES	An organization of individuals who have ideas, but dare not try them out

Double Blocks

9.	P and O 'DIRECTING' block: Self-sealing policy	Operations and policy emerge and evolve separately
10.	O and A 'MANAGING' block: Dependence on the 'informal' organization	Where individuals muddle on despite, rather than because of, the operational plan
11.	I and A 'LEARNING' block: Switched-off work	An organization of people who have given up applying their ideas
12.	I and P 'PARTICIPATION' block: Kitchen cabinet policy	Policy is made in isolation from dialogue and feedback from members

Conclusion

Unlike the more descriptive model of the 11 Characteristics of the Learning Company, the E-Flow model is a means for interpreting the *idea* of the Learning Company in whatever way seems to fit best for those concerned. Although it may appear deceptively simple, when searched and looked for, more and more processes and interpretations are revealed in organizational settings. Perhaps more mandala than model, the E-Flow repays imaginative input. It is a diagnostic framework to embrace members' observations and evidence, including intuitions and anecdotal examples, to make judgements and decide on possible actions in the company.

Many of the questions raised are those included in the diagnostic activities in this chapter – what blocks and biases are occurring here? What is causing them and holding them in place? What are the costs and consequences for the company? What might be done to overcome the blocks and biases? What might be the benefits and how could we know they were occurring?

As a diagnostic model, the E-Flow is designed primarily for the members of a company using it and its language of diagnosis as part of conscious review of their ways of working. We are enthusiastic about this, because using the participation process itself for collective self-diagnosis in a corporate setting fits true with the E-Flow model. Only through this process can consciously reflexive, self-aware Learning Companies be created. However, there is also a case for consultants or organization development specialists to use the E-Flow to plan and guide their influencing attempts. An initial consultant-led diagnosis can be given back to company members to own and take on.

Insightful sessions can be based on labelling the corners of a room, or even laying out a floor plan of the E-Flow model, and inviting people to stand where they think they are mainly active, or walk the part with the pattern they are usually involved with, then discuss with others doing the same how they are working together. Other ways of using the E-flow model are described in *The Learning Company Groupwork Guide to E-Flow (Energy Flow)*, Learning Company Guides No. 2, which can be obtained from Learning Company Project (see address on p.239). Among other methods this includes a simple questionnaire to be used for surveying organizational members to get an idea of perceived biases.

RERERENCES

Bohm, D. (1980) *Wholeness and the Implicate Order*, Routledge & Kegan Paul, London.
Dixon, N. (1994) *The Organizational Learning Cycle*, McGraw-Hill, Maidenhead.
Drath, W.H. and Palus, C.J. (1994) *Making Common Sense*, Center for Creative Leadership, Greensboro, NC.
Morgan, G. (1986) *Images of Organization*, Sage, London.

6. The biography of your company

Seen as organisms, companies are dynamic. Every year thousands are brought to life by hopeful founders, and each year many also die through bankruptcy, takeover or ceasing to trade. Infant mortality can be very high – up to 40 to 50 per cent in the first year – and even established companies do not stay the same for long. As companies change and grow they can be seen to pass through a number of stages from birth to maturity and, just as human beings encounter problems as they pass from childhood into adolescence, from adulthood into old age, these passages in the life of the company are often stormy, marked by crisis and turbulence.

This chapter provides a way of looking at the effect of the second of the three forces that shape companies – the *life stage*.

The notion of the company life cycle is a very old one. This organic or biological metaphor sees the company as a collective, living organism, which is dynamic, changing and developing over time in a series of phases. So, for example, a company may go through:

a free-form, *infant* phase ...   (when it first starts)
a more autocratic, *pioneer* phase ...   (where the founder(s) dominates)
a more bureaucratic, *rational* phase ...   (where rational management
                                               systems replace the personal,
                                               idiosyncratic control of the
                                               founder(s))

and...
one or more *post-rational* phases ...   (where systems are loosened up,
                                               people are developed and trusted
                                               to work on their own initiative and
                                               in partnership with others, etc.)

Although every organization is unique, meeting particular problems and circumstances, we can look at the company as passing through a series of such phases meeting certain questions at certain times, which are to some extent predictable. For example, the early creative pioneer phase of a company

50

often ends in a crisis of leadership in which the young company, full of the founders' drive and vision, struggles when they leave, retire or lose their way.

Developmental management

In this view the development of a company takes place via a progression of phases that are irreversible. Development is discontinuous, an old pattern is broken by the crisis and a new one forms over time, and involves qualitative transformation. Each succeeding phase is different in quality from the old and is characterized by a different principle (Greiner, 1972; Lievegoed, 1973).

Some companies spend huge amounts on change programmes which don't appear to have much long-term impact. Why is this? Perhaps because changes only have a lasting effect when they address an underlying need. A developmental approach asks not only: 'Does this help us deal with our current problems?', but also:

'Does this help us take *our next step* as a company?'

This implies conscious developmental management. The company is seen as a continuous system over time with a past, a present and a future. Developmental management requires a present state of readiness to take the next step and an optimistic future orientation to provide vision and courage. This means recognizing where the company is in terms of the developmental sequence, in recognizing the nature of the crisis when it comes, and in seeing the opportunities to develop inherent in that crisis.

There is some evidence that people who see things this way do behave differently. For example, a study of CEOs in the USA showed that those with most awareness of past events also looked further into the future (Kouzes and Posner, 1991, p.95).

The biography of your company: an activity

You can do this activity on your own but it is better to recruit a small group to work with you. This group could include the directors, as a biography exercise is a most valuable preparation for strategic discussions, or it could be a representative or cross-sectional group from the whole company – as in the *Whole Systems Development* design (see Glimpse 14 and Chapter 23).

Step 1 The past

What are the past events which have made your company the organization it is today? Pick out five or six *Key Learning Events* – learning experiences which have had an important effect on the company:

1.

2.

3.

4.

5.

6.

Now mark these on a 'lifeline' like the one below. Individuals (or each small group if many people are involved) could create their own lifeline on a fresh sheet of paper, and then come together to create a composite picture such as that shown in Figure 6.1.

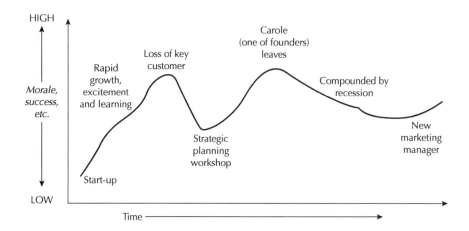

Figure 6.1 A company lifeline

In this small company, everything went well until the loss of an important market, which threw them into a spin until they pulled themselves together and changed strategy. Another crisis occurred when Carole left to live overseas ....

What does your company lifeline look like?

Now that you have a picture of the company's life to date, spend some time thinking about or discussing the Key Learning Events which have shaped your company ...

- How do those events live on in the character or personality of your company as it is today?
- Which were the especially influential events – those which strongly affected the direction of the company?
- Which events were:
  (a) changes that happened to us?
  (b) developments that we chose?

- How might things be different if one or more of these events had not taken place?
- What alternative paths are open to the company from now on?

In turbulent times, the company's ability to experiment and change appropriately is vital – part of what it means to be a Learning Company. But, diversifications, new systems, new products, new markets, often turn out to be mistakes or mere fads and fashions. These are a failure to take a long view – of the company as a being in the process of becoming. In the study of Chief Executives mentioned earlier, being able to learn from the past is an important step in moving to the present and into the future.

Step 2 The present

Now, either alone or in small groups, think about where your company is at present. What is the company's *life stage*?

To help with this, Figure 6.2 shows a generic model of the life stages of the company followed by some suggested key questions to help you think through the likely directions and strategies open to you.

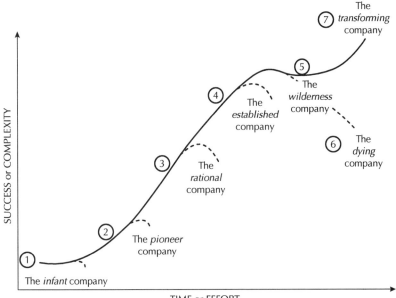

Figure 6.2 The life stages of a company

Although all companies are unique, they can learn from comparison with a generalized model. Though Figure 6.2 shows a tidy, linear sequence, in actuality you may skip stages or visit them in a different order – for example, a company can be faced with the *dying* or *transforming* stages at almost any time.

So, where is your company now? If there are enough people, divide up and consider this with the aid of the key questions below, before returning to reach consensus.

1. The *infant* company is a brand new start-up by an individual entrepreneur or group or it can be a new project, department or section in an existing company, or a joint venture between existing companies.

Key questions at this stage are:

- what is our vision of the company?
- what does the company exist for; what is its purpose?
- what does the company look like and feel like?
- how can the vision be turned into reality?
- what resources – people, money, equipment, etc., are needed?
- what are our products and how are they marketed?

2. The *pioneer* company is small and fast-growing with a central, powerful figure or group driving it.

Key questions at this stage are:

- do we stay small or get bigger?
- if we grow, what new systems do we need to cope with expansion?
- what new people do we need and how will they be integrated?
- who can replace the leader(s) and what plans do we have for succession?
- do we need a new leadership style?

3. The *rational* company has outgrown its initiators and become independent, bigger and more complex.

Key questions at this stage are:

- are the founders really in touch with the business needs now?
- is the management style too authoritarian, too personal?
- how can we use systems to bring order, rationality, consistency and fairness?
- what new procedures are needed to manage our people?
- what specialist functions do we need, e.g. sales, personnel, R & D?

4. The *established* company is just that – well set up with formal procedures and scientific management applied to most aspects of its functioning.

Key questions at this stage are:

- how can we encourage entrepreneurship, risk-taking and motivation?
- how can we minimize red tape, rigidity and bureaucracy?
- what can be done about the barriers between departments and functions?
- can we decentralize and give more autonomy to front-line departments?
- are we getting bored with our business?

5. The *wilderness* company has lost its way and got out of touch.

Key questions at this stage are:

- how can we change our relationship with our customers and suppliers?
- do we have the right clients?
- how can we change our view of the outside world from one that is full of enemies and threats to one which is full of opportunities and potential allies?
- what are we here for?
- what should our new purpose be?

6. The *dying* company is one that is failing or bankrupt or where the purpose of its being has been completed.

Key questions at this stage are:

- is it time for the company to die?
- should we make a good end or try to create new life through merger, 'surgery', management buyout, etc.?
- what are our moral obligations to stakeholders – shareholders, employees, customers, suppliers and the community?
- what new seeds can spring from the husk of the company?

7. The *transforming* company is one that has decided that now is not the time to die and has found new purpose, new identity, new life.

Key questions at this stage are similar to those for the infant company, except that they have a conscious awareness of the past:

- what is our new vision and what is our purpose for being in business now?
- who are our new customers and what new services are we offering our old ones?
- how are we going to work differently to accomplish our vision and goals?
- how can we learn from what we are doing?
- how do we organize ourselves for learning?

Of course there are many other ways to work on taking stock of where your company stands at the present time.

- You can do a SWOT analysis – what are our *Strengths*, *Weaknesses*, *Opportunities* and *Threats* at present?
- You could map your stakeholders – your *staff, users or customers, suppliers, service and business partners, local communities*, and so on – and ask yourself 'What do each of these want from us?' and 'What questions are they posing us?' (See Glimpse 29)

You could even involve some of these stakeholders in a strategy workshop to get a 360° picture of the company. And there are plenty of other ideas elsewhere in this book – such as setting up a management challenge for yourselves (Glimpse 1). The important thing is to get a good picture of the *present* – just as we did earlier with the past – before moving on.

Step 3 The future

There has been so much emphasis on 'vision' recently that some companies are in danger of being blinded by them. As we said at the outset of this chapter, developmental management means not only asking whether this idea of the future will help us deal with our current problems, but also whether it helps us to take *our next step* as a company.

With this in mind – building on a clear sense of what we want to preserve from our past and present, as well as what we want to change in future – now move into the future and do some future search and vision building. It is at this stage more than any other that the difficulties on proceeding alone will be most obvious. You need a group of other people, as diverse a group as possible, to help you think forwards into possible futures. Getting this diversity into the room is a key principle of 'Whole Systems Development' (Glimpse 14 and Chapter 23) mentioned earlier. An alternative to this is to hold a vision building workshop, and you can find a design for this in Glimpse 2 'Stars to Steer By'. The other Glimpses in Chapter 9 will also be useful.

As with the present, there are many ways of attempting to look into the future. Artistic and non-verbal methods are particularly useful – painting, modelling, music, dance, mime – for freeing the vision. You can have groups work up their ideas in an architectural competition of likely scenarios of the future, rewarding them with an exhibitor's newsletter, prizes and a party.

It is important at this stage not to let the rational self dominate or the scientific way of knowing block the artistic. Whether these visions are sensible is not the point – as far as we know no one can actually predict the future. More important, as the advocates of scenario planning tell us, is that it develops flexibility of thought and response; it helps prepare you for any eventuality.

You *can* apply rational planning to the outcomes of your vision building. Glimpse 3 'The Strategic Staircase' will help you do this. Working backwards from your preferred vision, what do we need to accomplish and by when? What are the small, first steps on this road?

What will demonstrate, in a way that everyone can join in, that the journey to the future has begun?

Finally

We've reached the end – at least of this cycle – of the company biography. This is a process that can be worked through somewhat hastily, in a day or can be spread over a much longer period. Whichever way suits your purpose, the company biography activity is worth some investment of your time in order that your plans for the future can be built on a firm understanding of who we are and where we have come from.

Company biography work serves as a foundation for the future in another way. In the past, some companies have commissioned outsiders to write – usually rather eulogistic – company histories. However, just as individual biographies of the past were for the rich and famous, so company histories were restricted to those of the great and good. Now we are in the age when the biography of *every* person is a story worth telling. The biography of every *company* is worth telling too, as a story of creativity, of development, of collective identity and shared purpose.

REFERENCES

Greiner, L.E. (1972) 'Evolution and Revolution as Organizations Grow', *Harvard Business Review*, **50**(4), 37-46.

Kouzes, J.M. and Posner, B.Z. (1991) *The Leadership Challenge: How to get Extraordinary Things done in Organizations*, Jossey Bass, San Francisco.

Lievegoed, B.C.G. (1990) *The Developing Organization*, Blackwell, Oxford.

7. Era spotting

Some companies make changes, some companies react to changes and some just wonder what happened. Which category does yours fall into?

However proactive, all companies are shaped by, and must fit with, their era. For some developing countries this means coming to terms with the rapid shift from agriculture to manufacturing, whereas in the West the decline of industrialism figures strongly. Other trends are not so bound by geography or the current phase of economic development. The emergence of the 'Knowledge Age', the advance of communications technology and increasingly urgent ecological issues are forces that shape the era for all of us.

To talk of eras is to talk in vast generalizations. A 'post-industrial society' may still need companies that extract raw materials or manufacture them into useful products. Terms such as 'post-industrial' or 'knowledge-based' are more to do with broad shifts or tendencies where we seek to put our finger on the essence and values of the new. Whatever your company does, whoever it serves, it must take account of these new values. Paying attention to the operations *within* the organization is in many ways a manufacturing era preoccupation; looking *outwards* and onwards is a keynote of the new age. Spotting the era we are in, sensing what it means in our organization, and trying to anticipate future trends, is a vital aspect of Learning Company functioning.

In this chapter we look at the ways in which definitions of learning are changing, and take a long and speculative view of how companies have learned from their experience in different eras. The notion of 'Transitional Myths' (sets of social beliefs and practices that support appropriate change) are one explanation for movement in this big picture. Finally, we offer a simple framework for 'Era spotting', so that you can build this into the way your company does things – always looking inwards, outwards and onwards.

Four types of learning

In a 1963 undergraduate psychology lecture, learning was defined as 'a relatively enduring change in actual or potential behaviour as a result of experience' – a definition that reflected the positivist, behaviourist theories holding sway at that time. Contrast this with Illich's (1971) iconoclastic counter: 'learning is unhampered participation in a meaningful situation'. This contrast characterizes the shift that we believe has occurred over the last few decades. This shift is from seeing learning as an individual phenomenon to seeing it as something that happens in people in relationship with others; from the individual making isolated sense in a concrete world to the person immersed in a collective social process of sense making and meaning creation.

In the Learning Company four kinds or types of learning are important (Pedler and Aspinwall, 1996, p.25). These are shown in Figure 7.1.

We can learn ...

1.	... *about* things	or	**Knowledge**
2.	... to *do* things	or	**Skills, Abilities, Competences**
3.	... to *become ourselves,* *to achieve our full potential*	or	**Personal development**

and ...

4.	... to *achieve things together*	or	**Collaborative enquiry**

Figure 7.1 Four types of learning (Pedler and Aspinwall, 1996, p.25)

The first two of these types – Knowledge and Skills, Abilities, Competences – are familiar and have been recognized as important in the best companies for many years. The third type – Personal development – has been valued outside work, in schools and in adult education, but is now becoming increasingly important in organizations. The fourth type – Collaborative enquiry – is less familiar, yet it is one of the keys to organizational learning, which we are only just beginning to recognize. In the first three types, learning is seen as something that individuals do, on their own, happening, somehow, inside them. In the fourth, learning can also take place *between* people in a relationship of persons acting collaboratively. In this last type of learning, outcomes cannot be fully measured in terms of what individuals take away, but by the new meaning which is created together.

Eras and Transitional Myths

At times of major change our ability to learn from experience assumes great importance as existing, pre-formed or programmed knowledge loses its value. In such circumstances, relying upon existing knowledge – upon what has worked until now – is dangerously misleading. It follows that the educational, training and developmental practices in place to support learning from experience in rapidly changing times, are crucial to making the transition.

Table 7.1 shows the Transitional Myths that have shaped the nature of learning from experience in companies. As we move from an economy dominated by agriculture, through manufacture, to mentofacture (made by the mind) in the knowledge era and on to spiroculture (the development of spirit or the creation of meaning and identity), changes are made possible by particular Transitional Myths. The essence of Transitional Myths is that they make sense in both the old and the new orders, and hence make the transition possible (Pym, 1979).

Our argument here is that in recent times, the methods for learning from experience have changed from being based on the Transitional Myth of self-responsibility, self-development, initiative and enterprise to being based on the Transitional Myth of quality, excellence and collective learning. This brings about a fundamental change in how we see learning from experience – from seeing it as individual discovery to seeing it as a collective construction of meaning.

Table 7.1 Transitional Myths in context (Burgoyne, 1995, pp.61–72)

Economic frontier	Transitional Myth	Political dogma	Managing principle	Culture
Agriculture		Feudalism		Romanticism
	Protestant ethic		Hierarchy and control	
Manufacture		Centralism		Modernity
	Initiative Enterprise Self-development		Autonomy and contract	
Mentofacture		Free market		
	Quality, Excellence Collective learning		Culture and mind control	Post-modernity Ecological Holism New Age …?
Spiroculture				

Thus the Protestant ethic was the Transitional Myth for the industrial revolution, and self-responsibility, initiative and enterprise serves the transition from manufacture to mentofacture in the same way. Now, shaped by a move from the Transitional Myth of *initiative, enterprise* and *self development* to one based on *quality excellence* and *collective learning* our understanding of the idea of learning is undergoing a radical change from the individual learning from concrete experience to the collective learning of persons in social contexts. In terms of human resource development this is a shift on from a concern with facilitating self-development (Pedler *et al.*, 1994 (1st edn, 1978)), to a focus on creating learning companies and organizations (Pedler *et al.*, 1991; Burgoyne *et al.*, 1994).

Hard work and deferred gratification (reward in heaven not on earth) were the principles supporting the transition of work from the field to the factory. Individualism, enterprise and self-development were the principles supporting the development of everyday capitalism, as knowledge workers found themselves the owners of the means of production (knowledge) rather than simply providing the labour factor. *Quality, excellence* and *collective learning* have the essential two-faced characteristic of Transitional Myths: they look back to quality systems (statistical process control, etc., continuous improvement), but also beg the questions of: Excellence at what? Learning for what? Fit for the purpose, but what purpose?

At the frontier, work is becoming both a source of meaning for life for those doing work, and the means of providing meaning via what is produced, for the consumer.

Table 7.1 also suggests that the guiding political principles have evolved from feudalism through centralism to free-market. There is a general sense of political philosophy lagging behind the era. So, arguably, early industrialization was supported more by colonial states with captive raw material sources and markets protected by military power, through centralist governments, rather than through free market competition. Interestingly, at the time of writing, the American sociologist Etzioni is promoting through various newspaper articles 'communitarianism' as a new approach based on a philosophy of collective responsibility, which would fit well with our general proposition.

Managerial principles have also evolved alongside Transitional Myths. Hierarchy and control is seen as the principle on which industrial firms first established advantage (Williamson, 1975). Autonomy and contract describes the 'networking' world of the autonomous, initiative-taking individual in the enterprise culture. Finally, culture and mind control represents the most recent trend in management, with the strong interest in culture management (Deal and Kennedy, 1988). In contrast to the external controls of job descriptions, objectives and appraisal characteristic of previous eras (Ouchi, 1980), the mission–vision–empowerment movement seeks to manage through inner control, capturing 'hearts and minds', offering 'freedom' and personal responsibility.

Culturally, Gergen's (1991) categories of romanticism, modernity and post-modernity can also be mapped on to the eras. Modernity represents the belief in, and application of, science, technology and rationality to the project to manage the world for humanity's own ends, and to define and achieve 'progress'. Modernity is certainly tied up with industrialization and the rationality of mentofacture. The term 'facture', to make, implies the modernist attitude of construction and control. Modernity in many ways replaced religious, mystical, less 'rational' beliefs and practices – though not completely. In that sense the modernist project has never come to full fruition, though it has been extremely influential in shaping the world, and is still likely to be so in large parts of the world expecting the benefits of 'modernizing'.

The post-modern thesis is that there has been a significant loss of faith in the modernist agenda. Science and rationality no longer offer a universally accepted formula for life and how to live it. The 'successes' of science and technology throw into stark relief the questions of what to do with them. Coupled with information technology, the moral and aesthetic nature of these choices creates the conditions for the easy dissemination of diverse opinions to create multiple rather than unitary meta-narratives – underlying belief systems that unite or fragment ideas and behaviour (Lyotard, 1984). As Gergen points out the post-modern situation can be taken in at least two ways: a relatively pessimistic view of the breakdown of meaning, or a more optimistic or liberating view that the constraints are off on the creation of new meanings, and the revaluing of old ones. In current times, the Transitional Myth of collective learning allows for the transition from work as knowledge production to work as meaning making.

Era spotting: a planning activity

Of course, although it may help to put strategic choices into long-term context, the theory of Transitional Myths doesn't help much with managing our affairs now. Here is a simple diagnostic activity which you can do with a group of colleagues – or, better still, with a representative Whole Systems Development conference (see Chapter 23).

1. First, how can we anticipate new requirements or motivations from inside or outside the company? What are the issues that are affecting and will affect your company in the current era? What are the wider, peripheral and apparently nebulous signals that point to the onset of the new?

With a group of colleagues, or with a representative cross-section of the company and its service partners, construct a list of all the 'issues in the air'. Here are some to get you started:

- demographics – fewer children, fewer school leavers, fewer workers, more retired people
- greater freedoms – of thought, lifestyle, leisure time, travel
- imbalance of rich and poor – at home and abroad
- increasing speed of new product/service development and differentiation
- people demanding more from work in terms of personal fulfilment and meaning
- 'new world order' – post cold war rise of fundamentalism, terrorism
- rise of vegetarianism
- increasing use of information technology and telemating
- people's desire for development outstrips traditional forms of provision
- pressure to reduce car and road use
- increasing instability – in people, in companies, in countries
- increasing diversity – of people and their life styles
- more one-person and more multi-family homes
- governance issues – representing all stakeholders

- ethics issues – knowing right from wrong actions, being social responsible, a 'good company'
- environmental pollution – more environmental laws, re-cycling, etc.
- organizational structures – patriarchal hierarchies less and less functional
- limits to growth – shift from quantitative growth to qualitative, sustainable development
- welfare state – from 'cradle to grave' provision to enabling services plus 'safety net'?

There will be many others, including those which are more specific to your particular area of interest. Try to collect as many as you can via perusing reports and papers, by brainstorming, by asking clients, competitors and so on. You should include any wild possibilities which come up. A SWOT analysis of your company is another good way to pick up some of the specific issues that are affecting you now or are likely to affect you in the future.

2. When you have a good, long list, classify each item in one of three bands:

- Band 1 – of central importance to us now
- Band 2 – increasing pressure in this direction, likely to be of importance in the future
- Band 3 – still too 'up in the air', 'off the wall' but keep an eye on this

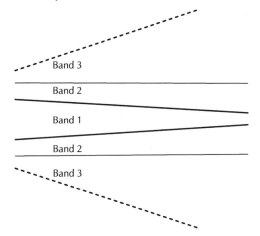

Figure 7.2 Classifying important issues in the era

3. Take your Band 1 items and compare them with your SWOT analysis. Which of the items are:

Strengths?	– how are you planning to build on these?
Weaknesses?	– what steps are you taking to deal with these?
Opportunities?	– how many of these are being picked up?
Threats?	– how can we monitor and avoid these?

Band 1 items are the easiest to predict so they should be familiar to you and, indeed, should already have been taken into account in your existing thinking. Band 2 items could make all the difference and you may have missed some of these in planning for the future. Band 3 includes many speculative items which you may want to keep an eye on; it will be interesting to see – if you repeat this exercise in a year or two's time – whether any have moved into Band 2 or even into Band 1.

If you are one of the companies that make the changes, you have either done your era spotting well or been lucky; if you are a company that has tended to react to changes or even 'just wonder what happened' – here's a chance to start moving into the era in a purposeful way.

REFERENCES

Burgoyne, J.G. (1995) 'Learning from experience: From individual discovery to meta-dialogue via the evolution of transitional myths', *Personnel Review*, **24**(6), 61–72.

Burgoyne, J.G., Pedler, M. and Boydell, T. (eds) (1994) *Towards the Learning Company: Concepts and Practices*. McGraw-Hill, Maidenhead.

Deal, T. and Kennedy, A. (1988) *Corporate Cultures: The Rites and Rituals of Corporate Life*, Penguin, Harmondsworth.

Gergen, K.J. (1991) *The Saturated Self: Dilemmas of Identity in Contemporary Life*, Basic Books, Harper Collins, New York.

Illich, I. (1971) *Deschooling Society*, Calder and Boyars, London.

Lyotard, J.-F. (1984) *The Postmodern Condition: A Report on Knowledge*, Manchester University Press, Manchester.

Ouchi, W.G. (1980) 'Markets, bureaucracies and clans', *Administrative Science Quarterly*, **25**, 129–141.

Pedler, M. and Aspinwall, K. (1996) *'Perfect plc?': The Purpose and Practice of Organizational Learning*, McGraw-Hill, Maidenhead.

Pedler, M., Burgoyne, J.G. and Boydell, T. (1991) *The Learning Company: A Strategy for Sustainable Development*, McGraw-Hill, Maidenhead.

Pedler, M., Burgoyne, J.G. and Boydell, T. (1994) *A Manager's Guide to Self-Development*, 3rd edn, McGraw-Hill, Maidenhead.

Pym, D. (1979) 'Work is good employment is bad', *Employee Relations*, **1**(1), 16–18.

Williamson, O.E. (1975) *Markets and Hierarchies*, Free Press, New York.

PART 3 ACTION
– CREATING THE LEARNING COMPANY

In Parts 1 and 2 we looked at the *Idea* of the Learning Company and suggested some methods for seeing how your organization measured up as a Learning Company (*Diagnosis*). Part 3 – *Action* – contains examples, illustrations and 80 Glimpses of different organizations putting the Learning Company into practice, each in their own particular way. While no company we know measures up to the Learning Company in all respects, many organizations have captured particular aspects and facets and made them their own. Here are a few of these examples of the Learning Company in action, and we hope they encourage you to get into action to begin to realize the idea in your particular organization.

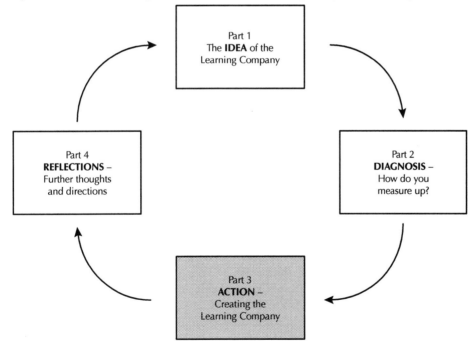

Figure P3.1 The Learning Cycle

Getting started

This can be a daunting task for all sorts of reasons. Having taken a good look at the idea of the Learning Company, having decided that this idea fits in with the aspirations of people in your company, and having done some thinking and diagnosis about the aspects of your company that are more developed and less developed in terms of the Learning Company idea, you might still be asking yourself:

How do we get started?

Given that there are no blueprints and that transformation comes partly from an alteration of what is already there, we think that you can start anywhere that seems possible and appropriate. To the extent that organizations are organisms, then each small part, every department or section, has some capacity to affect the whole. So, anywhere you can make a start has the potential to affect the other parts. Of course, a 'Learning Department' might be expected to flourish best in a Learning Company, which might also flourish best in the 'Learning Society', and so on, but it has to start somewhere.

Here are ten different starting points for pursuing a Learning Company strategy in your company. They are not mutually exclusive and you can follow more than one or even all of these. However, the Learning Company is about aligning and attuning flows of energy, so you need to start where the energy is – if none of these quite fits your situation, what would?

- **Work with the board of directors**   In some ways the obvious place to start. Sooner or later these people will have to support and live out the idea if it is to spread throughout the company. If the directors begin to practise the ideas and demonstrate their learning with those with whom they come into contact, then it will have a most powerful effect.
- **Begin with diagnosis**   All good organization development interventions begin with data collection of some sort – and the Learning Company Questionnaire discussed in Chapter 4 is one way of starting. However, as a word of warning, paralysis by analysis is all too common, either because those who might want to hold up the process keep calling for more and more information, or because you get swamped with data as a result of not thinking clearly and selectively enough about what data are needed. The best approach is perhaps an action research or action learning process that includes data gathering as part of taking action and learning.
- **Start with a 'Big Event'**   The Whole Systems Development approach described in Glimpse 14 and Chapter 23 includes a community conferencing process aimed at 'getting everyone in the room at the same time'. A conference or a teach-in with everyone in the company who is involved with a particular issue – and who is therefore potentially a part of the change process – generates a great deal of new ideas, energy and commitment. However, they can be quite testing for leaders or directors who may need help in preparing for such 'public learning' forums. Also, as with development

programmes (see below), such energy-raising activities need careful and persistent follow through.

- **Run a development programme to raise consciousness**   In pursuit of 'cultural change' many companies have mounted large-scale campaigns to get their message across, including training programmes for all staff such as 'Putting people first' or 'Quality means getting it right first time'. Needing board backing, this can be very effective in the short term, but it must be backed up by a sustained development strategy, otherwise the high energy and expectations generated may turn sour.

- **Work out from the human resources department**   This starting place has the advantage of being where the people management systems are located. For example, if there is a goal setting and performance review process then the ideas of the Learning Company can be linked into this. People in this function may be relatively knowledgeable about ideas of learning and development. This may help, but paradoxically it can also block new initiatives.

- **A joint union and management initiative**   There is a great developmental potential in any alliance of adversaries, working from their respective concerns to challenge and transform existing assumptions and methods of working. The ability to organize for productivity and well-being depends upon our ability to think creatively, and dialogue with those with whom we have differences helps to break up old positions and thinking. Any Learning Company initiative in a unionized company must confront this question of partnership (see 'The BICC Story', Chapter 19). Rather like human resources departments, trade unions can have great strengths in both supporting and blocking.

- **Set up a series of task forces**   Task forces can function like action learning groups and work best with sponsors to whom they are accountable. As temporary structures, they do not threaten the powers that be too much and can mobilize large amounts of energy and creativity. Task forces could be set up to look at a number of the dimensions of the Learning Company that you wish to pursue. A 'meta' task force could be charged with overseeing the whole Learning Company process. They should dissolve themselves with a suitable celebration when they have achieved their goals.

- **Work with the strategic planning cycle**   Where there is a strong commitment to a cyclical planning process, this might be a good point to attach a Learning Company orientation. The link here is to see planning as a learning process and to build in feedback loops and opportunities for all members of the company to have a say and make a contribution to future directions.

- **Major on a priority Characteristic**   A company wishing to follow a Learning Company strategy could start by focusing on its biggest priority and forget about the others for the time being. The development of a high-quality *Learning Climate* or using technology and software throughout the company to encourage *Informating* are two possible examples.

- **Start with one department**   If the energy and vision is there, why not start here? Supposing the finance department were to pick up and run with the idea. If they succeeded in changing themselves and the way they worked, perhaps taking a different approach to accounting responsibility, then this would affect their relationships with their 'internal customers' – with all the other parts of the company. Obviously, for the Learning Company impulse to be exported to the whole would require some wider recognition and sanction, but this is a very practical place to start.

The place to start is where it makes most sense to you to do so. We hope these ten possibilities stimulate your imagination and enthusiasm. Chapters 8 to 18 offer many other ideas, diagnostic methods, activities and Glimpses of the Learning Company based on our model of the 11 Characteristics of the Learning Company. Chapter 19 – 'The BICC Story' – illustrates how these come together in a two-year organization development effort.

8. A Learning Approach to Strategy
No. 1 of the 11 Characteristics of the Learning Company

This implies that deciding what to do in terms of the collective direction of the company and implementing this, has itself to be a learning process. The processes of strategy-making and of implementation, evaluation and improvement are consciously structured to produce learning.

One example of a non-Learning Approach to Strategy is the 'gung-ho', 'Charge of the Light Brigade', blind approach, where the organization commits its energy and effort to the policy without checking whether it is working or not. A Learning Company approach implies that the organization:

- takes controlled risks in terms of new ideas by trying them out in pilot form before full commitment
- measures, monitors and obtains feedback to check whether any plan is working and receives early signs of warning if it is not
- is regularly conducting small-scale experimentation in many parts of the business.

One example of this approach is 'the management challenge' used by Shell where every three years the managers of a plant receive a week's visit from some fellow managers. The visitors are free to examine and observe all aspects of the business and at the end of the week confront the plant managers with their questions, aimed particularly at challenging operating norms and assumptions. After the meeting the plant managers must publish the questions and their answers to them.

THE MANAGEMENT CHALLENGE

Glimpse 1

Challenging your own norms and assumptions is difficult. As the terms imply, these everyday structures of individual and corporate lives are taken for granted, not noticed, in effect, invisible to those who follow or hold them. They are much more obvious to others who follow different norms and assumptions who, while similarly blind to their own taken for granted norms and assumptions, can ask penetrating and provoking questions about those of others.

Royal Dutch Shell have tried to incorporate this potentially valuable process into their company operations with what they call 'the management challenge'. Every three years, a senior executive from another plant, and usually another country, visits a given location to deliver a challenge to management. He or she spends a week or so at the site, wandering around, reading reports, talking to people before challenging the managing team. The challenge itself involves presenting observations, impressions, making suggestions but, above all, asking 'naive' questions, questions that an insider would not ask because the answers are obvious. These questions are basically of the nature 'Why do you do such and such?' or 'How does this and that contribute to plant efficiency?' The local managers must publish the challenge and their responses to it.

The management challenge is one way of ensuring that the 'hidden' fundamentals of 'how we do things round here' are questioned on a regular basis. Such questioning seems to be an essential component of 'double loop learning' or the reframing essential to organizational transformation. You could institute your own management challenge and put in place this vital aspect of organizational learning by inviting different people in to question your operations. Why not start by inviting fellow managers from a sister plant? If you feel up to being more challenged than this you could invite a customer, a supplier or a stakeholder from the local community.

The management challenge at Shell illustrates one way in which current operating assumptions can be tested. This sort of action should help stave off complacency – as long as the people concerned do not collude with each other.

Challenge is one thing; vision is another. To survive and develop every organization needs the capacity to create and dream up better futures for itself. Better still if as many as possible of the people in the company can be involved in this.

Glimpse 2

STARS TO STEER BY

Since ancient times people have dreamed of better futures. Often these visions have served as stars to steer by when things are difficult or uncertain. Now, as our previous over-reliance upon scientific thinking is ebbing, we are turning to some of the ancient mysteries in order to rediscover the art of leadership to add to the principles of management.

'Only connect', E.M. Forster's famous epigram, is perhaps the most succinct way of describing the path to the Learning Company. Because we tend to think of organizations as man-made constructions, it is hard to think of them as whole, developing organisms, yet, we are beginning to be able to see companies as groupings of interdependent people trading in an environment and these can be said to learn through trial and error, questioning and re-formulating goals, purposes and values, So, to the extent that we connect – form a whole, are mutually dependent, share a common life – we can be together, organize together and, indeed, learn together.

Even so, it's still hard to see the company as a whole being. Here's an activity that you can try by yourself, with a small group or even at a large conference, but with a large group you may need some help to organize it appropriately.

Imagine your company as a person and ask the questions

- What sort of a person is it?
- Is it female or male?
- How old is it?
- Is it thin or fat?
- What temperament is it – lively, fiery and explosive or earthy, strong and slow-moving or light, full of ideas and quick or flowing, endlessly weaving and flexible?
- What is its name?
- What is your company good at? What are its strengths? What are the weaknesses?

We define vision as your hope for and belief in a desired future. To do this requires the ability to rise above your current, everyday reality in order to dream up a picture of how things *could* be and how you would *like* them to be. Your picture of the Learning Company comes from many sources as shown in Figure G2.1.

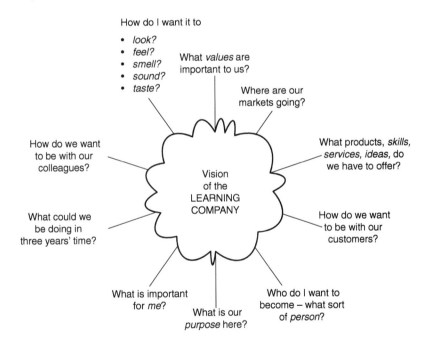

Figure G2.1 The elements forming a vision of the Learning Company

Next find a way of presenting your findings back to the whole group. Do think about some of the less obvious ways of doing it. A poster can be very effective, as can someone telling a short story about how the old company turned into the new. A job advertisement for the new company would give a strong flavour, while the dramatically inclined might choose to offer a poem, a play or a mime to get the message over. Why not use video if you have it?

Whatever you do, find a way of getting people to listen, watch, see in the right way – turn the lights off while you talk, hang your posters like a picture gallery and walk people round or give a speech outside.

The next stage is to create something out of the whole group. Again there are various ways of doing this. Which pictures or messages were particularly exciting? Which directions look most promising? Which presentations did people enthuse about?

Select one or more ideas to do some further work on and form into teams around these ideas (perhaps this would be a good time to have a social break to reintegrate the whole and allow for people to give up their individual ownership of ideas to the whole group).

Each team could then work together to create symbols, images or designs to embody the picture or a key aspect of it. There will be concrete ways of doing this, some of which may suit your particular organization. For example, people have made badges, coats of arms, T-shirts, logos, mock-ups of shop fronts, vehicle paint designs, brochures or letterheads.

It is important to make time to let people get on which this creative work. Most of us, especially in the company of a few colleagues, have more creative and artistic potential than we ever use. Being creative – in concrete form – is a key aspect of creating stars to steer by.

Exhibit the finished works and have an appropriate celebration. What comes next depends on your situation, whether it be commissioning a team to act on a chosen vision or publishing the exhibits to a wider audience. What's the next step?

Once you have a vision, the next thing is to turn this into a strategy.

Glimpse 3   **THE STRATEGIC STAIRCASE**

Strategy works backwards. Once you have a vision, a star to steer by, you can construct a strategy to get you there. The essential thing to grasp is that you work out your strategy going *backwards* from your vision and not from here forwards.

In this very simple four-step version of the strategic staircase (Figure G3.1), you start with your vision of your company as a Learning Company – what does it look like to you? Now put a time frame on it – when do you want to arrive there? Now come backwards 'down the stairs' – to get to your vision by then, what do you have to do by this date, and this date? Finally, where are you now in terms of your vision? At the moment you are on the bottom step.

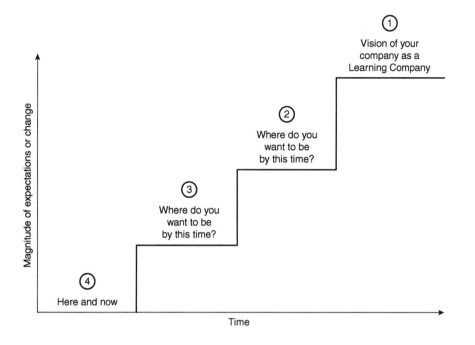

Figure G3.1 The strategic staircase

Glimpse 3 makes strategy making look very straightforward. In practice, it is often difficult to see far enough ahead to create a viable strategic plan, and the process of making strategic decisions can be tortuous, especially when you are a big public company and a potential 'news item'. Take Pilkington's decision on the site of their new glass plant, for example. Glimpse 4 shows that the question: 'What really happened here?' is unlikely ever to receive a single, straightforward answer.

Glimpse 4

PILKINGTON'S NEW GLASS PLANT
There is a debate in the corporate strategy literature as to whether strategy formation is a regular, systematic process of taking stock, reviewing and setting new directions or whether it is a process that happens only when 'big decisions' have to be made.

When Pilkington's made a 'big decision' about where to locate a new float glass plant, the options were St Helens, Pilkington's traditional home base, or Kent, to take advantage of the Channel tunnel and the continental European market. There were plenty of arguments on both sides. The business logic was for Kent, but land and labour are cheaper in Lancashire. If the company did not site in Kent, perhaps a continental manufacturer would operate from the other end of the tunnel and get a competitive advantage in the lucrative southern UK market. On the other hand,

Pilkington's have a long tradition, with some ups and downs, of being a big and good local employer, taking their social responsibility seriously.

The issue was widely debated internally to get the widest possible view and gain commitment, especially during internal management programmes and other gatherings. On the whole, the Kent option gained ground – it made more business sense, even if it did create local difficulties – and then a funny thing happened.

The Board announced that the plant would be built in St Helens and, indeed, that implementation plans were well advanced and would go forward quickly. It was an odd experience for those who had endlessly discussed the pros and cons and who had come to accept that it might have to be Kent. Had it been the tradition or cheapness of St Helens that had tipped the balance?

As with many such tales, we are never likely to arrive at a single truth or even a balanced account of the experiences and perceptions of making a big decision. In a sense that doesn't matter because what we have here is an illustration of the complexities of strategic decision making and the dilemmas that can follow the Learning Company approach of consulting and involving as many people as possible. Three points emerge, however, from this story that are of particular importance for those who are concerned in realizing the Learning Company:

- There is a very real dilemma in balancing the wish to be a 'good company', as an employer and a contributor to the local economy, with the need to be a successful and competitive company.
- There is a conflict between the demands for openness and for broad participation in decision making with the inevitable need for some confidentiality and secrecy about strategic plans in a competitive situation.
- Participation takes time and people must be given time to work out what they think in consultation with others; equally there are times when there is a need to be decisive and to act quickly in order to 'hit the ground running'.

The challenge for the Learning Company is to find ways of combining a commitment to broad participation and consultation with both the necessary confidentiality and the need for speed.

Pilkington's has the problems of trying to make decisions while involving its people, while living in a very competitive market and while being in the public eye. The problems for smaller organizations can be different. At G & G Fans (Glimpse 5) the people in the company were very inwardly focused, but this didn't stop them having a vivid picture of what the environment surrounding them was like.

G & G Fans' relationship with their environment can be described as 'autopoietic' (Morgan, 1986, Ch. 8). Autopoiesis means the capacity for self-production and orignated with two Chilean scientists, Humberto Maturana and Francisco Varela, who have challenged the taken-for-granted view that change is something that comes from outside the organization. They argue against 'open systems theory', seeing organizations as closed, autonomous systems of interactions, making reference only to themselves. This autonomy, circularity and self-reference allows living systems to self-renew or self-produce. In this view, the organization and identity of the company is its most important product.

An autopoietic standpoint on the company turns the world upside down. Instead of seeing the company as at the mercy of its environment, the environment is seen as a reflection of and as part of the organization. Thus, a company produces itself and its own 'environment' as part of its identity. You can see this clearly at G & G Fans.

G & G FANS

Glimpse 5

G & G Fans is a small engineering concern with 20 employees selling over 70 per cent of its output to an air-conditioning company. When its main customer was taken over by another business, who had their own supplier of fans, G & G faced extinction – unless they could find new customers quickly.

On the day their new marketing consultant arrived, she noticed that the neat little factory was almost half full of packed fans ready for delivery. However, what surprised her was that Barney, the owner, in his blue overalls, was over in the corner excitedly discussing a new prototype fan on wheels for garage fume extraction, with most of the workforce clustered round him. 'Who's responsible for sales?', she asked. 'Well, I do the invoices, like', came the reply.

On being told by the consultant that she would only work with him if he went on to marketing full-time, Barney refused point blank, saying, 'I'm an engineer, you see, I make things, invent things. I can't sell, that's a job for folks like you with smart suits and silver tongues.' Further discussion revealed that Barney and his people never went outside the factory if they could help it, they always got customers to come to them, they were unsure of themselves off their own patch and saw the world outside as vast and scary. They wanted the consultant to find them a new customer so they could get back to their fan on wheels.

Here are people 'producing' their own organization and its 'environment' every day. Their picture of the world outside the factory and their experience of life inside are part of the same whole. The consultant can start at either end, but if the firm is to survive, both inside and outside perceptions and actions have to change.

Of course, this 'production' of inside and outside worlds is not just a small-company phenomenon. When managers in large concerns talk up the 'opposition', the 'global marketplace', or the need to 'fight for survival' the same process is being enacted. These managers know only too well what it's like out there in that jungle – it's so tough that you'd never think of approaching 'competitors' to see what you could learn, to open up a new market together, to pool resources to develop a much-needed new product.

One way of making strategy a learning process is to ensure that it is examined and critiqued periodically by creative people in the company. These are the people who 'produce' the organization on a daily basis and the management or people development process can be used not only to train and educate individuals, but also to help form corporate strategy. Glimpse 6 describes how management development in any organization may function at one of six levels; the learning company would certainly be aiming at levels 5 and 6.

Glimpse 6

MANAGEMENT DEVELOPMENT FOR POLICY MAKING

Management development activities include *structural* interventions, such as succession planning, career appraisal, career structuring, and *developmental* interventions, courses, provision of open learning materials and mentoring arrangements. However, unless these individual level tactics contribute to, and form part of, corporate policy they will only be locally or remedially useful. Management development policy is concerned with the coordination of these structural and developmental management development interventions with corporate policy.

A six-level model of management development policy (Burgoyne, 1988) suggests that only companies operating at the fifth or sixth levels are likely to be able to function as Learning Companies.

- At **level 1** there is essentially no planned management development. People develop to some extent, of course, as a result of living and working, but this is natural or by chance. According to surveys, half of UK companies are at this level. Only very small and dynamic companies are likely to have people who develop to make their best contribution under these circumstances.
- At **level 2** there are isolated and piecemeal structural or developmental tactics, probably to meet some crisis such as a skills shortage, a succession problem or a failure in business performance due to a lack of collective competence such as financial awareness or customer care. When people are given development opportunities or career planning at this level they usually bear no relation to one another.
- At **level 3** structural and developmental tactics are coordinated. Development needs identified at appraisals are followed up and career plans take potential into account and incorporate planned development to realize it. A formal paperwork system exists. The snag here is that companies do not stay the same for long. When changes come as a result of policy initiatives or crises, the well-laid management development plans are obsolete.
- At **level 4** management development policy and planning is closely linked to corporate planning. This includes what is known and planned and also what is uncertain and what the main contingencies are. Management development practice is based on judgements about what will stay the same and what will change or is uncertain about future jobs, roles and tasks.
- **Level 5** includes the processes we saw at levels 2 to 4, but now with an input to corporate policy formation. Data on the company's collective competence, creative visions of possible alternative futures arising from career planning or development workshops using key policy issues as live case material contribute to the policy debate. Human resource directors make a critical input to the

company's strategic opportunities based on their reading of the cumulative abilities, potentials and vision of staff alongside their marketing, technical and financial colleagues.

- At **level 6** a management development perspective not only makes inputs to corporate policy, but also illuminates the policy-forming process. Previous policy and its implementation is reviewed, critiqued and learned from; new directions are chosen with exploratory or experimental objectives in mind; new ventures have built-in monitoring and evaluation mechanisms. When the company takes a risk, it does everything it can to maximize the learning from that initiative, whatever the business outcome.

This six-step ladder offers a possible agenda for the people development function and a way of making a contribution to becoming a Learning Company. The ladder can be used to take stock of where you are now (in our experience, people in the human resource function always believe they are higher on the ladder than do people in the operating arms of the company). This sort of debate can usefully contribute to emerging corporate strategy and also create opportunities for people to participate in policy making and to see their career futures in the corporate context.

Of course, some companies do learn to move very rapidly in response to environmental changes. Sometimes this is for rather dubious ends and gives rise to the question: 'What is this learning for?' Consider Building Designs Systems (Glimpse 7). Is this a Learning Company? It is certainly flexible and adaptable and has learned one way of dealing with market fluctuations, but is it a Learning Company?

IS THIS A LEARNING COMPANY?

Glimpse 7

Building Designs Systems (BDS) is a company employing some 60 people, making and installing windows, doors, double glazing and conservatories. Trade fluctuates with the demand for home improvements, which varies considerably with the level of interest rates. In the last few years, rates have risen and fallen and currently stand at a very high level.

One day, the caretaker was asked to come in at the very early hour of 5.00 a.m. to open the offices and workshops. Outside were three large vans and all the staff were on hand to help with the removal of 90 per cent of the stock and work in progress, together with most of the office equipment and furniture. At 6.45 a.m. the vans drove away and the staff dispersed to have breakfast. At 8.00 a.m. the liquidator arrived to value the inventory and the company. At 10.30 a.m. the liquidator left and at 12.00 noon the vans returned and were unloaded by the staff.

By 1.00 p.m. BDS was trading as Cosmopolitan Homes Ltd, a new company with new directors. All the staff were working as normal on their customary low wages and with the usual warnings of dismissal if they contemplated joining a trade union – nothing had changed.

During the afternoon, the caretaker discovered from one of the older hands that this was not the first time this had happened. A similar exercise had taken place 5 years previously and some 20 staff had lost their jobs. Then the company had been called Grosvenor Windows Ltd, but the management – as in the current change of company – had stayed the same throughout. The caretaker suddenly understood why it was often difficult to get supplies and why different workers were sent considerable distances to open new accounts.

REFERENCES

Burgoyne, J.G. (1988) 'Management development for the individual and the organization', *Personnel Management*, June, 40–44.

Morgan, G. (1986) *Images of Organization*, Sage, London.

9. Participative Policy Making
No. 2. of the 11 Characteristics of the Learning Company

This characteristic means that more, rather than less, people are involved in the policy or strategy-making process. It suggests that where all members of the company (including, where possible, stakeholders such as suppliers, customers and business partners) have a chance to contribute to and debate major policy decisions, then these will be better decisions.

This is based on three observations:

- First, compared with Western firms, it is suggested that in Japanese firms new organizational moves are discussed across the company, in greater depth, for as long as seems necessary for all to understand. Obviously this takes longer than having policy set by a small, élite group, but it helps consensus to emerge. The argument is that what you lose on the discussion, you gain on the implementation – not least because all sorts of small snags have been spotted and dealt with.
- Second, change is 'smoothed' in as much as the more people who are involved in looking at the proposed move and its implications for their areas of work, the more they are likely to be preparing plans for implementing it, should it become policy.
- Third, with participation there is more commitment, ownership and willingness to go along with the plan.

An illustration of Participative Policy Making in practice is from a book by Womack et. al. (1990) which suggests that Toyota can get a car from concept to showroom in five or six years compared to General Motors' seven or eight. Despite this Toyota actually spends more time planning – GM rushes the planning and sorts the teething troubles on the line; Toyota are more likely to be right first time.

Another illustration is the Brazilian company SEMCO.

SEMCO
Semco's vision of the Learning Company operates on the three principles of participation – or the increased involvement of people, a fair share of rewards and a free flow of information. Each of these requires the other two – participation is only possible with full information; full information means that the sharing of rewards has to be fair and *seen* to be fair; and fair shares is central to the company's way of employee self-management and motivation.

A Brazilian machinery manufacturer, this unusual company believes that size and hierarchy are the main enemies of Participative Policy Making so they have no plant with more than 150 employees. There is also a maximum of three layers of management, because Ricardo Semler (and his father who founded the company) believes that managers and management often end up blocking what they are there in theory to facilitate. Actually Semco has no 'managers' – the three levels being called 'counsellors', 'partners' and 'coordinators' – and all employees are 'associates'.

The company tries to treat everyone as responsible adults, believing that clear information about how the organization is doing will lead to the best results for the company. As Semler puts it:

> That's all there is to it. Participation gives people control of their work, profit-sharing gives them a reason to do it better, information tells them what's working and what isn't. ... We are very, very rigorous about numbers. ... We want them in on the fourth day of the month so that we can have them back by the fifth. And because we're so strict with the financial controls, we can be lax about everything else. Employees can paint the walls any colour they like.

FOLLOW UP
Semler, R. (1993) *Maverick!* Century, New York.

Obviously Semco has some very clear principles for operating as a company. These stem from the founder but have been developed by his son and other people in the company. Over time, the original beliefs of the Austrian exile Curt Semler, were modified with experience. Yet there were the not uncommon tensions between father and son, founder and successor. Ricardo Semler saw his father as very traditional and paternalistic and set out to change the company radically. Even so some of the old values remain. As new people join the company, they add something of their own ideas.

In this way the company builds up a set of collective values that underlie the more visible ways in which things are done.

LEARNING COMPANY VALUES

Rather as you'd find in the 'excellent' company or the 'quality' company, values are at the centre of the Learning Company. Because of the need to adapt and change intelligently and to be consciously developing as a whole organism, the Learning Company does not put its faith in enduring structures and processes but sees these as temporary. Values are more enduring and though changing over time do so rather more slowly. One of the key tasks is to try to embrace the values of all its members, who all wish to be valued.

This is a tough one. However, a useful start can be made with this simple activity that can be done with small and large groups of people, although larger groups will require a more sophisticated data gathering and analysis process than that described here.

- Begin by suggesting that a certain agreed set of values is central to the idea of the Learning Company and that the purpose of this activity is to determine what these values might be for this company.
- In pairs or small groups, members answer the question: 'What values would a Learning Company hold to be of central importance?' Each person should take a little time to think for themselves first before discussing their list.
- Lists are taken from pairs or small groups and collated centrally. A flipchart will suffice for a smallish number of people. For larger groups or whole companies, polling and computer analysis may be useful. As an example, here is a recent list from a group of 23 people:

  experimentation
  learning
  participation
  creativity
  feminine
  differences
  development
  self-control
  self-management
  information
  feedback
  equality
  collaboration
  contingency
  win:win
  freedom
  listening
  celebration
  self-denial
- How are these values displayed in what we do: in our mission statement, in the way we manage, in the way we treat customers, and so on?

The information generated from this activity can be used to review all aspects of company functioning as well as providing the most solid ground available for deciding what structures and procedures to establish.

Valuing differences

To enquire into values in this way is to find that there are important differences between people. In the case of 'first generation' enterprises like Semco, these will often be found between father and son, traditionalists and radicals. But there are many other dimensions on which the members of a company will differ. While the organization's product, processes and output are simple and uniform, these differences tend to be ignored; but as service differentiation, user-friendliness and quality become crucial, they matter more.

Glimpse 10   **DEVELOPING DIFFERENCES**

All learning proceeds from differences. When we notice what is different from what we expected, there is the learning opportunity. Science progresses via hypothesis, experiment and observation – new ideas come from the differences between what was expected and what was actually found. In everyday life we proceed on the same basis of assumptions about what will happen if I do this or that. Often we are annoyed if our hypotheses are disproved – 'something went wrong!' This judgement can stop learning.

In companies there are other barriers to learning. For example, they are political entities in that people hold different views and often seek to influence others to adopt their way of thinking. This process can inhibit open expression of differences and the proper debate of issues that might lead to learning. The Learning Company finds ways of becoming aware of differences – perhaps between women and men, old and young, black and white, northerners and southerners and so on – in order to give people permission to be different, and to learn from these differences within the company.

Surfacing and discussing differences means accepting and dealing with the underlying conflict. As Richard Pascale (1991) has pointed out, significant learning is often accompanied by the energy and heat of such questioning, debate and conflict. Here's a simple activity for developing differences within a group or company.

- Becoming aware. List all the differences between people in the room in relation to, say, company business strategy. Some of these differences might be:
  - product orientation versus service/customer orientation
  - like to be told what to do versus like to be their own boss
  - women versus men
  - wants new job versus happy with existing job
  - wants more responsibility versus wants less responsibility
  - feels listened to versus doesn't feel listened to
  - thinks all should be involved in strategy forming versus best left to 'top management'
  - happy with existing skills/knowledge versus would like to learn new skills
  - expression of conflict causes more harm than good versus conflict is a rich source of learning.
- Choose a suitable difference to debate, set a fixed time and elect a referee. Encourage people to take a position on this difference by, say, getting people to

negotiate their positions on a line across the room or asking people to form groups on the basis of their basic position (A or B or 'It all depends').
- Debate the difference and its impact on, in this case, business strategy. What differences are not being taken into account? Whose interest does the present strategy serve? How could it be improved? What opportunities are we missing?
- After the debate, make sure all participants have an opportunity to debrief in smaller groups. Learning from differences can be a stressful process that may start things off in people which cannot be dealt with in the debating chamber. Counselling facilities could also be available to those who take part. These facilities may be especially useful where people are not used to expressing different opinions and experiencing the strong and complicated emotions that these give rise to. This is something that becomes more familiar, if not easier, with practice.

The Learning Company is not created without deep questioning and the inevitable accompanying conflict. Differences are essential to transformation – becoming aware, debating, learning and deciding are part of this process. These are new skills for many company members and finding the structures to open up yet contain differences is a key part of the art.

FOLLOW UP
Pascale, R.T. (1991) *Managing on the Edge*, Penguin, Harmondsworth.

Embracing diversity

Diversity is important in the Learning Company, not least because, in the cause of encouraging learning and of harvesting the contribution of each member, it is the differences between us in our thinking, outlook, talents, skills and actions that is increasingly the potential source of advantage for the organization as a whole.

Diversity owes its current popularity as an idea to 'complexity theory' – an effort by physicists and other scientists to divine order in a seemingly chaotic cosmos. Complexity is about a new way of thinking about the *collective* behaviour of many small interacting units such as atoms, whose joint 'behaviour' over time can be seen to form certain emergent patterns. As a painting is made up of many brushstrokes, none of which makes sense on its own, these patterns do not appear at the level of the individual unit and analysis at this level is meaningless.

By analogy this idea can also be applied to people. Human resource management practices, for example, isolate us as individuals and habitually treat us as single units for the purposes of selection, recruitment, testing, training, appraisal, payment and retirement (Townley, 1993). To what extent does trying to understand us in this way at the individual level make sense?

Glimpse 11

WORKING WITH DIVERSITY

Diversity is one of the most vital aspects of the Learning Company. How a company manages to work with the diversity it has is one of the keys to learning and productivity. For many years companies have tried to suppress diversity, preferring sameness and uniformity because this is easier to manage. Acknowledging diversity or differences can lead to loss of control, which is something we always fear when we are in charge of something.

How can we not only recognize and acknowledge diversity, but positively use the differences between us to create power in the Learning Company? The whole cannot be enhanced without first splitting; division is needed before greater synthesis and synergy can be brought about; learning begins in difference – between me and you, between what I expected and what happened, between what is and what could be.

We all need practice in working with the potentially explosive diversity of ourselves. While suppressing differences is one way of avoiding an explosion, it is not the learning way. Organizations have to create within themselves a vessel strong enough to survive the occasional explosion so that learning, not just to acknowledge but to celebrate and capitalize on diversity, can take place.

Here is a simple but powerful activity for a group of people of any size that will need skilled facilitation.

- Elicit from a group of people the key differences that they see among them. List these. Obvious examples might be:

women and men	over 40 and under 40
Asian and white	part-time and full-time workers
engineering and others	administrative and others
managers and others	

- Choose a dimension of difference and ask the group concerned to split along these lines and stand in a different part of the room. (This activity can also be done remotely with a whole company by questionnaire and feedback means if a state of readiness exists – rather like postal chess.) In each of the two groups, separate into pairs. In each of the pairs complete these three sentences with your partner:

  What's important to me about being a _____ , is ....

  As a _____ I bring to this company ....

  The extent to which this company empowers me to live out and make use of my potential as a _____ is ....

- When each person has completed these in their pair, form a plenary session in each of the two groups and summarize the responses to the three sentences as briefly but as fully as possible.
- In the middle of the room, each group reads out its collective responses to the other, who listen in silence.
- Now split along another difference and repeat the last three steps as before. Continue until three or four major aspects of diversity have been explored.

This can be a powerful and rewarding activity. It is also capable of being adapted in various ways, including the whole company vision suggested above. You will need to judge for yourself what level of diversity and difference your company is ready to deal with and, indeed, whether this potent avenue of learning and development is open or whether you have to keep the lid firmly on at this time. There is a spectrum of developmental responses to diversity that starts with recognition (in many companies differences between the way, say, men and women are treated simply go unnoticed, they are invisible to most) and moves through acceptance to valuing this difference:

Spectrum of developmental responses to diversity

0	1	2	3	4	5
Unnoticed	Recognize	Become aware	Tolerate/ accept	Respect	Value

Managing conflict

Participative Policy Making is one of the most difficult challenges for the Learning Company to pick up, because it creates problems for simple authority structures and for those who – for whatever reason – want to concentrate power, hang on to it and limit the number of forms of power regarded as legitimate in the company.

Encouraging differences and diversity is simply bound to cause 'trouble' and lead to conflict. As managers we are naturally going to try to avoid this at all costs. And yet, in this respect, the Learning Company is counter-intuitive. Trouble – conflict, questions, disagreements, alternative suggestions – as well as being something we want to keep in check, is also an important source of learning.

LEARNING FROM CONFLICT

Glimpse 12

Many managerial problems turn out to be messy and poorly defined. It is sometimes hard to tell the problem from the symptoms or to pick out the relevant information from the vast mass available. Matters seem to be full of contradictions and paradoxes. There are different values among members that lead to political and emotional clashes.

The stresses of managing ambiguity are enormous. In such situations we are tempted to go for quick fixes or to contain the conflict and mess in some way – if only for the sake of our own health. Learning Companies have to do better than this. Conflict is stressful but it is also a source of creativity, of testing old ideas and generating new ones. An organization that structures out conflict will also cut out challenge, risk, creativity and learning.

Michael McCaskey (1988) describes a way of using three groups taken from the organization to conduct a dialectic in order to try to get the benefits of conflict without the destruction:

- Three groups, A, B and C, are set up to tackle an agreed problem area. The most senior person is put into group C.
- Group A goes off and develops an analysis and a plan for action on the problem using any agreed method.
- A's list of key assumptions is then turned over to group B that has the job of preparing counter-assumptions and an antithesis to A's plan.
- Next, group C facilitates a structured debate. A and B take turns to give spirited presentations, outlining their assumptions and the key data that they consider of importance. Each then probes the weaknesses in each other's plans using wit and humour as well as logic and analysis. A sense of the dramatic is helpful here. The facilitator(s) must work to balance combativeness with goodwill and prevent personal attacks. The rest of group C note significant points and omissions.
- Once the arguments begin to be repeated, the facilitator ends the debate and calls a break for members to socialize and re-connect at a personal level.
- Then the whole conference, led by members of group C, generates a list of agreed assumptions, a set of key data and a plan for action.

This harnessing of the dialectic can lead to a constructive use of conflict. It can bring to the surface existing differences, tensions and values. The clash of views can create something new – a third position from the opposing two – that may contain aspects of both together with higher validity or acceptability than either. It is a good way to test a plan and a method for involving more people and more parts of the organization in policy making.

FOLLOW UP
McCaskey, M. (1988) 'The challenge of managing ambiguity and change' in Pondy, Boland and Thomas (eds), *Managing Ambiguity and Change*, Wiley, Chichester.

Conflict and transformation

Encouraging and facilitating these outward expressions of difference and conflict can lead to big changes which literally transform the enterprise. Continuous improvement is now an everyday activity for many organizations, but it cannot lead to those major shifts that are important from time to time to jump into a new way of operation. This sort of major change often becomes necessary when the company is facing a crisis – as was the case at Semco – and also at Billiton Metals.

Glimpse 13

TRANSFORMATION AT BILLITON METALS
Unlike problem solving or trouble shooting, organizational transformation means that *everyone* changes the way they do things. Transformation poses the questions: 'Why are we in business?' and 'What is our purpose together?'

The process of asking these questions is likely to be unsettling, exciting, disturbing, energizing and disruptive. Such questions, if really asked in the company, cannot be answered by superficial changes of the 'redesign the logos and the letterheads' variety. Transformation in individuals and companies requires space, time and proper support. It does not happen overnight, nor without the necessary thinking through before, during and after, nor without the necessary skills of supporting, challenging and developing. Here is an example of transformation in practice.

Billiton, a Shell subsidiary and an international metals company with a turnover of $1.5bn had accumulated losses of $750m and was being considered for disposal by its multi-national parent. A new CEO decided that one last chance was possible.

He ordered a rigorous analysis of 'the businesses we are in and why we are in them'. Product divisions were replaced by 'core businesses' and power was devolved from head office to operating companies. Head office would lose half its establishment and change its role from 'command centre' to 'service provider' to the operating companies and 'monitor/auditor' for the shareholders.

Top-down prescription of the detailed way of working in head office was resisted and left to emerge from a planned consultation process. Over 18 months this programme included:

- attitude surveys of all 250 head office staff at six-month intervals (the first showed that people saw themselves in a tense and stressful situation)
- departmental work groups set up after the first survey to consider local needs and whole company issues – initially this took 30 per cent of staff time
- a multi-disciplinary task force to coordinate the work groups and the management team, supported by consultants
- specific consultancy skills were deployed to individuals and departments who asked for them; a full advisory and counselling service was offered to those who were to leave or who might opt to do so
- the second and third surveys gave progress reports, identifying positive changes and continuing concerns; training, team-building and other resource inputs were based on this data.

The results for the business were good: return on capital went from 2 per cent to 17 per cent over two years and the second year showed a profit after tax of $262m. For individuals it had often been traumatic, although group and team work meant difficulties could be shared. The managing team, who had remained throughout, felt they had changed significantly – personally and in the way they did business together.

Nietzsche's dramatic, 'that which does not kill me makes me strong' is worth pondering for those contemplating transformation. Change of this type, whether personally or organizationally cannot be done without upheaval on such a scale that many of us will require support and help to come through it. When and if we do come through, however, we are likely to be strengthened, fitter and perhaps wiser.

FOLLOW UP
Benjamin, G. and Mabey, C. (1990) 'Organizational transformation and the self', *Management Education and Development*, **21**(5), 327–334.

But do we have to wait for a crisis before we can enlist the services of the great variety of people in the company, with their different values and questioning insight? Some companies seem to lurch from crisis to crisis – like the drunk in the hospital corridor, stumbling and hitting each wall, somehow making an unsteady progress – as the only way they know to change.

Whole Systems Development is an idea for a specific process of Participative Policy Making which creates policy and plans through bringing the whole diversity of the organization together into the same 'room'.

Glimpse 14

WHOLE SYSTEMS DEVELOPMENT (See also Chapter 23.)

Participative Policy Making means getting more rather than fewer people involved in discussing and deciding on the goals, strategies, policies and procedures of the organization. One of the excuses for not extending policy making beyond the 'big boys' at the top is that of practicality – how do you involve everyone in making decisions?

This is a good question and one that is addressed by the idea of Whole Systems Development. Grown out of 'search conferencing' originated by Fred Emery as a methodology for collaborative ecological planning, this is a process for searching possible futures and generating desirable strategies for action. In 'social island' conditions – that is isolated away from work and home – search conferences proceed by a mixture of plenary and small, task group sessions.

Working with future, past and present, with the present always dealt with last, the search conference 'is an expression of participatory democracy, and seeks to lead individuals and groups in the direction of greater purposefulness and enhanced self-management' (Crombie, 1985). Search conferences or Whole Systems Development can operate in big groups – Herbst (1978) gives an example from northern Norway where a community of 3600 people sent representatives to a three-day conference to decide on plans for the future of the community. More recently, Weisbord (1992; 1995) has caught the imagination of many with his 'Future Search' conferences.

A hotel chain held a two-day conference with 300 people representing its 2700 employees and key stakeholders. The theme was 'Attracting, keeping and developing our people'. Groups of people are invited to represent the main stakeholders in the organizational community, in this case, for example:

- owners and managers
- customers, individual and corporate
- staff group from small hotels
- catering and housekeeping staff
- community representatives, e.g. suppliers, local government planners and economic development officers, school careers staff
- new staff joining within the last six months.

The two days, held in a university hall of residence, are chaired and facilitated by two consultants responsible for the structure but not the content of the sessions. The conference moves in two directions:

- divergent – identifying the range of desired goals and present problems

- convergent – clarifying and prioritizing problems and seeking lines of collaborative action.

On Day 1, after a statement of current policies and aspirations from the Leadership Team including several members of the Board, people work in homogeneous groups on the questions: 'What major changes have taken place in the company from the past until the present?' and 'Are these positive or negative?' Following a plenary before lunch to collect the data generated so far, they look next at the questions 'What changes do you expect in the future?' and 'Are these positive or negative?'

On Day 2, in heterogeneous groups – the representative groups now being mixed – people work on clarifying problems; then meet in plenary to negotiate an agreed list of priorities with the Leadership Team. In the plenary session it is clear that there are disagreements about priorities and a critical stage is reached when the Leadership Team acknowledges their intention to accept the decision of the conference. After this climax people return to the small mixed groups to prepare strategies of practical action for each of the chosen problems.

A final plenary session agrees several proposals for action and refers two that involve considerable expense to the board of directors. The personnel director gets the job of establishing task forces to be responsible for planning and executing the agreed changes.

Also, most importantly, the conference decides on what and how to report back to the other members of the organization. Apart from the agreed list of actions, it is agreed that one person in each of the groups will write ten lines on their personal experience of the search conference and that one of the consultants will include these in a short account of the conference's purposes, methods of working and results to be published in the company newspaper.

Whole Systems Development works on the basis of two important principles – 'getting the whole organization into the room together', which requires that the full diversity and complexity of the organization is represented, and 'public learning' in which everyone, especially the formal leaders of the organization, is subjected to feedback and questioning, and commitments to changed direction are publicly acknowledged.

FOLLOW UP

Crombie, A. (1985) 'The nature and types of Search Conferences', *International Journal of Life-long Education*, **4**(1), 3–33.

Herbst, P.G. (1978) *Community Conference Design: Skjervoy Yesterday, Today and Tomorrow*, Work Research Institute, Oslo.

Wilkinson, D. and Pedler, M. (1996) 'Whole Systems Development in public service', *Journal of Management Development*, **15**(2), 38–53.

Weisbord, M.R. (1992) *Discovering Common Ground: How Future Search Conferences Bring People Together to Achieve Breakthrough, Innovation, Empowerment, Shared Vision and Collaborative Action*, Berrett-Koehler, San Francisco.

Weisbord, M.R. and Janoff, S. (1995) *Future Search*, Berrett-Koehler, San Francisco.

Stakeholder diversity

Whole Systems Development is a way of involving all the people in the company and also for including important stakeholders. Companies can be seen as relatively 'self-centred' or 'other-centred' (Pedler and Aspinwall, 1996, pp.4–5) depending upon how ambitious they are in seeking to satisfy the purposes of all stakeholders. Some organizations exist largely for the benefit of their owners; others seek to address the needs of an ever-widening ring of those who have a stake or who are affected by the company's activities.

Glimpse 15

THE GOOD COMPANY?

Is a Learning Company a good company? When Peters and Waterman (1982) produced a list of 'excellent' companies, they were criticized among other things for using financial performance or profit as the sole criterion of 'excellence'. By this definition, it doesn't count if a company pays low wages and provides poor working conditions for employees; it doesn't matter whether its operations damage the environment or that it uses its buying power to force its suppliers' prices down in poor countries. In fact, on financial performance alone, doing these things would make it an even more 'excellent' company.

We know that many of our best-known firms engage in business practices that they would rather we didn't know about. It seems increasingly commonplace for companies to be involved in supplying arms or essential supplies to regimes with bad human rights records. Companies making cigarettes, alcohol, pharmaceuticals, nuclear power and so on not only turn a blind eye to research findings for years, but also actively seek to have the research stopped or, at the very least, to overcome such findings by heavy counter-advertising.

'That's business' we say. For some people 'business' and ethical values belong to different worlds. Yet businesses exert enormous influence over the shape of our lives and of our social and natural environments:

> Whether we do well, whether we like ourselves, whether we lead happy and productive lives, depends to a large extent on the companies we choose. (Solomon, 1993, p.148)

John Morris has suggested that a company really committed to quality is continuously striving for a better service for all stakeholders – to customers, in terms of working life for employees, of investment to shareholders and of being a good neighbour and citizen in the wider community (1987, pp.103–115). This means developing a method for 'Social Accounting' – auditing the impact of the company on all stakeholders, however remote. An increasing number of companies are taking this route, for example, Traidcraft in the UK and Tom's of Maine in the USA (Pedler and Aspinwall, 1996, Ch. 8).

So, is a Learning Company automatically a good company? Almost certainly not. A company could be well aware of its learning processes and leveraging a good return from them and yet still be pursuing narrow and 'selfish' ends. A good company is one that strives to be aware of all its possible stakeholders and their needs and to balance these against its own needs to survive and develop.

Where would you place your company on the grid in Figure G15.1?

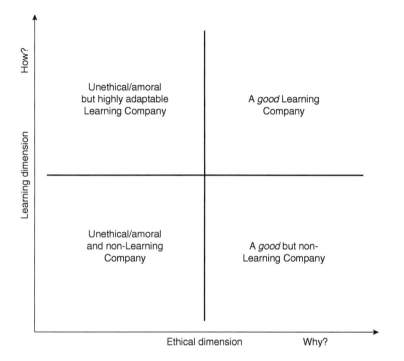

Figure G15.1 Finding out where a company stands on ethical and learning fronts

FOLLOW UP

Morris, J. (1987) 'Good company', *Management Education and Development*, **18**(2), 103–115.
Pedler, M.J. and Aspinwall, K.A. (1996) *'Perfect plc?': The Purpose and Practice of Organizational Learning*, McGraw-Hill, Maidenhead.
Peters, T.J. and Waterman, R.H. (1982) *In Search of Excellence*, Harper & Row, New York.
Solomon, R. (1993) *Ethics and Excellence: Cooperation and Integrity in Business*, Oxford University Press, Oxford.

REFERENCES

Pedler, M.J. and Aspinwall, K.A. (1996) *'Perfect plc?': The Purpose and Practice of Organizational Learning*, McGraw-Hill, Maidenhead.
Townley, B. (1993) 'Foucault, Power/Knowledge and its Relevance for Human Resource Management', *Academy of Management Review*, **18**(2) 518–545.
Womack, J.P., Jones, D.T. and Roos, D. (1990) *The Machine that Changed the World*, Rawson Associates/Macmillan, New York.

10. Informating
No. 3 of the 11 Characteristics of the Learning Company

Information technology (IT) is used here to aid the free flow of information and to inform and empower all members of the company to ask questions and take decisions based on available data. There is a contrast with *automating* where IT is used to take human intelligence out of a process and perhaps to disempower people. Informating systems:

- provide people with access to all relevant information held by the company to speed action
- create 'public domain' databases which speeds information flow to the point in the organization – often the front line worker relating to the customer – where it is needed
- are designed to encourage learning, are user-friendly, interesting and, preferably, fun to use.

British Airways told us in one of our data-gathering sessions that they would rather sell their aeroplanes than their computer system, because while you can always lease a plane, the computer system is at the heart of the business. With its tentacles, like the roots of a tree, reaching out to all travel agents, it sucks in business; on the operations side (the branches and twigs) it reaches out and coordinates the flights, planes, aircrews, catering and so on.

There are many other organizations that are increasingly structured around their information systems, which are tending to replace middle managers. Informating supports Participative Policy Making by making the company transparent. A romantic view sees working in the informated organization as being like a live business game – where people tap into corporate data, make sense of it and analyse it, have a view of what is going on and what should happen. This is sometimes how Consulting Engineer Helen James sees it.

WORKING IN THE ELECTRONIC LEARNING NET

Computer Mediated Communications Systems (CMCS) exploit the storage, processing and retrieval capabilities of the company mainframe for internal and external communications. Database, texts, articles, reports, manuals, directories and so on can be held for quick and easy access by members. Communications software including e-mail, bulletin boards and conferencing allows for interaction between members both person-to-person and among dispersed groups. CMCS provides an electronic learning environment where all members have equal access to data and are able to communicate freely.

Any member can take part and all the company PCs are networked through the mainframe with relevant external systems. Thus remote access to national and international knowledge networks are available within the company at any time. CMCS is increasingly being used to deliver all kinds of education and training programmes in which users typically report higher levels of interest, involvement and personal control than with conventional delivery methods. CMCS also provide for the distributed knowledge networks that are at the heart of up-to-date professional practice, known as Executive Information Systems (EIS), as well as providing groupware such as Lotus Notes for on-line conferencing and project work.

Helen James works for a large international firm of consulting engineers as an internal management adviser. She is currently involved with an important project team that is advising on the building of an integrated steel plant in Belarus.

As part of her work with the project team Helen puts out regular progress reports of the project on the internal network bulletin board. On arriving at work on Monday she finds various e-mail items delivered over the weekend. One is from a manager in new product development asking for details of the project planning methods being used. Another is a request from an engineer for a short attachment for personal learning purposes with the project team. Helen prints these off to present to her project team meeting later in the week.

Helen also belongs to a professional association and has been taking part in an on-line seminar on new organizational structures. This morning she logs into the seminar and finds that since she last took part several members have been exchanging ideas about temporary structures and 'opportunity structures'. After scanning the summaries, she downloads the full texts for later study. Meanwhile she makes some notes and prepares some questions to add to the discussion section of the conference later on. She then logs into the Papernet held by her association to see whether there are any items relevant to the steel plant project. She notes the names and numbers of two members offering papers on project management and cross-cultural issues to follow up later. Finally, before going to her 10.00 a.m. meeting she sends travel warrant requests and last month's expenses through to the relevant section via e-mail.

Returning some two hours later, Helen deals with a query about her travel requirements before logging on again and instructing her PC to send the previously noted comments to the Organizational Structures Conference and to send requests for the Papernet offerings. She has also received an invitation from Vienna to contribute to an electronic journal on managing in a unified Europe that addresses comparisons and contrasts between Western and Eastern approaches. She makes notes in her computer diary to remind her to clear some papers on the Belarus project with the project team before offering them to the journal.

FOLLOW UP

McConnell, D. and Hodgson, V. (1990) 'Computer Mediated Communications Systems (CMCS) electronic networking and education', *Management Education and Development*, **21**(1), Spring.

Orlikowski, W.J. (1992) 'Learning from Notes; Organizational issues in groupware implementation', CSCW 92 Proceedings, Sloan School of Management, MIT, Cambridge, MA.

Knowledge versus authority?

There is much excitement over the potential for applications of information technology. One obvious impact can be on the speed of response of the informated organization. However, there are many barriers to be overcome in benefiting from this apparent potential. Some of these are to do with cost, technical difficulties and 'technophobia', others are less visible, more subversive. For example, knowledge and authority are on a collision course in the informated organization.

Glimpse 17

THE INFORMATED MANUFACTURING COMPANY

Shoshana Zuboff (1988) gives us the word 'informating' and recognizes the profound possibilities of information technology as applied to work processes. Her thesis is that IT has often been used to automate, whereas companies concerned to increase learning must informate. Automating strategies are designed to take the skill and intelligence out of processes, designing managerially controlled, closed-loop systems designed to minimize costs; informating strategies provide knowledge to operators in order that they can learn from feedback about their actions, and go on to improve the production process.

Informating encourages people to reflect critically on their actions and to question what goes on around them – qualities essential to learning. According to Zuboff, where conditions place a premium on innovation and learning companies are most likely to choose an informating approach. These conditions include:

- market conditions, here there is a need for responsiveness, flexibilty and continuous improvement
- competitive conditions, which offer opportunities for value-added products or services
- wide variations in customer or user needs
- short production cycles
- variability in raw materials
- interdependence among production operations
- interdependence between production operations and other business functions
- 'unknowns' in core production processes

- opportunities for increased quality or decreased costs of services
- the need to develop and maintain a highly committed and motivated workforce.

Where these conditions are not seen to apply, companies are more likely to automate rather than informate (Zuboff, 1988, p.305). Informating is, however, highly subversive to traditional forms of managerial control – where people are encouraged to ask questions, other changes follow, as a corporate vice-president at American Paper Company notes, reflecting on the emerging manufacturing environment:

> Traditionally we have thought that such data can only be managed by certain people with certain accountabilities and, I hesitate to say, endowed with certain skills or capabilities. But with the new technology it seems there is an almost inevitable kind of development if you have as a goal maximizing all business variables and maximizing the entire organization's ability to contribute to that effort. I don't think you can choose not to distribute information and authority in a new way if you want to achieve that. If you do, you will give up an important component of being competitive. (Zuboff, 1988, p.289)

FOLLOW UP
Zuboff, S. (1988) *In the Age of the Smart Machine: The Future of Work and Power*, Basic Books, New York.

Despite the difficulties there seems to be little doubt that the search to gain advantage or to keep up with user requirements, means that most organizations will be seeking to use information technology to increase learning processes within and without the company. There is much hype about the current IT 'revolution' and many suggestions that it is likely to lead to major shifts in the way we see ourselves and in the way we organize, much in the way that Caxton's printing press is credited with bringing about the development of the modern era in Europe.

Currently we are struggling with the technology and its implications, but it seems clear that this is a phase in the development of the possibilities. In discussions with several companies involved in the Learning Company Project's Consortium on Enhancing Company Learning through Information Technology, Chris Blantern (1995) reports the following typical comments:

- 'we know networked IT and groupware are going to be very important but how can we use them to build learning companies?'
- 'we've got the technology but we're not making the best use of it for our collective learning – I'm sure there's more we could be doing'
- 'we simply need to increase the flow of information exchange around the organization which shouldn't be constrained by the structure of our existing systems'
- 'we want an arena where we can readily share our individual and collective learning in a "no-fuss" way'

- 'we need instant and continuous feedback about how, as well as what, our company is learning'
- 'I want to find a way of getting people to contribute who are currently not doing so'
- 'We heard about an experimental project which we are thinking of repeating in our organization. If we could "informate" that – that is make it available to everyone and get them to participate in some way, it would be a real breakthrough'.

ABB is perhaps a forerunner of the new type of organization that will take these sort of applications of information technology for granted.

Glimpse 18

ABB – A NETWORKED LEARNING ORGANIZATION?

The Swedish–Swiss electrical engineering multi-national ABB was created in 1987 to transform two national institutions into a new kind of organization that could operate successfully in world markets.

With over 200 000 people across the world, ABB set out to decentralize radically while still operating globally. Recognizing that most people's commitment was to their local company, ABB made each of its 1200 local companies a separate legal and trading entity, and further subdivided these companies into 4500 profit centres – each with an average of only 45 people.

Like the much smaller Semco, at ABB strong, centralized reporting goes hand in hand with local autonomy. Various powerful structures and processes link the network; 'Global Networking Hubs' of managers operate on two foci – by business area and country. A rigorous, monthly reporting system 'Abacus' provides performance data on all profit centres, which is instantly communicated via electronic data interchange. Huge efforts are made to communicate via overlapping information systems.

One of the core values is to promote the continuous exchange of learning and each unit is expected both to learn from elsewhere in the group and to make contributions to the learning of other companies. Benchmarking within business areas is easy because of the widely available reporting data and it is an important job for both Business Area leaders and country CEOs to facilitate learning between units and companies.

Another core value is to try and minimize cultural barriers. The ABB CEO Percy Barnevik notes that European managers in particular tend to be selective about sharing information and there is clearly plenty of work to be done in combating such habits where these conflict with the vision of the company to speed and facilitate communication and to learn.

FOLLOW UP
Taylor, W. (1991) 'The logic of global business: An interview with ABB's Percy Barnevik', *Harvard Business Review*, March–April, pp.92–105.

We *may* soon take the current possibilities of informating for granted, but there is still plenty that can go wrong, even where information technology is being well used:

SOCK ON THE WRONG FOOT?

Thanks to information technology, the Sock Shop is reputedly able to inspect the day's trading figures from all its branches two hours after the close of business. Visions of lorry loads of socks being despatched to snow-bound areas? But Sock Shop, along with other niche marketeers, got into financial troubles through a combination of rapid growth, high rental outlets and a fall in impulse purchasing with the downturn in disposable income.

With the 20 : 20 vision of hindsight, what kind of management information system might help to anticipate these sorts of trends and identify appropriate courses of action to avert disaster?

Clearly one that looks outside as well as in – but it's easy to be wise after the event. One way in which IT can contribute to learning in the organization is to add value to existing processes. Linking individual and collective learning is a critical task in ensuring that each person's learning is made available to all, and that each person can draw upon the accumulated wisdom of everyone in dealing with the problems and tasks facing them. How can IT help with this? Can it help harmonize the cyclical processes of learning and business?

PERSONAL AND COMPANY LEARNING CYCLES

It is interesting to note how many processes in organizations are described in cycles.

- The learning cycle (Kolb, 1984) of concrete experience, reflective observation, abstract conceptualization and active experimentation.
- The task performance cycle – aim, plan, do and review.
- The training cycle of identifying needs, designs, deliver and evaluate.
- The appraisal or performance review cycle – agree targets, perform, appraise and reset targets.
- Budgeting and operational planning cycles of plan/forecast, perform, monitor, review and re-plan.
- The strategic planning cycle of collect data, review situation, consider options, choose direction, direct operations, monitor and re-direct.

These cycles can be represented as circles as shown in Figure G20.1.

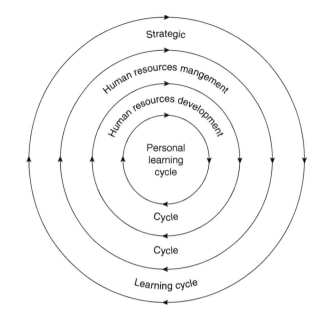

Figure G20.1 Personal and company learning cycles

One way of thinking about the Learning Company is to see it as one in which all these cycles work in harmony. In highly competitive, 'war machine'-type organizations, there is often a good deal of alignment but not much attunement. In many companies these cycles may be working independently of one another and they may even be working against each other.

FOLLOW UP
Kolb, D.A. (1984) *Experiential Learning*, Prentice-Hall, New York.

Harmonizing these cycles offers a role to the human resources department, previously criticized for focusing entirely on the individual as the unit of analysis and not upon the collective company.

Glimpse 21

THE COMPANY CLUTCH PLATE
In Glimpse 20 we described some common cycles in corporate life and remarked on the great similarity between them. A Learning Company might be one in which these cycles are sensitively attuned with one another as well as appropriately aligned.

Here is a possible 'conductor' role for the human resources development people – to orchestrate these cycles, individually and severally, to bring the company in tune, performing at its best.

Looked at this way, human resource development can occupy a strategic role, mediating between personal and organizational processes, linking them and acting as 'the company clutch plate' (Figure G21.1) in bringing the energy and direction of the two kinds of processes into alignment with one another and to the point when they are properly attuned. Without the strategic clutch, the cycles of individual learning and performance are unconnected with the cycles of strategic planning and operations management with a consequent massive loss of potential and power.

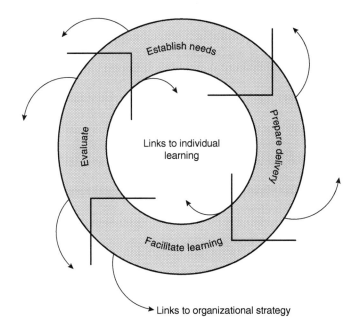

Figure G21.1 The company clutch plate.

REFERENCE

Blantern, C. (1995) 'The Learning Organization and the Emerging Contribution of Computer Networks', *Learning Company Project*, Sheffield.

11. Formative Accounting and Control
No. 4 of the 11 Characteristics of the Learning Company

With Formative Accounting and Control the essential control systems of accounting budgeting and reporting are structured to assist learning from the consequences of managerial decisions. These systems promote self-control by encouraging individuals and units to act as small autonomous businesses within a regulated environment. The emphasis is upon auditing, controlling and accounting for one's own actions.

While this may sound simple, it requires a huge shift in perspective for many of the people who currently run the accounting systems of our big organizations. It means that these people ask themselves the question: 'Who are the customers for this system and what do they want?'

Many people make rather rude jokes about accountants. One of the politer ones is that when accountants are in charge of the business it is like playing in a cricket match in which you don't know the score until the end of the game! People are keeping the score but they don't tell you what it is until the game is over. Producing the year-end results is important for audit purposes but what we need is the equivalent of the 'ball-by-ball commentary'. We need up-to-the-minute information about the financial situation of the company and of the potential consequences of our actions in order to make judgements and decisions.

An illustration of Formative Accounting and Control comes from a double glazing company Mercian Windows which has country-wide branches and a tight central financial control system. After realizing that the branch managers did not understand how money was used in the company, the finance director organized a 'roadshow'.

ACCOUNTING ROADSHOWS AT MERCIAN WINDOWS

Glimpse 22

After a series of customer care programmes, and following several requests, the finance department at Mercian Windows set up a 'roadshow'. This was designed to go at fairly short notice to any of the 38 branch offices of the company.

As an operationally decentralized but financially centralized organization, Mercian Windows needed to ensure that branch management teams understood the way money worked in the business in order to make better deals with customers without the need to refer back continually to head office for permission. In particular, the company wanted to encourage its branch management to take appropriate risks.

The roadshow consists of the branch accountant from head office, the factory accountant, the internal auditor and an attached management trainee. It includes a video, some short presentations, self-development activities, designed to illustrate the workings of the money system, and opportunities for personal one-to-one or small group coaching to work through specific issues. Following a roadshow visit, branch managers are encouraged to set up a further learning contract with the head office which can involve further study, visits and contacts.

The accounting roadshow has certainly shown head office to be responsive and resulted in some branch managers being better informed. In the Learning Company a further question is important: 'Has it resulted in any changes to the way finance is done in the company?' The finance director was cautious on this point, saying 'It has certainly resulted in people being better informed and in some changes to the way we present financial information in the company' – this was as far as he would go.

An example of almost instantaneous financial feedback which acted to informate the operators is at Beetham Paper Mill where costs were cut and batch quality improved through the installation of digital displays giving operators instantaneous feedback on paper specification and quality. Now the operators can make their own adjustments rather than wait to be instructed. 'It's like playing Space Invaders', said one.

BEETHAM PAPER MILL

Glimpse 23

Beetham Paper Mill in Lancashire boasts a very special and expensive piece of paper-making equipment. As well as being able to make an unusually wide range of products, it can be reset easily to different specifications and therefore has a great ability to meet customers' urgent small batch demands. However, the catch is that if the machine does not reach quality standards, then the economic consequences are dire. You can't afford the wastage that is normal on the slow learning curve of a long-run standard product. This was a major problem for operators as they tried to check the quality specifications early in each new batch. It took several minutes to go round all the dials and gauges in order to make adjustments.

The company decided to install new monitoring equipment to give an instant digital display of the quality and specification of the paper coming off the machine. This step cut waste to negligible proportions, but also dramatically changes the experience of the operators. They can now see the effects of adjustments as they make them. Another consequence is that they are much more aware of the financial implications of meeting quality standards as quickly as possible. Interestingly, as well as current data, the monitors keep a cumulative score of quality output – the sought-for, ball-by-ball commentary; although the operators use a different sporting analogy – they say it's like playing space invaders.

This is a simple illustration of the rewards that can come – in both financial and quality of working life terms – from applying information technology to provide feedback of financial data for quick learning, greater productivity and job satisfaction.

This example of Formative Accounting at Beetham Paper Mill involved some hi-tech wizardry and some considerable expense – although this was not excessive by the standards of the paper making machine and was quickly recouped. However, the application of these principles need not be expensive or complicated – take the examples of Richardsons (Glimpse 24).

It is a common experience in many companies that the people who do the selling do not have the same interests and priorities as those who produce the goods or supply the services. A less-celebrated but equally common situation is where the salespeople do not understand the financial implications of particular orders. Where it is important to the survival and success of the company for the front line to make rapid and flexible decisions without the tedious and initiative-sapping process of referring back to base for authority, such knowledge is vital.

Glimpse 24

SAVED BY A FORM

Everyone works hard at Richardsons and gives every appearance of enjoying life, including the two owners, who are always around, always accessible. Yet, although this small office supplies firm was expanding, they never seemed to be able to hang on to enough revenue to get the new warehouse they sorely needed.

Discussions showed that they didn't really know which orders they made money on: they couldn't tell the high value-added orders from the ones that made little or no contribution. If the accountant didn't know, then how could anyone else?

After some thought, a new order form was produced for the representatives. Based on the known fixed cost of any delivery and the cost of assembling the order (roughly proportional to the variety of items in it), three lines were added to the order form.

The new form enabled the representative to work out the business value of any order they took. There was no rule about not accepting orders below a certain value, because the firm was committed to a long-term view of the customer relationship and would deliver what was asked for, it was simply that the new form made the representatives and everyone else aware of their most valuable customers, actually and potentially.

It was very simple. It was very 'low-tech'. It worked.

Of course, IT does offer great possibilities for Formative Accounting – perhaps before long Richardsons' reps will have lap-top computers just like their counterparts in Mercian Windows – a company met already in Glimpse 22.

LAPPING UP THE BUSINESS   Glimpse 25
Representatives at Mercian Windows carry lap-top computers that they take with them on sales calls. These have a tailor-made programme that enables the representative to quote immediately for any job by entering the product dimensions and installation conditions.

Before they had the lap-tops, they either had to guess and take a risk, delve into thick manuals and work out a back-of-the-envelope calculation or go away and prepare a proper proposal.

Now they can not only cost any job on the spot, they can also show a series of alternatives. One drawback which the representatives report is that some customers distrust the 'magic box', so that it can require careful handling.

Learning from accountability

Although Formative Accounting is usually about learning from how money works in the business, it can go much further than this. Especially in the public services there is a requirement to be accountable not only managerially and to customers or users, but also to political masters, professional bodies and codes of ethics. In the National Health Service, for example, the statutory Code of Practice for NHS Trust Boards lays down standards of accountability, probity and openness or transparency between staff, patients and the public.

Of course, these are very tough standards to live up to – failures from time to time will be inevitable. However, for those who wish to provide the highest standards of service quality (and who doesn't these days?), holding the company accountable in various ways is a powerful source of learning. There is a growing body of work that seeks to widen the normal limits of accounting practice. For example, the notion of the 'balanced scorecard' implies that performance measures based solely on returns to capital are unbalanced. Measures of customer satisfaction, internal operations and organizational learning and innovation are suggested as balancing factors (Kaplan and Norton 1992, 1993).

In Traidcraft plc, a 'social accounting' process takes this even further in the quest for ethical trading.

SOCIAL ACCOUNTING AT TRAIDCRAFT PLC

Traidcraft plc is an unusual business based on Christian values while operating to best commercial practice ... and beyond. Founded in 1979 with a mission of spreading the message and practice of fair trade, it works with over 100 overseas suppliers in Asia, Africa and Latin America. Employing 150 people at its head office and warehouse in Gateshead, it sells imported handicrafts, clothing, books, cards and paper products, tea and coffee through a network of some 2000 volunteer representatives and retailers. By March 1994 sales turnover had reached £6.6m (up 13 per cent on the year), profit after tax was £51 000 and the board declared a nil dividend to shareholders.

Traidcraft's key vehicle for learning is the Social Accounting Report, an annual account of the social, economic and ethical impact of its business activities. The 1993/4 Report examines the perspectives of key stakeholders, including: producers or suppliers (because of costs, a sample of producer groups are surveyed each year); staff or employees; voluntary representatives and retailers; the wider public; and environmental issues. Shareholders were surveyed in the 1992/3 report and consumers are included in the plan for the 1994/5 report.

Social accounting at Traidcraft is not just an outstanding effort at corporate responsibility, it has an important strategic value to the company. Through consulting with all the groups of people involved in or affected by Traidcraft's activities, the social accounting process creates policy and helps shape the future direction of the business:

> The social accounting process recognises that the Traidcraft dynamic is not about a few good and great trying to work out what it means to do fair trade, but it is about listening to the people who are the Fair Trade movement and finding ways of hearing their expectations and reflections of what Traidcraft is doing and balancing that with our inherited quality framework and the inherited values, and the foundation principles.

The distinctive features of social accounting include the key role played by stakeholders in defining what performance indicators are used, and comparing performance with other organizations as much as possible. The report seeks to be 'polyvocal' – recording the views and accounts of stakeholders themselves, and to recognize the role of spiritual values in the management of the life of the company. It is a regular, externally validated process with full disclosure to all. Social accounting is an essential tool for Traidcraft as a learning company, and seeks to extends this learning in a reciprocal partnership with all stakeholders.

Source: Pedler, M.J. and Aspinwall, K. (1996) *'Perfect plc?': The Purpose and Practice of Organizational Learning*, pp.161–167, McGraw-Hill, Maidenhead.

REFERENCES

Kaplan, R.S. and Norton, D.P. (1992) 'The balanced scorecard: measures that drive performance', *Harvard Business Review*, **70**(1), 71–79, January–February.

Kaplan, R.S. and Norton, D.P. (1993) 'Putting the balanced scorecard to work', *Harvard Business Review*, **71**(5), 134–147, September–October.

12. Internal Exchange
No. 5 of the 11 Characteristics of the Learning Company

Internal Exchange owes much to Total Quality ideas and involves internal units and departments seeing themselves as customers and suppliers contracting with each other in a partly regulated market economy. Rather than top-down management control, in the flatter, leaner organization, cooperation and coordination are achieved via mutual adjustment and negotiation.

Individuals, groups, departments and divisions exchange information on expectations and give feedback on goods and services received. Since the company's ability to operate effectively outside reflects the internal ability to relate and collaborate, units aim to please their internal customers and suppliers, even 'delight' them. To do this a regular dialogue on matters of importance is essential.

However, this dialogue can also include elements of competition and debate as a medium of exchange. Deliberate redundancy of functions can stimulate the development of ideas and innovation as part of organizational learning.

An example of internal exchange comes from Kodak at Macclesfield which moved to a chain of departments, laterally regulating supply, quality, output, timing and so on, rather than having middle managers to do this. The displaced managers were redirected to learn on behalf of the organization by investigating new products and procedures. Their job became to help implement these rather than spend their time coordinating operations – so this was a double move towards the Learning Company.

Many of the ideas on which internal exchange is based can be traced back to W. Edwards Deming.

DEMING'S PROVOCATIVE SAYINGS

Deming began as a statistician and ended up as an iconoclast with some radical ideas about management thinking. A number of Deming's one-liners offer very different messages from the orthodoxy of much management practice. However, like many great teachers, the meaning behind some of his sayings needs puzzling out – what do you make of these?

- 'Crushed by their best efforts'
- 'All new knowledge always comes from outside'
- 'Because nothing's wrong, doesn't mean everything is right'
- 'Competition does not help the development of people'
- 'We're being ruined by people doing their best'
- 'Anyone can save money; what does it do for the company?'
- 'Exchange of ideas doesn't mean developing knowledge'
- 'Competition always leads to people being crushed'
- 'The best players don't join orchestras'
- 'Survival is not compulsory'

You can use these as an activity to try out on your colleagues or any group of people in the company – perhaps as part of a meeting or a training session to heighten awareness and share experience of Total Quality ideas.

To do this write each of Deming's provocative sayings on to a file card. (You can add to those above if you wish by using statements from Deming's 14 points – see Deming, 1986.)

Then each person in the group takes a card and takes it in turn to interpret its meaning in the context of their experience in the company.

What are the implications for relationships between the departments and different parts of the company?

FOLLOW UP
Deming, W.E. (1986) *Out of the Crisis*, Cambridge University Press, Cambridge.
Price, F. (1989) *Right Every Time*, Gower, Aldershot.

Although Deming developed many of his ideas in Japan, not everyone there agrees with his strictures on the effects of competition. Nonaka (1991) describes a distinctive way of developing internal exchange to Japanese companies. Deliberate 'redundancy' in organizational design – 'the conscious overlapping of company information, business activities and managerial responsibilities' is a critical step for the 'knowledge-creating company'. Canon provides an example of this which links to the process described in Glimpse 12 'Learning from conflict', and also with Toyota's planning strategies noted in Chapter 9.

Glimpse 28	**CANON'S COMPETITIVE TEAMS**

In Canon, product development teams are organized on the basis of internal competition. Teams are divided into different groups who develop different approaches to the same project and who then argue for their own ideas. The team as a whole therefore has the advantage of looking at a given project from a variety of viewpoints and is able, through team leadership, to develop a common understanding of the best way forward.

Redundancy in Canon is also applied in other ways. There is the expectation that every employee should hold at least three different jobs in any ten years; thus spreading ideas and making organizational knowledge more 'fluid'. Freedom of information is another crucial element to encourage everyone to search for different interpretations of existing knowledge. Canon is similar to another Japanese company in this respect – in Kao all company information, except personnel records, is stored on a single, integrated database, open to all employees regardless of rank.

One aim of these ideas is to try to prevent some of the pernicious aspects of the cult of the expert. No one person or group should 'own' an aspect of knowledge and be the sole arbiters in that field. The knowledge-creating company creates deliberate overlap and redundancy in order to learn from the resulting profusion and collision of ideas.

FOLLOW UP
Nonaka, I. (1991) 'The Knowledge-creating company', *Harvard Business Review*, pp.96–104, November–December.

Of course, there is another side to the notion of redundancy. Earlier in this chapter we saw that the Kodak managers, whose purpose was to coordinate sub-units in conformance with classical management theory, ended up by getting in the way of fast, flexible operations. This sort of redundancy is an inevitable consequence of learning organizations who are actively seeking new ways of doing things.

Many of the old assumptions that have underpinned the manager's job are being made redundant in this way. For example, Deming's supply chain notion asumes that if you treat people as responsible citizens, then they will take the authority to sort out their relationships with each other as colleagues. A way of describing this is to see colleagues as 'internal customers' who are similar in their needs and demands to external ones. This is important for the Learning Company, not only because it needs good customers, but because it does much of its work through high-quality relationships with others both inside and outside.

DELIGHTING CUSTOMERS

To follow this seven-step activity you need to recruit one of your customers – internal or external – with whom to work. It will help you improve things with that customer and the others, and also help you build up valuable skills in creating and improving good relationships. Rosabeth Kanter has called this 'becoming PALS – Pooling, Allying and Linking Systems across Companies'.

Step 1: Who are our customers?
- Identify your main customers, naming them as specifically as possible.
- Choose six of these and write their names in segments of the first ring of the customer map, given in Figure G29.1.

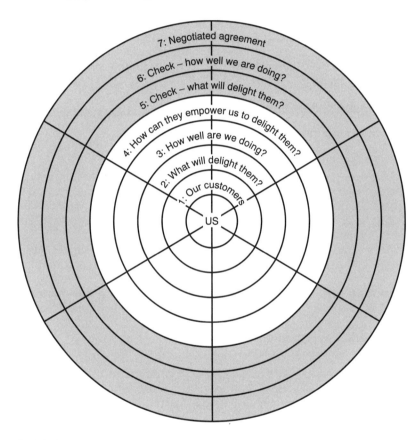

Figure G29.1 A customer map

Step 2: What will delight them?
- For each customer ask yourself, 'What do they want from me?' and 'What will delight them?'
- Write your perceptions for each customer in the segments of the second ring on the map.

Step 3: How well are we doing?

- Estimate how well you think you are doing regarding each of the things that you think will delight your customers and put this in the third ring.
- Try to make this measurable, e.g. 'we are taking 20 days to turn around our orders', or with a simple scale, from 'doing rather badly' through to 'doing very well', even 'exceeding customer expectations'.

Step 4: How can our customers help us to do better?

- Although they are often 'always right'– as a supplier you have needs and rights too – to delight the customer you need a partnership that works well for both.
- Work through the following three questions, perhaps using your colleagues to help you brainstorm responses:

  - What do your customers do already that helps you (and that you would therefore like them to continue to do or to do even more of)?
  - What do they do that makes it harder for you to delight them (and that you would like them to do less of, indeed, stop altogether if possible)?
  - What don't they do that would help you delight them (and that you would like them to start doing)?

Enter these into the fourth ring on the diagram.

Step 5: Checking out what will delight your customers

- From now on the diagram rings are shaded – this means that you can only do these in partnership with your customers.
- Arrange a meeting with one of your customers, explaining carefully why you want the meeting, namely, to explore how you could improve your service to them. You could use the format from Step 4 above but asking the questions from their perspective, e.g. 'What is it that you do that delights them and that they would like you to continue and do more of?', etc.
- Check the responses out with your own assessment from Step 2. At this point just listen; don't get into discussion or negotiation, let alone argument.

Step 6: Checking out how well we are doing at delighting our customers

- Check out your earlier judgements at Step 3 with the new data from Step 5.

Step 7: Negotiating an agreement

- If the customer agrees, you can negotiate a new contract to cover the following:

  - aims what you will do/will not do to delight them
  - support what they will do/will not do to help you in these
  - review the programme you will follow for monitoring and review. It goes without saying that this negotiating must be carried out in a win:win spirit. The aim is to improve a relationship that might already be good but could even be better.

Negotiating partnerships with key stakeholders is crucial for would-be Learning Companies; a critical aspect of this is in facilitating networks of production and supply.

FOLLOW UP
Kanter, R.M. (1989) *When Giants Learn to Dance*, Simon & Schuster, New York.

Much attention has been given recently to external alliances or making PALS – an attractive option for people who want to stay small while thinking big. Schools can link with other schools to employ music specialists; hospitals can share scanning equipment; specialist manufacturers can exchange expertise. But the notion of 'internal partnerships' has received less attention.

One way of working on this notion is that of Lazertek, an organization faced with the need to retain and develop their best people in the face of competition from larger employers. Using the idea of 'internal partners' Lazertek transformed some of its employees and the company's relationship with them.

LAZERTEK

Lazertek, a small but rapidly expanding specialist engineer, realized that, apart from the three founding directors, everyone else was just an employee – well-paid, trusted and highly-valued to be sure – but an employee just the same. The directors owned the shares and had an interest and commitment not shared by anyone else, yet Lazertek's ambitious plans meant that they must not only keep the people they had, but keep them all growing and learning in order to take up the opportunities available. Can people stay, develop along with the business and be rewarded for commitment on a weekly wage? Perhaps.

Consultants helped Lazertek directors think through the concept of 'internal partners' compared with employees. A partner is someone who 'shares', who 'carries responsibility and risk' they decided. This led to some brainstorming about the possibilities:

- equity stakes/share options in Lazertek
- franchise opportunities
- 'buy your own machine'
- 'run your own business in which we'll buy a stake if you wish'
- become a managing partner – attend Board meetings and still be a machinist
- set up consultancies
- sell Lazertek part of your time.

The directors decided to investigate these ideas and find out what sort of a stake their people wanted. Some people might indeed be content with being well-paid, valued employees; others might want to be partners.

The Lazertek directors soon realized that internal partnerships offered as many development opportunities as external ones. Via equity stakes, franchises, own machine ownership and a number of other options, the changes in ownership led to very considerable and parallel changes in relationships between people and sub-units.

The Lazertek story illustrates just how important relationships are to the effective organization. The quality of relationships has a very marked effect on how much learning is likely to happen in the company. Without good relationships the dialogue required between the different parts of the organization, in order to deliver the best product or service, will not take place. Behind good quality dialogue is a sense of the whole company.

THE COMPANY MOBILE

A family therapist we know has a mobile of a family hanging in her consulting room. There's mum and dad, the kids, grandma, aunt and dad's brother. When you pull on any one of them, the rest of them jump up and down.

Companies resemble families in that they are patterns of interaction, communication and relationship. Anything that disturbs or excites one part of the company can be felt in all the other parts. When things are going well in the company – when we find a new customer or reach a long-sought ambition – then it is a cause of celebration for all of us. When a valued person leaves, it is a loss to us all and we remember them and mark the point. When things are going less well, we care less that department B is in trouble – perhaps we don't get on with them or they are making life hard for us – but, just as in the family, if we say or do something mean to them, it spreads out insidiously, and jumps up and down among the rest of us.

As an individual it's very hard to be conscious of the whole company. Most of the time our consciousness is limited to our own needs and those of our close colleagues. Peter Senge makes the 'I am my position' syndrome, the very first of his seven learning disabilities (1990, p.18).

One of the keys to the Learning Company is getting the whole into every part. Gareth Morgan's discussion of the 'holographic' idea of organizations is relevant here – holograms are images in which every piece contains the whole; if broken, it can be re-created from just one tiny piece (1986, Ch. 4). We need to be mindful of the whole company while getting on with our own job. The Learning Company takes time to become conscious of the whole. How are we? What's going on with everyone else? How are we organized for living and learning?

FOLLOW UP

Senge, P.M. (1990) *The Fifth Discipline: The Art and Practice of the Learning Organization*, Doubleday Currency, New York.
Morgan, G. (1986) *Images of Organization*, Sage, London.

One way to work with a notion of the whole organization is to involve everyone in deciding what is important for learning across the company. Usually most people have plenty of ideas about this – you only have to ask them.

DEVELOPING DIALOGUE

People in many organizations are not used to being asked for their opinions about how to improve relationships and learning. Here is a simple activity that involves asking people for their opinions, and having them work in groups to come up with agreed actions.

- Ask any number of people to divide into two groups – A and B. If there are more than, say, ten in each group, then ask them to split again, giving two group A's and B's. It doesn't matter how many of each there are.
- Now brainstorm as follows:

  - Group A: 'What would you do, or build in, to facilitate learning in this company?'
    List your responses, then score each of them on a scale from 0 to 7 on how well we are doing with regard to these as a company at the moment.
  - Group B: What would you do, or build in, if you were trying to inhibit learning in this company?
    List your responses, then score each of them on a scale from 0 to 7 on how well we are doing with regard to these as a company at the moment.

- Bring groups A and B together and have each present to the other. Give each ten minutes to discuss the findings of the other (or to add to them). Now create an agreed list of recommendations for action.
- What would be the next steps? Do you build on positives or act to remove inhibitors?

Another form of dialogue between internal partners is that of peer review and assessment. This is particularly important with professional workers who are often members of self-regulating professional bodies and trade associations. These professional bodies are national or international associations sometimes with strong academic links that create loyalties and networks which go far beyond any given organization for which the individual happens to be working. As economies become more based on knowledge-based industries and personal services, organizations tend to become more and more reliant on attracting the services of these potentially mobile professionals.

The Learning Company is flatter in hierarchical terms than its predecessors; we are professionals and co-workers for the most part. Relying less on line management and more on individual responsibility, autonomy and decision making, self and peer accountability and appraisal become more central. Appraisal systems often don't work when they are done by 'bosses' to 'subordinates', dishing out the merit awards or apportioning the blame, which Deming saw as so damaging to organizations. Self and Peer Assessment (SAPA) is also not without its difficulties, but it is about development and learning from actions at work.

'Clinical Audit' is the method chosen in the British National Health Service for encouraging doctors to learn with and from their colleagues. A quite different process to managerial appraisal, it is not mutually exclusive and you can run both systems side by side. Of course it is not easy to raise questions of competence and professional ethics with peers and tough questions are often dodged but SAPA is arguably a better way for professionals to collaborate on performance review because it focuses on improvement via learner control and self-direction.

Glimpse 33

SELF AND PEER ASSESSMENT (SAPA)

SAPA is an essential tool in Learning Companies. The process is simple to map out but requires considerable self and peer skills to do it. However skilful you are, it won't work without the right learning climate. Here is a step-by-step process you could try out with your colleagues.

- Invite a group of colleagues to join you in experimenting with SAPA.
- Each person chooses one or more areas of task responsibility on which they wish to improve their performance.
- The group brainstorms a list of criteria for all the areas of performance chosen by members.
- Each person chooses criteria from this list and makes a private assessment of their performance against them. (Try using both a qualitative description and a quantitative rating. However much you might want to escape from memories of the classroom, giving yourself four out of ten for a performance does rather concentrate the mind.)
- Each person then chooses some peer assessors. This can be the whole group, if it is small enough, or it may be one or two people. (Do you choose your friends or your critics?)
- In the meeting with their chosen peers, each person gives their own assessment of their own performance and asks for questions, feedback and suggestions for improvement.

    Each individual should be in charge of this process for themselves and should try to say what they want to receive. Sometimes I may want the whole truth, sometimes not; feedback may be only useful in so far as I am willing and able to act on it – otherwise it may be a waste of time at best. However, there is usually a surprise element in this strengthening process; sometimes you have to work hard to persuade people that it's safe to be honest with you; at other times you fear the worst and receive some generous gifts.
- Before their time is up, each person commits themselves to a line of action and a review date with named peers.

If you wish, and if you have the support of all concerned for doing so, you can have a system of reporting to the centre, whereby members log their improvement plans and report progress over time. This can be private or open to inspection, but if it ever becomes used for control purposes without each person's consent then the system will soon decay and become lifeless.

REFERENCE

Nonaka, I. (1991) 'The knowledge-creating company', *Harvard Business Review*, pp.96–104, November–December.

13. Reward Flexibility

This means trying to provide the rewards and conditions that reinforce learning for people in the company. This is not easy; research suggests that all plans and solutions should essentially be seen as temporary. The Learning Company aims at a fair sharing of rewards and explores alternative approaches to pay, attempting to create flexible packages for individuals.

This will involve the questioning of some assumptions. Why do we pay some people more than others? What values underlie the pay system? What do we pay people for? Whatever answers are agreed, the Learning Company will certainly aim to make sure that, if it does not exactly pay people to learn, the pay system is part of an environment that encourages learning, experiment, new ventures.

One principle is that of uncoupling the association of development with promotion. In many companies, 'hopping' might be more useful than 'climbing' as a career metaphor. Whatever else it does, the Learning Company works hard at legitimizing individual and collective learning efforts that are not aimed at promotion. The logic of the pyramid is that, taken as a work collective, most of the time we suffer more aggregate pain through not being promoted compared with the occasional joy when we are.

The Learning Company may break some taboos, with people 'lower down' earning more than some 'high ups'. Also, though we all tend to want more as a matter of course, it is not always recognized that people often want more control over their earnings – a quite different matter. Again as Deming has pointed out many times, individual incentive schemes can have very damaging effects on the relationships between people. Another key point is the value of non-pay rewards. In situations where pay is fixed or laid down by national agreement – and as long as the level is regarded by and large as 'fair' – people's concerns over whether they are being well-rewarded tend to be couched not in money terms but in different language.

Glimpse 34

REWARDING WORK IN THE CIVIL SERVICE

The staff of a large Civil Service department found themselves with fixed salary levels and limited promotion opportunities. They were fed up because a new fast-track management development scheme was soaking up all available promotions. The department has a policy for encouraging staff self-development and in a long and frank discussion it became clear that the link in people's minds between learning at work and promotion is hopelessly constraining.

When asked what they wanted in the way of better rewards, however, staff were able to come up with a long list including:

- the warmth, support and practical help of colleagues
- opportunities to learn new skills
- performance-related pay
- the right to leave of absence for short periods
- secondments to other departments or outside companies
- the change to work flexitime or part-time for spells
- equal opportunities
- workplace nurseries
- a sense of 'running your own business'
- security of employment
- royalties on their ideas
- more flexibility to change jobs
- individual bonuses
- less hierarchy – a sense of being in a good team
- learning and self-development opportunities.

Of course, there are money issues in the list, but they are far outweighed by other concerns. The first lesson for pay and reward system designers is not to make assumptions about what people want. Not having control over the pay system has its pros and cons for managers, but the advantages are considerable where the debate focuses on other aspects of the working experience. Focusing on pay and money is essential from time to time, but where it becomes habitual it can be very damaging to the relationships at work. There are few issues in any partnership guaranteed to produce as much dissatisfaction and falling out as money.

There are many examples of widely differing pay systems that work for particular companies. There are examples of organizations that try to minimize pay differentials such as Keatings described in Glimpse 35 below. In contrast, we found an engineering firm with a most complicated pay incentive system. A small proportion of pay is fixed, but there are separate and additional proportions for corporate, divisional, departmental and individual performance. This seems very complicated, but seems to work for them; they feel they have a good balance of incentives for individual and corporate performance.

In Keatings, everyone, including the directors, is paid the same, high flat rate. The main motive behind this is to avoid differentials, and the jealousy and lack of cooperation that these can create, but also to create a positive, committed workforce who all take responsibility for managing the business.

KEATINGS

Keatings of Mold, North Wales, a small but rapidly expanding company, engraves cylinders for the printing of packagings of household-name clients like Cadbury's and Marks & Spencer. Keatings is a breakaway from a larger company and owner Mike Keating is determined not to make some of the mistakes he experienced in the past. One view of his – echoed by many of the staff, who are all paid the same high, flat rate of pay – is that everybody should be doing the managing and that there should be no designated managers, apart from Mike and his fellow director, Phil.

Consultants carried out a survey that identified a list of ways in which the running of the company could be improved. These ranged from improving the labelling of cylinders to computerizing the ever-shifting operating schedule; from more people needing to deal with customers to designing the layout of the new building. Most of these 'needs' came from the staff and not from the directors.

As part of developing managing skills among the staff, the consultants suggested that everyone become a member of a task force with others from different parts of the factory. Although there were only 30 or so staff at this stage, there were significant differences in terms of jobs, knowledge about the whole factory and so on. Each person in each of the seven four-person task forces chose a task for themselves and sometimes the whole team took on a given task, such as designing a new building. The consultants set each group off with a two-hour session on how to work in a team and helped each task force to choose a coordinator, agree meeting times, target dates for completing tasks and so on. The task forces then met as and when they wished.

After three months, most of the tasks had been completed. A party was held to hear summary reports and to celebrate. The results were impressive – not only in terms of improved supplier quality, better customer contact, computerized planning and the other tasks, but also in terms of people's abilities and willingness to take responsibility for managing. Most people now felt that they could take on jobs and responsibilities that were outside their job definitions and make a valuable contribution.

Larger organizations probably have to have some full-time managers and more complex pay systems than Keatings, but they can often still be clearly differentiated on the basis of whether or not they reward their staff well.

YOUR CAREER AT M & S

A group of human resource managers on a development programme went out on to the high street to gather some first-hand evidence about work, rewards and careers. Not surprisingly, given the nature of the exercise, most of them ended up talking with shop assistants and shop managers, many of them female.

Most expectations showed low expectations and low awareness of the business: 'It's really just a bit of work for money, I don't expect to get much else out of it', said a full-timer with a number of years' service. 'It's just part-time work when they need us, we only find out what's going on when they put up notices for customers', said another. 'We are having a lot of sales – are we closing or having a new range of products?' queried a third, and added, 'They don't want to know about the problems which customers bring to us.' 'Managers come and go with no apparent reason or explanation', observed an assistant in a well-known high street chain.

Marks & Spencer were different; assistants were aware of their options – part-time, full-time, becoming a supervisor. Managers and supervisors would talk to them about what was involved in these various options. Staff welfare facilities were in evidence – proper breaks, staff rooms, some taking of personal preferences into account in deciding rosters; training and on-the-job development in new products and procedures happening on a regular basis. It was appreciated.

Some of the human resource managers sniffed paternalism, even indoctrination to the party line, yet even these could not resist feeling that here were some of the basics of best practice as far as rewards are concerned.

So part of M & S's success is based on good employment policies and practices, including how people are rewarded for working there. This clearly gives the company an advantage in what is a highly competitive situation. Michael Porter has suggested that there are three basic competitive strategies – innovation, quality enhancement and cost reduction – and that very different actions on the part of the people in the company are needed to support each of these.

For innovation, individual autonomy and a high level of risk taking are required, but for cost reduction you want tight control, no experiments and predictable behaviour. A Learning Company is always centrally concerned with innovation but may wish to pursue all three strategies at different times, or all three strategies at the same time in different parts of the operation.

REWARDING INNOVATION

Some companies have taken creative steps to encourage as many people as possible to take risks and innovate and to get out of the habit of asking for permission and waiting for instructions. For example, 3M developed an informal norm that workers 'bootlegged' 15 per cent of their time to work on their own projects. Honda have instituted a competition for inventions among employees.

Individuals or work groups submit schemes to a committee that awards time and resource budgets to projects and an annual 'Ideas Fair' is held to show off the projects and to award prizes.

In a large service business, 20 professional workers defined what they saw as essential for a climate of innovation:

- planning and review are critical activities
- no secrets, only openness
- general interest and understanding of what we're doing and what our products are
- a good methodology/capacity for self-diagnosis
- people set their own boundaries and choose their own work problems
- there is freedom not to learn
- a cooperative climate and equality of participation in decisions
- people take responsibility for decisions
- questions are encouraged
- people are encouraged to try things out
- people get supported for taking risks
- being excited about expanding myself – moving from spotty youth to mature human being
- no deviants!
- eliminate waste/recycle as much as possible
- lots of other people to learn with, learning partners, networks and teachers
- no punishments for asking questions.

Thinking about these conditions for encouraging and rewarding innovation . . .

- What is your competitive strategy?
  - Have you told other people what it is?
  - Have you asked them what conditions would best support their efforts to realize this strategy?

FOLLOW UP
Porter, M.E. (1980) *Competitive Strategy*, Free Press, Glencoe.
Porter, M.E. (1985) *Competitive Advantage*, Free Press, Glencoe.

These are the conditions that these professional people saw as enhancing their creativity and which were likely to lead to higher levels of innovation and learning. Such conditions probably wouldn't help much with cost reduction and only some of them would be useful in quality enhancement.

Returning to the issue of pay and to the particularly knotty question of whether you should reward individual performance or not, one way to think about this is to consider what we are paying people for. It may be, as the cynics have it, that the most important phrase in management is WIFM ('What's in it for ME?'), but do your pay and rewards packages encourage people to put 'ME' first and see themselves in 'I am my job' terms or to think about their contribution to the overall purpose of the whole company?

| Glimpse 38 | **PAYING FOR CONTRIBUTIONS TO THE WHOLE** |

One of the hardest things to do in the Learning Company is to get everyone active, taking individual initiatives and so on, while also being mindful of the whole. To be able to do this, we have to *know* what's going on in the rest of the company, we have to *care* about what happens in the rest of the company and we have to feel able to *contribute* to the whole as well as to improving performance in our own job.

Rewards are important in the Learning Company, and pay is as important here as elsewhere, but the Learning Company pays people to learn and those who join are expected to carry on learning as an implied part of their employment contract. Beyond this, however, the Learning Company also develops the capacity to transform itself, so that, as well as rewarding people for doing their jobs better, it rewards people who make contributions to the whole over and above their own job performance.

This can be built into the normal salary review processes and merit- or performance-related pay given under two headings:

- pay for performance in own job
- pay for contribution over and above own job performance, e.g. for assignment and special project work; for learning new skills useful to the company; for reorganizing work processes; for making successful suggestions; for 'above and beyond' work with customers and so on.

A word of warning: all pay systems degrade over time and in the Learning Company the best systems are those that have been put out to the widest possible consultation. *What* is rewarded under the second heading above, should be agreed by the company as a whole.

The basic principle in encouraging people to feel part of the whole enterprise is to treat them that way. This is what Reward Flexibility is all about – recognizing individual differences, but less in terms of pay differentials and more in terms of giving people as much control as possible over their work including their pay as part of creating working conditions to reward innovation and contribution.

The idea of 'gainsharing' is one which helps to treat people as part of the whole enterprise. The idea has been suggested in various guises many times – but we seem to forget it equally often.

GAINSHARING

People in work expect to get paid well: 'a fair day's pay for a fair day's work' is still an ideal objective for many. In the Learning Company we're asking for greater commitment, for people to keep on learning, to pool that learning with others and to act on the basis of this collective learning in order to transform the business – this calls for more than a hired hand or wage-earner relationship. In consciously linking their own learning and development with that of the company, people are entering into a deeper contract and one that is, essentially, *moral*.

Alan Fox (1974) wrote about this need for a new moral involvement in work in the early 1970s and now is the time of its realization. Pay, of course, is only one aspect of this deeper contract, which must cover rights and obligations of all sorts on both sides, including access to training and development opportunities, a variety of ways of joining, leaving and belonging, etc., that go to make up the new 'partnership' agreement. For the moment, let us stick with pay, for *form* of which – even more than the amount – must acknowledge this new relationship.

Rosabeth Kanter (1989) has suggested that there is a trend in the USA away from basic pay increases towards performance pay, profit sharing, employee ownership and gainsharing (a form of profit sharing). She gives as an example the US airline industry, forced to cut costs due to deregulation. Western Airlines, after four years of losses, gave almost a third of the company to its employees, together with two seats on the board for 10 to 18 per cent wage cuts. Western employees did well on their shares when the company was sold to Delta, but, at Eastern Airlines, where a similar scheme was adopted, the business continued to lose money and employees' stock declined in value, leaving them embittered.

In this example it was 'survival bargaining' that led to more employee partnership. Our own research suggests that many companies will seek to follow a Learning Company strategy because of increased competition and the need for continuous improvement in order to survive. Other people may have more time, more luck or more foresight. Whatever the conditions, a Learning Company strategy includes finding a way to reward people for being part of something that has been collectively created. The Learning Company, if you like, is shared intellectual, emotional and physical property and the belonging or partnership contract – which replaces the old 'employment contract' must reflect this.

FOLLOW UP

Fox, A. (1974) *Beyond Contract: Work, Power and Trust Relationships*, Faber & Faber, London.

Kanter, R.M. (1989) *When Giants Learn to Dance*, Simon & Schuster, New York.

Pedler, M.J., Burgoyne, J.G. and Boydell, T.H. (1988) *Towards the Learning Company*, Final Report to the Training Agency, Moorfoot, Sheffield, May.

14. Enabling Structures

No. 7 of the 11 Characteristics of the Learning Company

Enabling Structures provide opportunities for individual and business development as well as the frameworks for functioning together as a company – the necessary bureaucracy. The emphasis is upon adaptability and flexibility.

The idea of 'scaffolding' that stands and supports while something else is built or emerges can be seen as a temporary structure. A simple example of a temporary structure might be a building that has movable partitions to allow for different configurations of rooms. An example from the organizational world comes from Semco (Glimpse 8) where, according to the company handbook, organization charts are always drawn in pencil because they change so often.

Following this analogy, roles can be loosely rather than tightly defined, in line with both current customer requirements and with individual needs to learn and develop. Departmental boundaries may overlap and cross over with project groups. This is an organizational architecture that gives space and headroom for meeting current needs and responding to future events.

John quotes his old teacher on organizational design, Tom Lupton, who said:

> Designing an organization is like a three-sided Rubik Cube. You've got to get the Technical logic right, and the Financial logic, adding value at each stage, and you've got to get the Human logic right.

His favourite example was a Walls Pork factory near Manchester:

> Pigs go in one end and sausages and pork pies come out the other and there's not a lot of waste.

There was a very tight technical process; cost control was a fine art and they understood and used their local labour market well. It was a tight, profitable operation until changing fashions and health concerns knocked the bottom out of the sausages and pork pies market when they then found they could not adapt or change their operation. What they needed was a fourth logic – the ability to change structures and procedures cheaply and quickly.

THE FOURTH DIMENSION

According to Tom Lupton, designing a company is a bit like doing a three-sided Rubik Cube – there are three 'logics' to get right simultaneously:

- **Technical logic** means that things have to facilitate the work flow to produce goods and services. This includes the production process, the delivery of supplies and the despatch of finished goods or, in the case of a service, the logical steps to deliver that service to the customer. Material and information flow between work units and departments have to be arranged in the best pattern.
- **Financial logic** means that the costs incurred and the value added at each stage of production have to be arranged to maximize income and minimize cost. As we know, financial logic is often different from technical, and both can be very different from the third type of logic, human.
- **Human logic** decrees that work has to be arranged to make it possible for people to do it – jobs defined and linked, people selected and trained with the appropriate skills, and the right working conditions established. The effort/reward equation has to be right in the short and long term to match the labour market and meet people's expectations for money, variety, career progression.

These three logics can be quite tightly designed and controlled. Indeed, mature companies are often so 'tight' that they can become rigid and inflexible, lacking that element of novelty or randomness that can lead to change and learning.

The Learning Company has a fourth logic... a...

- ... **Learning logic**, which allows people, individually and as a company, to flow, adapt, change and develop. This means that those previously tight logics – technical, financial and human – have to flex to allow for learning, through adaptive structures, systems and procedures, which support and encourage rather than constrain.

Central to this learning logic is giving people the space to learn. This is a crucial task for leaders in the Learning Company, and is harder than it appears because we tend to manage the other three logics tightly.

A key managerial skill in the Learning Company is the ability to create enabling rather than disabling structures for learning. Peter Senge starts his book on the learning organization with a description of seven common learning disabilities (1990). The Learning Company aims to do away with these disabilities, such as restrictive job descriptions, over-controlled hierarchies, red tape procedures and rigid mind sets, in order to build a healthy, responsive organization. Often the old structures and practices are so entrenched that some special support is needed.

SCAFFOLDING
Enabling structures can be:

- physical, like buildings, offices, room layouts
- procedural, like policy statements, action plans, training schemes
- mental and cultural structures of 'how we do things around here', what is done and what is not, what is taken for granted and so on.

The idea of scaffolding can help refurbish old structures. Don't tear them down and put up the first thing that comes into your head – that's how we got all those speculative office buildings. Scaffolding is something erected around an existing structure so that the necessary building or re-building can be done. Scaffolding is a temporary structure that is not the change itself.

In trying to bring about changes it is very useful to have such a temporary structure to enable those involved in the change to have access to the familiar and to hold things together until the change is completed. So, you don't have to go straight from old to new, you can use temporary scaffolding around a difficult or contentious change that allows for the debate, discussion and revision of plans necessary before you commit yourselves irrevocably to a new system or structure.

In the Learning Company, dedicated as it is to learning, adaptation and flexibility, it may be that most structures are temporary and seen as such by people in the company. Scaffolding can also help in setting up joint ventures with other companies where such partnerships can be risky. We can dismantle and move them about any time we like, but, at the same time they have to be strong enough to take the weight and strain of company operations as well as reassure us all that the structure itself is safe and sound. A good way of maintaining creativity, flexibility and responsiveness is to structure the company in such a way that this is available in some parts and not in others.

Temporary parts in permanent wholes are a good way of managing innovation. 'Behind the Beat' is a black music programme screened on BBC 2 and, though 'Aunty BBC' is an old, permanent company with many bureaucratic features, the production team for 'Behind the Beat' is very temporary and fluid. There are great advantages for the BBC in this arrangement, the BtB team is assembled carefully, lovingly nurtured, fed and looked after and, once the task is completed, quickly disassembled. However, to be able to do that requires considerable skills and organizational capability in this care and feeding of infant systems.

TEMPORARY ORGANIZATIONS

The 17 team members of 'Behind the Beat' are recruited on three-month contracts – 11 of them new to the programme, 6 entirely new to TV. Terry, the creator of the programme is 26 and a good people manager and developer. To help him he has Jenny, an executive director in her 40s, to provide some wisdom and links to the parent BBC. There is ample evidence of parental feeding – people who bring telephones, photocopiers, people who provide studios and technicians, managers who provide budgets and other managers who buy the finished programmes.

The team don't have time to worry about all this. They have to learn very quickly how to do their jobs of researcher, production assistant, director or office support. They are also very aware that 'by Christmas they'll be on the streets'. They must do good work and develop their existing skills for the future. Everyone lives and works together in a big open-plan room, clustered into little groups of two and three desks. People move about frequently, try ideas out on each other, ask for contacts, call for help. On the morning after the programme goes out, Terry calls a two-hour review meeting – the only team meeting – in which the programme is picked over. Apart from initiating discussion, Terry doesn't say a lot. People who were responsible for clips ask for feedback, get praised and criticized and think about how they could do it differently.

Throughout the three months, everyone is acutely aware of time. The time of the day, the day of the week and the 'long' cycle of birth, maturity and death of the team. By Christmas the team has had its celebration and also mourned the tragic and unexpected death of one of its members.

The 'Behind the Beat' team learn quickly and naturally because there is so much that is new – people, product, processes and ideas. It is almost an organization designed for learning because so much of this is essential to get the job done. Many new, small organizations seem able to learn quickly because this is necessary for survival, but having made it through the first few years can fall prey to rigidity and lose their 'natural' learning ability.

Then the wise leader has to find the space to create that learning anew. Usually this 'space' is about time, often it involves social and psychological elements and sometimes it is simply about physical space.

At Wisewood School they were so short of physical space for staff that there was not even a private room where meetings could take place. The head and five senior staff decided to improve their team work by moving into one office together. As well as helping them as a team, this action had all sorts of beneficial knock-on effects round the school.

CREATING HEADROOM

At Wisewood School in Sheffield, the headteacher, his three deputies and two senior teachers act together and think of themselves as a team. They wanted to demonstrate this and to make a strong and clear statement about this way of managing. They decided to move out of their separate offices and share the biggest room available. This met a second objective of creating five new spaces for other activities.

What the senior management team had not anticipated was the knock-on effects of their action. They began to notice small and incremental changes in the positioning of furniture and work spaces taking place all over the school. Bookcases, previously used as screens, were put against walls; filing cabinets used to block the view and create privacy were moved out of the way. A ripple effect of the teams' actions seemed to spread throughout the school. The overall impression was of taking down barriers and opening access and communications. The five offices previously filled by the senior teachers became much needed private interview and meeting rooms used on a bookable basis.

In making space for learning in an organization, there is a similarity with the task renovating and converting old buildings. Here architects work to create large, open areas, removing dividing walls, even parts of floors, letting in light through larger windows, softening the inside/outside boundary further by bringing in lots of greenery and so on.

> Architecture means the thoughtful housing of the human spirit in the physical world. (William Meyer, Contemporary Architects)

Clearing space in over-supervised, over-regulated regions of our working world in order to encourage more rather than fewer organization members to boldly go where they have not gone before is an exciting task. Space making – gaps, breaks, openings, windows, elbow room, and so on – is opportunity making. As a managerial task it is a striking reversal of the bureaucratic concern with space filling via job descriptions, key results areas, departmental boundaries and organization charts.

Yet this is no task for modern Cromwells laying waste with ball and chain. The old walls and floors provide security and the unbounded sense of space – void, abyss or infinity, will not so much offer opportunity as terror to those long confined by the bureaucratic form. Too much space and we lose our bearings and are unable to learn.

CREATING ORGANIZATIONS FIT FOR THE HUMAN SPIRIT

Some architectural devices are becoming common in space making in companies. Here are some examples from architectural practice with their possible organizational interpretations:

- removal of dividing walls
- partial removal of floors
- outside staircases; putting service pipes, etc. outside
- central courtyards, wells, atriums
- add balconies
- re-cycling old bricks, etc.
- use historical objects as sculpture
- lots of inside greenery
- put skylights in the roof
- put in bigger windows
- preserve historical objects
- demolish departmental boundaries
- removing levels of supervision
- hiving off service functions

- decentralize functions, remove central services
- encourage outside trading
- re-train people, encourage radical job changes
- celebrate differences, encourage expression
- blur home/work/community boundaries
- full disclosure; open up top management processes for inspection and comment
- encourage secondments outside
- bring back selected retirees

These examples help to illustrate that before people can take initiatives, either for their own development or for the development of the business, certain conditions are necessary. Giving yourself and others this headroom is part of a supportive learning climate. There are far too many examples of people under great pressure and stress of deadlines, quality standards and other overlapping and contradictory demands, who are also told to 'be innovative' or 'develop yourself'.

Managers in the Learning Company must become skilled practitioners in the art of making learning space for themselves and for their people.

LEARNING SPACE

Here are some ideas for creating learning space for people in the Learning Company – as a manager, facilitator, counsellor, chairperson, project leader:

- stop talking and listen actively instead
- don't always respond to requests for expert advice when expected
- allow and encourage small silences
- avoid teaching
- slow things down – people, discussions, processes
- question the relevance of tasks
- encourage reflection and deepen discussions
- sit within the group, not at the front

- leave the group to work on their own
- build on people's comments, make linkages, offer options
- look for normal practices and reverse them.

Most of us are better at filling things up with 'busyness' than at emptying and opening up space, so it is important to make a conscious effort to do so.

FOLLOW UP
Kemp, N. (1989) 'Self-development: practical issues for facilitators', *Journal of European Industrial Training*, **13**(5), 1–28.

Of course, structuring cleverly in terms of physical, social or psychological learning space can't resolve all the problems of creating Learning Companies. One of the most common errors in organizational development stems from the assumption that changing the structure will change how people in the company act.

There is much to be said for changing structures at appropriate times, but this is best done when the reasons for doing so have been carefully thought through. In particular it helps if all those affected by the changes are consulted and, preferably, after all of us have had a go at rehearsing or practising any changes in actions and behaviour that will be called for under the new structure.

As in all good architectural practice – form follows function.

Glimpse 46   **FORM FOLLOWS FUNCTION**
In their manual on making cultural changes, Marcia George, Peter Hawkins and Adrian McLean (1989) offer the model shown in Figure G46.1.

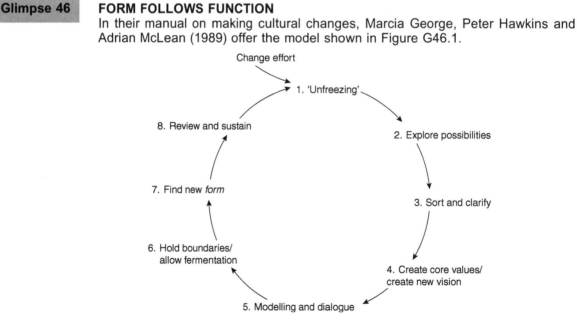

Figure G46.1 A model of cultural change

It is suggested by this model that before you make any changes to the form of your company, remember there are six steps to go through before you fix the new structure. Step 6 is particularly interesting because it suggests a very different role for the manager as leader from that of the 'gung ho' structure shifter.

Having gone through a careful sifting of the possibilities for how people want to behave and act in the future and having set up the opportunity for people to try this out, the leader holds the tension and allows the situation to remain fluid so that individual and collective learning can take place. First, people get a chance to rehearse and learn how to act in the new ways; second ideas are clarified and modified before the organizational commitment to a new structure takes place.

REFERENCE
George, M., Hawkins, P. and McLean A. (1989) *Organisation Culture Manual*, Bath Associates, Bath.

Prematurely abandoning new organizational forms before developing the new desired habits and actions is a mistake. So, choosing a good form for your unit, department or company can be a tricky problem. What is the right structure?

There is no one correct form for the Learning Company. Such an organization may cultivate a repertoire of forms that it can use or transform itself into – in whole or in part – to be best fitted for certain markets, products or people's wishes. Have you got the right forms in place? Have you a rich enough repertoire? Can you move from this into that form when it's appropriate or does change of form only come with each sweep of the new broom?

Many writers have addressed this theme. Glimpse 47 shows four of the basic possibilities in a continuum from hierarchy – the enduring and most mechanistic form – through matrix and cloverleaf, to network – the most nebulous and organic form. While going through these, ask yourself: 'Where is my company (or unit) on this continuum?' and 'What would be the best form(s) for my company?'

Glimpse 47   **FINDING GOOD FORM**

● *Hierarchy*

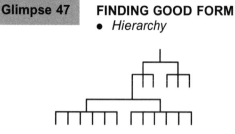

The classical, bureaucratic form promising order, control, predictability. Works best in stable conditions and is slow to change. All know their place and tend to be punished, or at least not rewarded, for innovating, taking risks or asking questions. Claims about the end of hierarchy are probably premature given that, on some reckonings, it has been around for 2000 years. This form, however, has some serious limitations for companies that need to adapt and flex quickly.

● *Matrix*

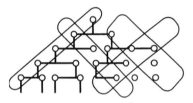

This is where a hierarchy remains but is overlain by project teams and groupings as a response to novel demands and problems. A matrix often has functional departments – marketing, production, R & D, etc. – with a product, brand or business area teams cutting across the vertical lines. In theory, the matrix gives strong alignment *and* task forces, which enables the company to draw widely on available functional skills and knowledge. A problem is that hierarchy tends to reassert itself, especially around 'crunch' resource issues such as budgets, members' careers or big risks. Some form of matrix is probably an operating necessity in most modern companies. An individual's ability to balance their several roles is a key skill.

● *Cloverleaf*

This form has done away with hierarchy – almost! Here there's a small, core team managing the radiating, often-changing work teams and functions. Often only the core are full-time or long service. Work groups may contain a lot of part-timers, self-employed or short-term contractors. Cloverleafs deal well with rapidly changing circumstances and short-life tasks. Highly skilled and professional workers may demand the sort of autonomy and variety of contracts that they offer. Companies may find it hard to operate in fashion markets without parts or the whole structured in this way.

- *Networks*

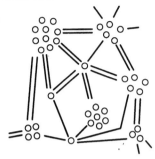

These are much more loosely coupled systems of people and groups that work together. Here there is no hierarchy or centre but more 'heterarchy' based on job leadership by the best-equipped group or the person who originates the project. People are in business and can be mobilized at a number of levels – as self-employed units, members of small firms and as part of the whole network. It is much harder to say where the network company starts and finishes; each member, group or node has many links inside and outside.

FOLLOW UP

Three writers who address the theme of form are:

Mintzberg, H. (1983) *Structure in Fives: Designing Effective Organizations*, Prentice-Hall, New York, and (1989) *Mintzberg on Management*, Free Press, New York.

Handy, C. (1989)*The Age of Unreason*, Basic Books, London.

Lievegoed, B.C.G. (1990) *The Developing Organization*, Blackwell, Oxford.

So finding the right form or forms is important, because inappropriate ones can constrain rather than support the action and learning of the people in the company. Moving from one form to another is a long-cycle process, best taken carefully and with due consideration, reflection, discussion and dialogue. In the day-to-day management of the organization, however, there are plenty of smaller measures that will communicate the idea and bring about the reality of the Enabling Structure.

Sometimes it is these apparently insignificant, small steps that, in retrospect, have created the biggest shifts. Distinguishing the fertile from the futile can be difficult and 'shifting the deckchairs on the Titanic' is a frequently-heard complaint against managers, yet the right small step can often be the transformation of an outdated set-up. A good place to get started on the idea of Enabling Structures is with your own meetings – everybody has these, and many of us like to complain about them – their number, frequency, interminableness, inconclusivity, etc.

Glimpse 48

BRIEFING THE POLICE

A friend in the police was promoted to chief superintendent in charge of a large patch containing several small towns. One of the first things he did was to introduce his new people to the idea of 'team briefing' – a 30-minute session on Monday mornings over coffee in his office for all managers. He was surprised about the difficulty that some people had over what to him was such a simple thing:

> What was most surprising – and touching in a way – was how I had to teach them to talk to each other in the work setting. They were fine talking ten to the dozen in the pub after work, but they didn't know how to talk to each other informally at work.

Because they are such a common and increasing feature of the workplace, meetings are a good place to start breaking patterns and introducing small changes.

What small changes could you introduce to your meetings? Here are a few ideas you might try:

- if you usually have an agenda, try doing without one (people may start talking about what's important to them)
- change the physical setting – the room, the seating, remove the tables, etc.
- hold your meeting off-site, but not necessarily in a hotel – try your home?
- end the meeting on the stroke of the agreed finishing time
- start with a poem, a story, a small meditation
- if you always have the same person in the chair, take it away from them (especially if the chair is also the boss)
- invite someone to the meeting who 'shouldn't' be there
- devise a penance for latecomers – one person we heard about keeps a plant spray in the office with which offenders are doused (especially senior ones), but a less boisterous idea is to have the last person make or buy the tea
- write the minutes before the meeting and only discuss the items that people want to argue about (an acquaintance who chairs several companies always follows this process and says that in his experience only 1 in 4 or 5 items is contentious yet we'll talk endlessly about them all!)
- use a 'talking stick' or similar so that only the person holding it may talk; everyone else listens.

And so on. With a couple of confederates you could think up a dozen other ideas. Meetings are a good place to start on creating the Learning Company. Make some time towards the end to ask people what difference the change has made. Reflecting on differences brings us to awareness and perhaps to learning. One of the rules of learning is that reviewing is just as important as doing.

One of the suggestions in Glimpse 48 is to change the layout of the room in some way. This can have a surprising effect on the way people communicate and relate to each other and this sometimes shows itself in a strong resistance to any change!

MUSICAL CHAIRS

Musical chairs is an exciting and cruel game played with equal gusto at children's parties and in the Prime Minister's Cabinet. As long as we have hierarchies in organizational life, we are likely to experience our own version of musical chairs from time to time. If you get the last seat, don't you feel, oh, so pleased – and relieved but, how crushing it is to find a full company with no place for you.

The idea of the Learning Company is that everyone finds a seat and gets a say, but what sort of a voice you have depends a lot on how the chairs are set. Figure G49.1 gives just four ways of arranging the chairs, which affect quite strongly how most of us are likely to participate.

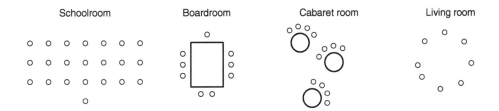

Figure G49.1 Seating plans

Jot down against each of these settings three ways in which you think your actions would be influenced by the way the furniture has been arranged.

Next time you organize a meeting with your project team or group, why not try a little organizational restructuring of your own?

- Try a new seating arrangement – there are lots of variations.
- Note the effect it has on people and how you do business together.
- Discuss why you made the change.

Finally in this chapter, let's visit that potentially most enabling – yet often so disabling – structure of all, the authority system in the organization. In the Brazilian company Semco, people are not just appraised by their superiors, they also have a say in reviewing the performance of their boss. This idea of managing upwards or 'upwards appraisal' is beginning to appear in organizations in a variety of guises, for example, attached to development programmes and called '360 degree feedback'.

For some 20 years now, Russell Ackoff has been advocating the notion that responsibility and authority in organizations are essentially circular processes – directors and managers are there to control and coordinate, yet in the last resort they do so on the say-so of those they manage.

Glimpse 50

ACKOFF'S CIRCULAR ORGANIZATION

Russell Ackoff has suggested that all people in authority in organizations, from the chief executive to the supervisor, should have boards made up of their immediate superiors and subordinates to create a circularity of responsibility and account-ability. He also advocates that, where they are recognized, trade unions should join the boards at all levels.

These boards are responsible for planning and coordinating the work for which that person is responsible and also for reviewing and evaluating his or her performance. The boards have considerable powers, including that of recommending the removal of the person from office. In Figure G50.1 people at various levels of authority are shown by the numbers 1 to 4: complete lines show the authority relationships and the dotted ones show board membership.

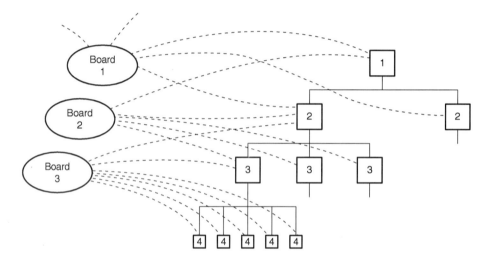

Figure G50.1 Ackoff's circular organization

Ackoff claims over ten years' experience with the circular organization in companies as diverse as Kodak, Alcoa, Anheuser-Busch and A & P Supermarkets. He stresses that the precise form varies from organization to organization, but that the evidence is that organizational democracy and operating efficiency go together.

The circular organization addresses three major organizational needs to increase:

- organizational democracy
- the readiness, willingness and ability of people in the organization to change
- the quality of working life in the organization via participation in managing at all levels.

FOLLOW UP
Ackoff, R. (1981) *Creating the Corporate Future*, Wiley, New York.
Ackoff, R. (1989) 'The circular organization: an update' *The Academy of Management Executive*, **3**(1), 11–16.

REFERENCE

Senge, P.M. (1990) *The Fifth Discipline: The Art and Practice of the Learning Organization*, Doubleday Currency, New York.

15. Boundary Workers as Environmental Scanners
No. 8 of the 11 Characteristics of the Learning Company

This characteristic is concerned with the critical question of how companies can learn from their environments. Rather than employing market research agencies and other consultancies, the Learning Company involves all its people – especially those in the front line with regular customer, supplier and outside contacts – in scanning the outside world for important data. There are three linked processes here:

- **Collecting** Boundary workers deliver goods and services and receive orders and supplies; they can also learn to search for and collect information, if the company is alert to this possibility and values their abilities and opinions.
- **Receiving** Once the information has been collected it must be welcomed into the company – managers seek this data on a regular basis.
- **Using** The data is analysed and disseminated to those who need it. One way in which the Learning Company measures its capability is through the rate of 'knowledge turn' – the speed at which new knowledge is discovered, understood, tested and turned into operating practices.

There are lots of bad examples of where companies don't do this, and where the knowledge of employees is undervalued. Most companies treat their van drivers simply as delivery people. Not so Harvest Bakeries.

Glimpse 51

ENVIRONMENTAL SCANNING AT HARVEST BAKERIES
At Harvest Bakeries, everyone with a boundary role – one with working contacts outside the company – is expected to pick up useful information and bring it back. Marketing people are used to doing this, but now the delivery people enquire about complaints and ask supermarket managers what new products they would like to see Harvest Bakeries offer.

This information is pooled at weekly 'intelligence gathering' meetings which include all those with outside contacts and are attended by the marketing manager and the general manager. Apart from producing vital information and ideas, the meeting has helped create a wide awareness of the company, its products and its market.

A bonus system rewards named individuals for useful ideas and the company newsletter prints a photograph and a news item.

It is obvious to an outsider that people like van drivers, people who come into contact with customers, suppliers, competitors, are picking up all sorts of reactions to their products or services – what is right and wrong, what is the best on the market for what particular requirement and so on, as well as all sorts of requests for different products or possibilities. However, all too often no one bothers to ask them about this.

The irony is that many companies spend a good deal of money on activities such as market research to find out less than their van drivers could tell them, information that the latter already know or could easily find out. To turn boundary workers into environmental scanners means convincing them that this is important and worth while. The system for collecting and using the information is vital and it helps to be able to recognize and reward the effort people put in. Using your people as intelligence gatherers could really open your eyes.

Of course it is sometimes difficult for big organizations operating with standard products and services to respond to anything out of the ordinary. Take the case of Ernest Jones, a milk deliverer working for a large national dairy. He noticed that one of his households had stopped ordering milk. He knocked on the door one morning to investigate ...

MILK ROUND | Glimpse 52 |

Border Dairies encourages its franchised milk deliverers to ask their customers from time to time what new products and services they would like from the dairy. In this way, over the years, Christmas and birthday cakes and Easter eggs have joined the long list of dairy and vegetable products that can now be bought from the milkman.

One day, Ernest Jones knocked at a door to enquire as to why there had been a drop in the milk order. He found out that two members of the household had become vegans and therefore drank soya milk only. Ernest said he would ask his sole supplier, Border, if they could get him the soya milk. But on asking his despatcher he was told: 'No. The quantities are far too small to make it worth our while.' In this case, Border decided that there was not enough demand to justify setting up supplies, so Ernest had to disappoint his customer.

Perhaps the dairy should have been a little more imaginative and tried to actively sell the new milk; perhaps they should have loosened their franchise agreement and let Ernest get his own supplies from elsewhere?

Perhaps there was a happy ending to this story. Perhaps this entrepreneurial soul was not satisfied with that answer and made his own arrangements despite a company rule forbidding this? Perhaps not. More likely perhaps that Ernest Jones stopped asking questions of his customers.

Apart from illustrating the vital importance of encouraging staff to ask these sorts of questions, this story also shows how invaluable are the customer contacts of staff in detecting new markets and opportunities. Those in contact with suppliers and competitors could do the same. Some firms are always on the lookout for ideas and practices that they can take back – it is a matter of attitude, frame of mind, of the cultural acceptance of the possibility of learning from others.

How open we are at learning from others depends upon how we see ourselves. It is a remarkable fact that even today some people and some organizations think they have little to learn from their colleagues and competitors. The idea of 'excellence' can be a trap here – if you believe your own propaganda about being the best, who can you learn from? Beneath this is how we view ourselves as a company – are we a separate unit, complete and self-sufficient or part of a much bigger system along with many others like ourselves?

Glimpse 53

WHAT IS AN ORGANIZATION?

The word 'organization' has at least two everyday meanings – first, a collection of people or a *bounded entity*; second, a *process* of ordering work.

In Glimpse 52, the milkman is linked to his supplier and if they don't deliver to him, he can't deliver to the customer. The organizing process reaches back from the customer, through the delivery system to the dairy and, ultimately, to the farmer and the cow. You could go even further in tracing the links, to the people who supply cattle feed, for example. This is to think of organization as *process*.

In the other sense – as bounded entities – the milk round is a small business, the dairy is another business and the farmer yet another. All these are organizations with different and unique members, boundaries, plant, property, legal liabilities and so on. You could draw a map of the organized process flows with circles showing the different individual organizations that specialize in various parts of the process.

What does this distinction mean for organizational learning?

The story of the milk round is of one bounded organization trying to learn and adapt and being blocked by another, the dairy. Both are part of the same organization as process, so this raises the question of whether you can have learning in one organization, as a bounded entity, without learning in the organization process?

To have learning in this particular process, the dairy would have to reconsider its identity – re-frame itself – as being in the dairy as opposed to the milk business. If you're in the dairy business, soya milk is outside your scope, but if you're in the milk business, it is your territory.

From this point of view, organizational learning means change and development in the 'process lines'. In our example, it is conceivable that ecological, public health and animal welfare concerns might combine in questioning the validity of the food chain from the production of vegetable proteins to the consumption of cow's milk. From here you might reach the conclusion that using the cow in the food chain is more extravagant than bypassing it! This sort of questioning, related to emerging trends, gives some idea of what is involved in learning in an organization-as-process.

This is an important point in terms of understanding organizational learning. To take the argument a stage further, organizations as entities often block learning in the organization-as-process. This is because of vested interest and concern for individual organizational survival. Food companies are often accused of perpetuating unhealthy practices or of holding back advances in public health and nutrition. Learning in the organization-as-process can, however, create all sorts of new opportunities for business. In our example, this would be for a soya milk wholesaler and distributor to do milk rounds. When we talk of collaborative learning between organizations it is precisely this process we have in mind – of people in the organization as process getting together to learn and look for new opportunities.

This analysis helps to explain why we chose the term Learning *Company* rather than Learning *Organization* for this book. We prefer 'company' because it means people working together in each other's company, not because we have a primary concern for the private, 'for profit' sector. If we see ourselves as working and learning 'in company' with others, both in the bounded entity sense and in the organization-as-process sense, then we can learn from organizing in both senses and not be blocked by the limits of the particular boundaries of our present company.

Who we see ourselves working with creates and limits our opportunities. What or who is your company? Thinking of company in the organization-as-process sense can extend the boundaries and help us to think outside our habitual frames of reference. You can see yourselves working in company with all sorts of people – it's a question of how you see it or conceptualize it.

The way we conceptualize things leads to why we do what we do and to how the notion of 'organization' is enacted by particular companies of people. For example, managerial culture has tended to stress excellence, competition and market forces in recent years yet contemporary cultural concerns are increasingly about ecology and health. Although organization-as-process may seem at first sight the weaker idea, it can become strong if it helps to visualize the world differently. Thinking differently leads to acting differently.

Doing new things is a way of life in the Learning Company. Inventing new products, exploring new markets, experimenting with new structures or methods of working, creating new relationships, having fresh insights – all these activities provide the food for learning. A critical element in all learning is that of difference. Once we notice a difference – in performance, in attitude, in outlook – it provides us with the question: 'Why?'

Glimpse 54

COMPETE *AND* LEARN

People outside our organization are a rich source of differences. In the Learning Company we don't just buy from suppliers, sell to our customers, compete with competitors; we set out to learn with and from them.

This requires quite a change of attitude. 'Learn with competitors – surely that's madness!' But think again – think of all those antique shops on the same street, or all those software houses in the same science park. These companies are competing in a serious way, but they also collaborate. They watch each other carefully, attempt to outdo each other certainly, but also get together from time to time to attempt projects that require the resources of two or three.

It's much the same story with customers and suppliers. If you're just seeing these people as buyers and sellers, you're missing something vital. They could be learning partners too. When Rover set up a 'Preferred Supplier' programme, it reduced the list of over 1000 suppliers by two-thirds. It also held 'Buyer-Supplier Negotiating Training Workshops' where people formerly regarded as 'the enemy' were given free places to learn how to negotiate better with Rover's buyers. Doesn't make sense does it?

Here are some questions that might help you improve your ability to learn from those outside your organization:

- What innovations, suggested by staff, have been implemented this year?
- What services and products have remained unchanged over the last five years?
- What did you learn from your last visit to a supplier?
- How many joint action teams do you have with existing clients?
- When was the last time you set up a joint venture with a competitor?
- What new markets have you created this year?
- With which of your suppliers do you have quality improvement projects?
- What changes have you made as a result of listening to your users' suggestions?
- How can you involve your customers in helping you with marketing and market research?
- What changes have you made in your own life in the last year?

The Learning Company doesn't just exist in an environment – it sets out to develop it's users, suppliers and even competitors in order to learn and to develop itself.

Using boundary workers to collect intelligence from the environment can help with two forms of learning in the Learning Company. First, it helps with the monitoring of current services and products and with the continuous improvement of these. Second, it can provide clues about what the future may hold in terms of major shifts. This is important because much of the organizing effort in companies is aimed at stability and continuity – at keeping things the same.

This applies to the skills and knowledge of people in the company. Organizations often attempt to define the competencies that are needed in certain jobs or for certain career paths. These tend to be oriented to the skills that are needed to allow the organization to continue to do what it is already doing well. Again, although this is a necessary and useful process, as a major component of a human resource development strategy it tends to fix or reinforce current or historical ways of doing things in a company.

FRACTURE LINES   Glimpse 55

There seem to be two ways out of the problem of being trapped by stability and continuity: recognizing learning as a competence and recognizing forecasting as a competence.

In our work on self-development we propose that the skills of learning itself are creativity, mental agility and balanced learning habits and offer various ways of developing these abilities. Developing learning competence in itself is an attractive option in the Learning Company because it offers the prospect of people becoming more flexible in their ability to take on and quickly master new tasks.

Another option is to develop the environmental scanning capability of the company; specifically the skills of forecasting. Gareth Morgan suggests that the skills of reading the future are a crucial area of managerial competence. He uses the notion of spotting 'fracture lines' – the emerging major discontinuities in the social and economic system of which any company is embedded, the reaction to which will significantly determine the company's future.

Such changes are easy to identify in retrospect – an oil crisis, an ecological crisis, major changes in political power, privatization – but what will future fracture lines be?

FOLLOW UP

Pedler, M., Burgoyne J. and Boydell, T. (1994) *A Manager's Guide to Self-Development*, 3rd edn, McGraw-Hill, Maidenhead.

Morgan, G. (1988) *Riding the Waves of Change*, Jossey Bass, New York.

Some companies, such as SmithKline Beecham, have instituted 'future skills' projects to try to identify the skills, competences and capabilities that will be required in the company in, say, ten years' time. This involves forecasting what skills will be required in the company itself and what will be 'bought' from outside (Pedler and Aspinwall, 1996, pp.83–87).

But how do you go about identifying these future skills and capabilities? One solution is to employ some forecasting 'experts'. Again, however, it is easy to fall into the trap of using outside agencies to tell you what your people already know – if you really listen to them. This does not mean that the expert reports are useless, of course, but it does suggest recruiting all those who work for the company to be part of the intelligence effort.

Glimpse 56

FUNNY STORY?

The shop assistant had to disappoint her customer ... 'Sorry dear, we don't stock that any more, there's no call for it.'

Then after a moment she said ...

'Mind you ... people do keep asking for it ....'

REFERENCE

Pedler, M.J. and Aspinwall, K.A. (1996) *'Perfect plc?': The Purpose and Practice of Organizational Learning*, McGraw-Hill, Maidenhead.

This refers to the way companies can learn with and from each other. The Learning Company is always on the lookout for opportunities to learn with others – especially with trading partners. Joint ventures, joint training, sharing investment in R & D and job exchanges are some of the ways in which companies can work together with a specific learning purpose.

Learning from companies in other industries can happen through 'benchmarking'. For example, when Rank Xerox wanted to learn about how to handle heavy equipment, it set out to learn from Caterpillar, who is regarded as being the best at this. In turn Rank Xerox encourages others to learn from it with their slogan 'come and steal shamelessly from us'.

Learning from competitors is another way. When Boots the Chemists introduced a free prescription delivery service in South Yorkshire, Weldricks, the local chemists' chain was quick off the mark in offering the same service to its customers. This sort of responsiveness is what learning in many companies is all about. Take the UK's Rover Cars for example.

THE ROVER LEARNING BUSINESS

Glimpse 57

As a minnow among whales, the Rover Group realized that it would soon be swallowed up if it did not change radically. The company began a collaboration with Honda from Japan that challenged many of the assumptions held by the people in Rover. It also eventually produced cars that were perceived as much better and more reliable than their predecessors.

Rover Group has a long and illustrious history with the Austin, Morris, MG and many other famous marques in its biography. Yet by the 1980s – like so many other household names – a new direction was needed. As the managing director said, the reason for the collaboration with Honda stemmed from a critical need to learn:

> As a company we desperately needed to learn. We thought there was only one way to run a car manufacturing plant. Our collaboration with Honda taught us differently.

One fruit of this learning is the Rover Learning Business, a business within a business, which has a brief to provide learning and development opportunities to all 40 000 members of the Group. All employees are entitled to a Personal Development Plan with the company and a Personal Development Budget. Publicizing the activities of the Rover Learning Business has been a key objective, both inside and outside the company, from the start. Learning has become an important part of the company image.

However, having learned a great deal from Honda, Rover switched its allegiance when it became part of the German company BMW in 1994. The BMW management valued Rover's niche market leaders such as the Landrover and Range Rover and saw synergy in the vehicle ranges of the two groups. Clearly this was another learning opportunity that Rover saw as meeting better their long-term objectives. However, their erstwhile partner, Honda was surprised and unhappy with this change of direction, it did not accord with its assumptions about long-term partnerships.

The urge to learning is sometimes opportunistic, impulsive, sudden. We commit ourselves without being able to fully evaluate the risk.

Some of the best inter-company learning comes from joint ventures and experiments. Various forms of strategic alliance have become an integral part of contemporary strategic thinking. The takeover boom of the 'Acquisitive '80s' has given way to a rising wave of cooperative agreements as, in the face of rising competition or increased demands from users, many public and private sector organizations are looking to share costs and resources to supply new services, acquire new technologies or enter new markets.

Some writers link joint venturing with the notion of the 'Virtual Organization' as

> an enterprise which can marshal more resources than it currently has on its own, using collaborations both inside and outside its boundaries (Byrne, 1993)

which links with the idea of the organization-as-process discussed in the last chapter. In many communities, local authorities, social services departments and health organizations are exploring how they can work together to pool already inadequate resources in the face of rising expectations and demands from clients and customers. Multi-agency collaboration and cross-boundary working will become the norm rather than the exception here. However, although such partnerships are often founded on the basis of sharing costs or exploring new markets, they may work best if they are based upon a mutual learning contract.

LEARNING PARTNERSHIPS

Glimpse 58

Creating a good partnership is clearly a more complex and long-term matter than making an acquisition. For Rosabeth Kanter, *collaborative advantage'* – a key corporate asset – stems from the ability to be a good partner. Such alliances are living systems that evolve progressively to enable partners to create new value together rather than just being a deal in which you get something in return for your investment. They cannot be controlled by formal systems but require:

> a dense web of interpersonal connections and internal infrastructures that enhance learning. (Kanter, 1994)

According to many research papers, joint ventures should be seen as long-term commitments rather than as a basis for short-term financial gain. While the choice of partner is often made on financial grounds, alliances based on strategic and operational synergy are likely to do best. Mutual trust and commitment can be hard to achieve but where it works the need for close cooperation with others imposes a distinct set of requirements on the firm, including the need for substantial delegation and an emphasis on organizational learning.

One paper suggests that alliances should be structured as:

> learning platforms to assimilate new technologies and skills to revitalise their core operations and find new uses for existing skills; guidelines for managing alliances are: (i) understand the firm's core competence and skills; (ii) choose partners with complementary skills and markets; (iii) match external alliances with internal strategic intent. (Lei, 1993)

FOLLOW UP

Kanter, R.M. (1994) 'Collaborative Advantage: The art of alliances', *Harvard Business Review*, July/August.

Lei, D. (1993) 'Offensive and defensive uses of alliances', *Long Range Planning*, **26**(4).

One example of a synergistic partnership based on complementary skills is that of Nissan and Pilkington's in Washington in the UK. Here the car plant includes a glass plant that makes the windscreens.

INTEGRATED OPERATIONS

Glimpse 59

The windscreen manufacturing plant is on the car assembly site, but it belongs to a glass firm and not to the motor manufacturer. Just-in-time delivery systems and a TQM regime stitch the two together pretty completely. Staff in the glass plant are employees of the glass firm but culturally and day-to-day are part of the car assembly plant. Career planning and other aspects of managing are dealt with jointly and both the glass firm and the car manufacturer learn from practices that they would not normally experience.

Some of this learning is 'exported' to other parts of their businesses. It's a bonus that was not anticipated when the integrated plant was set up. The Learning Company sets out deliberately to learn from such collaborative relationships.

In the process, Pilkington's were integrated with Nissan's management procedures, including the quality system. The Nissan culture also affected employment policies including career management, and one result was that pay and conditions were harmonized. The story is that Pilkington's learned many lessons from this experience that they were able to take back to their other plants.

Nissan and Pilkington's operate as equal partners, yet sometimes one partner learns more from the relationship. Marks & Spencer is well known for making high demands upon their suppliers and for spending a great deal of time in the plants of suppliers making sure that things work as they should.

Glimpse 60

MARKS AND SPENCER'S SUPPLIERS

M & S are reputed to have a strong and demanding influence on their suppliers. Rigorous quality control standards are applied and monitoring procedures reach deep into suppliers' operations.

Suppliers are said to have mixed reactions to this, though not too mixed or too public if they wish to stay suppliers. The exacting standards do improve their quality, but sometimes too much so for their other markets. There are feelings of loss of control and of being trapped into dependency, yet they have achieved the status of no. 1 supplier on the high street. Suppliers certainly learn things from M & S, but is there a flow of learning in the other direction?

These are some of the dynamics of interorganizational relationships and learning. Here M & S's famous quality control procedures reach deeply into the suppliers' organizations with the end-result that these companies become very effective and produce high-quality goods. In this case, because of the dominant size of one partner, there is the downside of the loss of control on the part of the supplier.

Nevertheless, the web of relationships that a company has with its suppliers, customers and business partners is a potentially rich source of learning.

Glimpse 61

STRIVING TO PLEASE OUR MEMBERS

In Glimpse 26, we saw how Traidcraft tries to be accountable to all its stakeholders. As well as being socially responsible this is also a good source of learning. The Learning Company aims to be successful in the long term by striving to meet the requirements of all stakeholders including suppliers, neighbours, owners, even competitors, as well as employees and customers. These are the members of the company in the widest sense of the word. Here is an activity to help you think through the learning potential of your membership network.

1. Brainstorm a list of the members of your company, as has been done below for

Totley Kitchen Designs. Your list may include specific names and also more general clusters of people.

- Suppliers   Woods Timber
                     Premier Transport
                     Hardcliff Catering
                     Hallamshire Bus Company
                     Yorkshire Electricity
- Owners   All shareholders
                     Jo Taylor Partners
                     Jean Mann
- Neighbours   Duplex Manufacturing (specific company)
                     Local people (group of residents)
                     River Don; Totley Woods (environment)
                     Statutory bodies representing neighbours
- Competitors   Beta Kitchens
                     Lancaster Paint Company.

2. As the full list may be quite long, the next step is to choose some priorities. Choose at least one from each group, and for each of the chosen members, discuss what you think would

- delight them
- please them
- satisfy them.

Give yourself a score out of ten as to how well you're doing at the moment on each of these points for each member. Then describe why you gave this score – what data did you use? (Rather than just talking, you and your colleagues could role play the various members and their views.)

3. Now identify and note some ways in which your stakeholders could help you using this classification:

- things you do that help me to please you – *please continue or do even more of these*
- things you do that make it difficult for me to please you – *please do less of these or stop altogether*
- things you don't do now that would help me to please you – *please start to do these*.

4. As the purpose of all this is to improve and to learn from your relationships with your members, you now need to grasp the nettle and go out to talk with them. This will involve describing the ideas behind the approach; sharing your views of what will delight, please or satisfy them; and, also sharing your picture of how well you think you are doing and getting their view is of this. Finally, you can tell them what you would find helpful from them.

Going through this process with some business partners might take several meetings, especially with tricky relationships such as competitors or those with a poor history. Yet a company's ability to make alliances and operate in networks is emerging as one of the key areas of organizational capability for the future.

While developing the competences for survival and learning is an important requirement for the individual organization, it is also part of a wider awareness of the interconnections between units. An ecological perspective on the Learning Company underlies the third level of the definition that we put forward in the early part of this book. At this level learning is not just for individual survival and adaptation but for mutually sustaining relationships in a stable ecology.

Glimpse 62

ECO-AUDITING

Esprit de Corp, the American casual clothing company, commissioned Fritjof Capra's Elmwood Institute in Berkeley, California, to carry out an 'eco-audit' of the business. This attempts to assess the impact of the business on its environment, and vice versa, and the internal relationships among the members. It also explores the links between these inner and outer relationships.

The eco-audit is a response to the perspective of organizational ecology and focuses on the collaborative as well as the competitive aspects of relationships between organizations. Ecologists in general are concerned about the effects of industrial pollution, and an ecological perspective on organizations sees the potentially destructive effects of individualistic and hyper-competitive actions of powerful companies that threaten the social world.

As the ethics of collaboration and partnership come more to the fore, organizational ecologists stress 'the survival of the fitting':

> Seen from a global viewpoint, the organization exists only as part of a larger reality, supported and nurtured by the larger system on which it depends. . . . From such a viewpoint, organizational purpose is not simply decided by its members, but is, in large part, 'given' by its membership of the larger system. . . . Adopting such a view requires a fundamental change in one's orientation to goals and the success or failure of one's plans. . . . [We can profitably] take the view that our organization has an appropriate place in the larger system, and that our task as managers and leaders is to attune our organization to its environment in order to discover what our part is and play it. The difficulties we experience are interpreted as signs and signals from the environment that we are somehow out of resonance with our true role. . . . According to this point of view it should not be difficult for an organization to survive and thrive, any more than an organ in a healthy body has to work especially hard to survive. When it plays its part it receives the nourishment it needs. From a system point of view, then, strategic thinking is a search for meaning, rather than a search for advantage. (Harrison, 1983)

FOLLOW UP

Harrison, R. (1983) 'Strategies for a New Age', *Human Resource Management*, **22**(3), 209–235.

Callenbach, E. et al. (1993) *Eco Management*, Berrett-Koehler, San Francisco.

REFERENCE

Byrne, J.A. (1993) 'The Futurists who fathered the ideas', *Business Week*, 3304, 8 February.

17. A Learning Climate

No. 10 of the 11 Characteristics of the Learning Company

The Learning Company aims to generate and maintain a culture and climate that encourages learning. Two hallmarks of this climate are:

- Managers see their primary task as facilitating the learning of their people – it is normal to take time out to reflect, to question and to seek feedback on ideas, understandings and actions. Senior managers set the tone by demonstrating their own learning habits, by requesting feedback and by questioning their own assumptions and actions.
- What happens when a mistake is made? The non-learning reaction is to cover up, not to admit fault, to try and 'pass the buck'. While not actually encouraged, mistakes in Learning Companies are more in the way of being experiments that didn't produce the right results. Why not? And how can we do better next time? How mistakes are handled is an instructive marker of the overall learning climate of the company.

Glimpse 63

A LEARNING COMPANY LITMUS TEST

There is an old story about the young person who, entrusted with a high-profile project, made a risky decision and ended up costing the organization a great deal of money. Expecting the worst, she was summoned to the boardroom and subjected to a painful interview. At the end of this she was amazed to be told that she was being offered the post of personal assistant to the chairman. 'Thank you ... ,' she gasped, 'but I expected to be sacked!' 'What, after all the investment we've made in you?' snapped the Chairman. 'What nonsense! I want value for my money from you, and soon.'

What's the reaction to failure in your company?

Do people deny their mistakes, bury the evidence and cover their backs?

Or do they say, 'I did it like this and it didn't work, but this is what I learned from it'?

The Learning Company strives to create the kind of climate where failures, accidents, breakdowns and mistakes are learned from so that they can be avoided in the future. This means making time for review, whatever the work pressures. It means that the leadership style and culture is about learning from experience and not one of allocating blame and punishment. Managers say things like, 'Do your best and if it doesn't work, let's talk about it and find out why'. Planning to collect information, to monitor, review and evaluate new ventures is part of the skill of operating the Learning Company.

This doesn't mean that we choose failure or take stupid risks – far from it. If you want a litmus paper test of where your company stands as a Learning Company, just look at the way the last three errors, breakdowns or failures were dealt with.

- Did people talk openly about them or did they hide away and avoid the subject?
- What was learned from the mistakes?
- Did people get blamed or did they feel empowered as a result of the postmortem?

In many companies it just isn't possible to talk about mistakes. When you make one you feel awful about it, it gets left with you, it isn't OK to talk about it and therefore for you to have a chance to redeem the error through learning and the knowledge that things will be different next time.

As ever, the Learning Company starts with little things. You can make a start today by talking about failure in a constructive spirit. Adopting a non-punitive – but not soft – leadership style is something any one person can do today to move us all that little bit along the road.

In a healthy learning climate it is commonplace for people to be learning to do new things. There is an atmosphere of continual improvement and constructive questioning. In Woodmill School, a new headteacher showed herself to be a leader of learning in the way she behaved. She was always learning herself and when she came across a new idea in teaching reading she broadcast this and demonstrated it in the school. She made learning normal and part of the daily round. Of course, this was a new tradition and some of the staff found it hard to cope with the new attitudes.

LEADING THE LEARNING COMPANY

Mr Thorncliffe, the head of Woodmill School, died at his post after 32 years in the job. Woodmill was a very private school – the teachers respected each other's space and didn't talk about work in the staffroom, sticking to subjects like homes and holidays. Probationers found it a tough school to learn in. If they asked for help, they were likely to be told 'We had to learn how to teach for ourselves!', or, 'Work it out for yourself' and they rarely stayed longer than their probationary year if they could help it.

The new head, Mrs Ashton, brought in one or two new teachers, but she also brought some new ways of behaving. She was taking an Open University course in the teaching of reading to young children and one day she burst excitedly into the

Glimpse 64

staffroom saying, 'Look at this! I've just discovered this research which shows that children look at the whole page of a book as a whole picture and not as lines of print. We have to teach them to follow each line along from left to right – isn't that amazing! It's so obvious! How could I have been teaching all these years without realizing that?'

While ashamed of herself for not knowing such an 'obvious' thing, Mrs Ashton was not embarrassed, she did not hide it or to let it dampen her enthusiasm for learning. This was typical of her and gradually she introduced a new atmosphere into the school.

Not everyone in the school thought she was wonderful. Some did not like her new ways and did not think that she behaved 'properly'. In particular, one senior, rather authoritarian, teacher consistently sought to undermine her efforts. Eventually this person was persuaded to retire early.

Four conditions for leadership in the Learning Company emerge from this story:

- *Do it yourself* you are always engaged in learning something – what's your current learning project?
- *Share and demonstrate your new learning* when did you last make it obvious to your colleagues that you've just learned something?
- *Make learning normal, legitimize it and encourage others to do it* learning is part of life and work in the Learning Company – look around you, is it obvious that those around you are learning from what they are doing?
- *Be tough and persistent in confirming learning as a central value* this is the clear sticking point. From time to time all of us need many opportunities and much help to learn what comes easily for others. Finally it is important to uphold the human right not to learn – being forced to learn is both a contradiction and an offence to personal dignity – although taking up this right is likely to carry certain consequences with it.

You can overdo it, of course. As a leader you can't always be asking for help, you can't behave as if you don't know anything. Openness to learning is not the same thing as incompetence, yet many people in leadership roles do feel a great deal of pressure to be competent all the time. That makes it very hard to learn anything – because highly competent people don't admit to needing to learn, and no one around them dares to teach them. Eventually you get a non-learning company – and there are too many of those already.

Leading the Learning Company demands lots of competence *especially* those of being able to admit ignorance, the ability to display incompetence and, occasionally, the capacity of being able to 'make a fool of yourself' in trying to learn something new.

Actually it is quite easy to measure the Learning Climate in your company. Anyone who has worked in an industry such as steel or heavy engineering knows how much it is second nature to walk around the plant being on the lookout for safety. Unguarded machines, uncoiled ropes, tools left out, materials blocking throughways are all immediately recognized by the trained eye.

It should go without saying that safety remains of paramount importance in these situations, but there may be less recognition that learning is a critical factor in survival of quite another kind. Measuring the Learning Climate in your company is a question of noticing how things are done from a learning point of view.

Here are two ways to measure the Learning Climate in your organization. The first of these – the Organizational Toxicity Index or OTI – started as a bit of fun really, but it attracted a lot of attention in the first edition of this book. People wrote and called up to say, 'where can I get the full version of this?' Clearly, they recognized the phenomenon.

ORGANIZATIONAL TOXICITY INDEX (OTI)

Glimpse 65

A Learning Company has a healthy climate fit for human beings to live and learn in. Many companies today are less than healthy, and some are downright toxic – or poisonous to developing people. You can take a climate check on your company with the Organizational Toxicity Index below.

For each of the following ten questions choose one of the responses – a, b or c – on the basis of which is truest, in your experience, most of the time.

ORGANIZATIONAL TOXICITY INDEX
'In my company ...

1. **sexist and racist remarks are commonplace and tolerated by management.'**

   a This is not a problem. ☐
   b This is something of a problem. ☐
   c This is a big problem for me and others. ☐

2. **praise is much rarer than criticism.'**

   a This is not a problem. ☐
   b This is something of a problem. ☐
   c This is a big problem for me and others. ☐

3. **you get little information about your own performance.'**

   a This is not a problem. ☐
   b This is something of a problem. ☐
   c This is a big problem for me and others. ☐

4. **there is competitive pressure from fellow employees to work long hours.'**

   a This is not a problem. ☐
   b This is something of a problem. ☐
   c This is a big problem for me and others. ☐

5. there is little concern shown for members' health and welfare.'

a This is not a problem.   ☐
b This is something of a problem.   ☐
c This is a big problem for me and others.   ☐

6. making admissions of mistakes or failure is "career limiting".'

a This is not a problem.   ☐
b This is something of a problem.   ☐
c This is a big problem for me and others.   ☐

7. all management decisions are justified in terms of the "bottom line", that is, solely on financial grounds.'

a This is not a problem.   ☐
b This is something of a problem.   ☐
c This is a big problem for me and others.   ☐

8. there are a lot of hierarchical distinctions made in terms of conditions, perks like cars and offices, canteens and so on.'

a This is not a problem.   ☐
b This is something of a problem.   ☐
c This is a big problem for me and others.   ☐

9. there is little diversity in management – most are male, white, etc.'

a This is not a problem.   ☐
b This is something of a problem.   ☐
c This is a big problem for me and others.   ☐

10. it's very hard to get people to listen to you and your ideas.'

a This is not a problem.   ☐
b This is something of a problem.   ☐
c This is a big problem for me and others.   ☐

Scoring

Score 0 for every a, 1 for every b and 2 for every c.
The minimum score is 0, the maximum 20.

- If you scored less than 5, then your company is comparatively healthy, although there may be some points that need attention.
- If you scored 6 to 12, then your company is quite toxic – to the point that many people's performance must be impaired.
- If you scored more than 12, your company is getting to the point where it is not fit for human beings to live and work in. Time to do the decent thing?

_____

Many important decisions are defined as much by the things they are trying to avoid as by what they are trying to bring about. The story of Keatings (Glimpse 35) shows how much strategy was set by the toxic factors that Mike Keating was determined to avoid. He was determined not to make some of the mistakes that he had experienced before in his career with a large company – the size of the company, the endless trouble over wage differentials; the endless squabbling of managers and trade unions. This is not a bad place to start from in working out what you want.

The OTI stresses the importance of detecting toxins that may damage or limit the learning processes in the company. Looking at the 'shadow side', of how things really are rather than how they ought to be according to the orthodox managerial interpretation, is often a useful way of examining organizational matters.

Glimpse 66 is another way to measure the Learning Climate of your organization and looks this time at the positive side.

ENCOURAGING THE LEARNING HABIT

Glimpse 66

One of the defining characteristics of the Learning Company is of being a place that encourages everyone who works in it or who has contact with it to learn. It has the 'learning habit' so that actions taken for reasons of production, marketing, problem solving or customer service also yield a harvest of reflections, insights and new ideas for action.

Here is a simple questionnaire that you can use to measure how well you encourage the learning habit in your company, department or team. Learning Companies aspire to scores in the 50 to 70 range as the best guarantee of future survival, maintenance and development. If your score comes to 30 or less, you have a poor learning climate.

THE LEARNING HABIT QUESTIONNAIRE
For each of the following ten dimensions, ring the number that you think best represents the quality of the Learning Climate in your company, 1 being very poor, 7 being excellent:

1. Physical environment
The amount and quality of space and privacy afforded to people; the temperature, noise, ventilation and comfort levels.

People are cramped little privacy and poor conditions	1 2 3 4 5 6 7	People have plenty of with space, privacy and good surroundings

2. Learning resources
Numbers, quality and availability of training and development staff, books, films, training packages, IT facilities, equipment, etc.

Very few or no trained people, poor resources and equipment	1 2 3 4 5 6 7	Many development people and lots of resources; very good facilities

3. Encouragement to learn
The extent to which people feel encouraged to have ideas, take risks, experiment and learn new ways of doing old tasks.

Little encouragement to learn; there are low expectations of people in terms of new skills and abilities	1 2 3 4 5 6 7	People are encouraged to learn at all times and to extend themselves and their knowledge

4. Communications
How open and free is the flow of information? Do people express ideas and opinions easily and openly?

Feelings kept to self; secretive; information is hoarded	1 2 3 4 5 6 7	People are usually ready to give their views and pass on information

5. Rewards
How well rewarded are people for effort? Is recognition given for good work or are people punished and blamed?

People are ignored but then blamed when things go wrong	1 2 3 4 5 6 7	People are recognized for good work and rewarded for effort and learning

6. Conformity
The extent to which people are expected to conform to rules, norms, regulations, policies rather than think for themselves.

There is conformity to rules and standards at all times – no personal responsibility taken or given	1 2 3 4 5 6 7	People manage themselves and do their work as they see fit; great emphasis on taking personal responsibility

7. Value placed on ideas
How much are ideas, opinions and suggestions sought out, encouraged and valued?

People are 'not paid to think'; their ideas are not valued	1 2 3 4 5 6 7	Efforts are made to get people to put ideas forward; there is a view that the future rests on people's ideas

8. Practical help available
The extent to which people help each other, lend a hand, offer skills, knowledge or support.

People don't help each other; there is unwillingness to pool or share resources	1 2 3 4 5 6 7	People very willing and helpful; pleasure is taken in the success of others

9. Warmth and support
How friendly are people in the company? Do people support, trust and like one another?

Little warmth and support; this is a cold, isolating place	1 2 3 4 5 6 7	Warm and friendly place; people enjoy coming to work; good relationships = good work

10. Standards
The emphasis placed upon quality in all things; people set challenging standards for themselves and each other.

Low standards and quality; no one really gives a damn	1 2 3 4 5 6 7	High standards; everyone cares and people pick each other up on work quality

In carrying out a survey of the company, it is usual to find differences in the various parts or sections. What is the explanation for this? The person in charge of a department usually has the biggest influence on the learning climate. Does that person have the development of an excellent learning climate as a key objective?

One of the characteristics of a Learning Company is that many of the members have acquired and value training and development skills. For example, a German department store in Bonn has 73 out of 450 employees – more than 1 in 7 people – who are professionally qualified trainers (Holland, 1986). How does your company compare on that standard?

Of course it is not just a question of how many of us have professional qualifications – although that would be a useful start – but of how seriously we take the issue of creating a learning climate which ensures that everyone acquires and keeps the learning habit. This is a key building block of the Learning Company and also, given the resources and the commitment, one which is relatively simple to enact.

Once managers accept their role as developers of their people and become interested in the skills involved, the next question is: how to go about it?

INSTRUCTOR, COACH OR MENTOR?

Glimpse 67

For the manager as developer there is always the question of what is the right, the most appropriate style for this type of skill, for this particular person, under these conditions? David Megginson has provided a useful summary of three styles together with a questionnaire to help you diagnose your own preferred style and to clarify the alternatives.

QUESTIONNAIRE

For each statement, circle the number that best represents your usual style in helping people to learn things.

1. 'Before telling people about a job I want them to do, I work out, stage by stage, what's involved in it.'

Seldom   0 1 2 3 4 5 6   Often

2. 'I actively seek out opportunities for people to develop themselves through doing new things at work.'

Seldom   0 1 2 3 4 5 6   Often

3. 'I listen to people's ideas and help them fit these into their broad plans for work and life.'

Seldom   0 1 2 3 4 5 6   Often

4. 'When I have something I want people to do, I give them very clear instructions.'

Seldom   0 1 2 3 4 5 6   Often

5. 'When helping people to learn, I help them plan how to meet challenges at work.'

Seldom   0 1 2 3 4 5 6   Often

6. 'I ask people questions that help them think through why they want to do things.'

Seldom   0 1 2 3 4 5 6   Often

7. 'I check that people have understood their instructions clearly.'

Seldom   0 1 2 3 4 5 6   Often

8. 'I am prepared to let people try new things, even if there is a risk that they may not do the job well.'

Seldom   0 1 2 3 4 5 6   Often

9. 'I am interested in what people do outside work and how this fits in or conflicts with work activities.'

Seldom   0 1 2 3 4 5 6   Often

10. 'I check up on things I've asked people to do, and let them know how they did.'

Seldom   0 1 2 3 4 5 6   Often

11. 'I encourage people to review how they perform and plan how to improve.'

Seldom   0 1 2 3 4 5 6   Often

12. 'I sit down with people and help them think through where they are going in their career.'

Seldom   0 1 2 3 4 5 6   Often

Scoring
To calculate your scores, total up the numbers for each of the questions in three columns as follows:

Instructor		Coach		Mentor	
Q1	☐	Q2	☐	Q3	☐
Q4	☐	Q5	☐	Q6	☐
Q7	☐	Q8	☐	Q9	☐
Q10	☐	Q11	☐	Q12	☐
Totals	__		__		__

The higher your score in any one column, the more you tend to that style of helping others to learn.

INTERPRETING YOUR SCORE
What is your style? A score of 15 or more for any of these shows quite a strong preference, while 5 or less would show a marked avoidance. If you have pursued a 'central tendency' on the questionnaire, your scores will average around 12 to 16.

Is this style good or bad? First, you can ask a colleague to do the questionnaire and compare your scoring with their's. Best of all, you could ask the people themselves – the learners. Why not do the questionnaire again now, and use the whole range of marks – let's say you can't use the 2, 3 and 4 more than twice each.

Table G67.1 describes the styles. This should help you to locate yourself more accurately and perhaps give you some ideas for things you might do differently or try out next time you are helping someone to learn.

Table G67.1 Three ways of helping people to learn

Dimension	Instructor	Coach	Mentor
Focus of help	Task	Results of job	Development of person throughout life
Timespan	A day or two	A month to a year	Career or lifetime
Approach to helping	'Show and tell' – give supervised practice	Explore problem together and set up opportunities to try out new skills	Act as friend willing to play 'devil's advocate', listen and question to enlarge awareness
Associated activities	Analysing task; clear instruction; supervised practice; give feedback on results at once	Jointly identify the problem; create development opportunity and review	Link work with other parts of life; clarify broad and long-term aims and purpose in life
Ownership	Helper	Shared	Learner
Attitude to ambiguity	Eliminate	Use it as a challenge – as a puzzle to be solved	Accept as being part of the exciting world
Benefits to the company	Standard, accurate performance	Goal-directed performance oriented to improving and being creative	Conscious questioning approach to the mission of the company

FOLLOW UP
Megginson, D.F. and Pedler, M.J. (1991) *Self-development: A Facilitator's Guide*, McGraw-Hill, Maidenhead.

Learning as a top priority for managers is a relatively recent development. Traditionally the manager's job is about coordinating and supervising people to ensure that people meet their job requirements and fit in with the overall operations plan. This task remains important although people who are better trained and educated are more autonomous and self-supervising, freeing the manager for what is increasingly the more vital work of facilitating learning in individuals and in the company as a whole.

Many large organizations are creating special structures to bring about climates of continuous learning. At Motorola, this work is so central to the manufacturing process that the company has created its own 'University'.

Glimpse 68

MOTOROLA U

Ten years ago Motorola realized that they needed people who would work for quality and output rather than the time clock. The rules of manufacturing were changing and yet the company was trying to compete globally in new technologies with people who often couldn't read adequately – only 40 per cent of the people in one plant could answer the question 'Ten is what per cent of 100?'

Motorola then launched an ambitious scheme of education and training for its employees – a scheme that they have now extended not only to all their people worldwide, but also to employees of suppliers, of principle customers and even to those of educational partners. This has built up over the ten years with many mistakes on the way, one of which was the attempt to put 400 executives through an MBA in four weeks!

Calling it a 'university' seemed ambitious, but Motorola operates with a wide range of educational partners who resource and credit the programmes and whose attitudes to collaboration with business had to change along the way. The definition of company training changed as it became not just for the company and the job but also for the person. The commitment is to:

> Creating an environment for learning, a continuous openness to new ideas. . . . We not only teach people how to respond to new technologies, we try to commit them to the goal of anticipating new technologies. . . . We not only teach skills, we try to breathe the very spiral of creativity and flexibility into manufacturing and management.

FOLLOW UP
Wiggenhorn, W. (1990) 'Motorola U: When training becomes an education', *Harvard Business Review*, July/August, pp.71–83.

Motorola's effort, like that of many other big organizations that have followed similar routes, is primarily aimed at individuals, in the hope that as more and more people become committed to the learning habit it will become a normal part of life in the company.

One of the enduring mysteries of the Learning Company idea is the question of whether the company can be said to learn as a single, whole organism, or whether it is actually just a company full of people who are learning. The latter is more sensible and understandable but it does not meet some of the tests of the idea – how can the company 'learn' its way through major changes and crises rather than fall behind at first and then, if it is to survive, endure abrupt and often brutal treatment? Lots of individuals learning does not necessarily mean that the company as a whole will act 'intelligently' and as one. This is the problem that Senge (1990, p.9) has referred to at a team level when he talks of a group of managers, each with an IQ of more than 120, producing a collective output with an IQ of 63!

It is most infuriating when, having finally resolved some expensive problem, someone from another part of the business says, 'Oh, we could have told you how to do that!' Yet, this is a common phenomenon: much needed know-how exists just around the corner, but you didn't know that and perhaps you didn't ask.

How can we get to know what is available in the way of knowledge, and skills, throughout the company? How can we avail people struggling with knotty problems of the immense array of know-how and expertise in the business? The idea of the 'learning community' is an elusive one, yet it underpins many hopes for the Learning Company idea.

THE LEARNING COMMUNITY

Glimpse 69

A learning community exercise may help to seed the idea for the organization as a whole. Twelve to thirty members meet on any given theme, for example, pay, motivation and morale, over two or three days, off-site. They identify and post up their needs – what they need to help them do their jobs better, to resolve the problems facing them, to overcome current blocks to progress and development. Members also work on and post up their offers – what they know, what they can do, that may be of value to others in this field and which they are prepared to put on offer.

Needs and offers are posted on a notice board and members may then make contracts to match their needs with appropriate offers. The structure is free-form and tends towards the chaotic. There is a 'free market' in needs and offers and market regulation is created only by the actions of members. Therefore, it helps to have a facilitator or two – encouraging people to be less bashful in putting forward offers, to be proactive in setting up meetings, picking up the lost and lonely and, also, once a day or so, calling a meeting to collectively review progress.

Surprising connections can be made in a learning community. Minor miracles such as going to fulfil a contract on an offer you have made and mysteriously finding that one of your own needs is met in so doing. Above all people become aware of the richness of the environment surrounding them – the knowledge, the skills, the opportunities.

However, people must be ready for the learning community – the prevailing climate has to be one where people are willing to be open and to share their ideas and experience. They also have to be able to cope with this level of messiness. Beyond and above any learning on the actual theme chosen, the learning community can help members learn to cope with 'chaos' and to be self-directing while also trying to be conscious of the whole.

FOLLOW UP
Megginson, D.F. and Pedler, M.J. (1976) 'Developing structures and technology for the learning community', *Journal of European Training*, **5**(5).

Creating a learning community off-site for a day or two is one thing; building it in the whole organization every day is another. However, practising this sort of working together may give a glimpse of what the analogous behaviour might be on the day-to-day basis. For example, the conflict between deciding whether to make an offer rather than get a need met, requires the sort of 'both' ... 'and' ... thinking needed to make the idea work company-wide. I want *both* to get my needs met, *and* to make myself available as a resource to others. In the organization I am *both* determined to fight for the resources that my department needs, *and* equally keen to meet the requirements of those others who are my clients, users and customers – my buyers and suppliers.

These dilemmas are both a source of conflict and of learning. The place of diversity, differences and conflict are discussed in Chapter 9 and especially in Glimpses 10, 11 and 12. It's clear that being in a Learning Company does not make for a quiet life. In adults and in mature organizations learning is always associated with a certain amount of upset, of giving up old ways to take on new ones. The Learning Company is one that, every now and again, is able to challenge its own operating assumptions, its very taken for granted ways of doing things and this cannot be done without conflict and argument.

However, we can only get learning out of constructive conflict, not out of endemic flare ups or habitual strife where the differences have become entrenched, repetitive, unresolved. Another important litmus test of a learning climate is whether we can talk about difficult things. Can we fight about the important things?

FIGHTING ABOUT WHAT'S IMPORTANT

Conflict can be creative, starting from differences among us and leading to all of us seeing things differently – when we manage to find the 'third position', or, the synthesis of the argument and counter-argument. Yet it can also be destructive, leading to unresolved difficulties, running battles, stand-offs or insidious under-currents that haunt us in the future. The Learning Company has to find ways of encouraging more of the former and less of the latter. Perhaps it's not so much a question of having 'constructive conflicts' as having the attitude that causes us to ask the questions: 'Why are we in conflict?' and 'What can we learn from it?' (see Figure G70.1). This takes maturity and learning in itself.

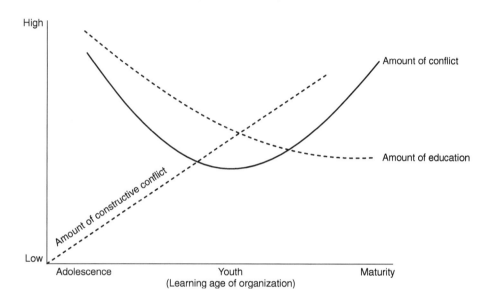

Figure G70.1 Learning from conflict

The level of conflict is high in 'adolescence', when shared understanding is low, and decreases with age. However, a sign of maturity in the company is that it can tolerate and cope with more conflict where differences are appropriately surfaced and worked on to produce new ideas and insights.

In this model, education plays a crucial part in converting conflict into learning. In 'adolescence', education focuses upon helping everyone learn the 'language' and skills of managing with others. This learning forms an essential infrastructure that enables learning and transformation from differences and conflict.

REFERENCES

Holland, G. (1986) 'Excellence in industry', Speech to Institute of Directors at the Dorchester Hotel, London, 11 February.
Senge, P.M. (1990) *The Fifth Discipline: The Art and Practice of the Learning Organization*, Doubleday Currency, New York.

18. Self-development Opportunities for All
No. 11 of the 11 Characteristics of the Learning Company

In the Learning Company opportunities, facilities and resources for learning are made available for all. People are encouraged to manage their own learning and career development rather than either being ignored or moved around in some hidden chess game, occasionally being sent on training courses if they're lucky.

Learning starts from the job itself which is designed to be developmental. Helping people learn from their work is a priority for all managers, and job swaps and job shadowing are encouraged. Special groups – project teams, task forces, action learning groups and quality circles can all produce good learning opportunities. Additionally there are self-learning materials and resources centres as well as courses, seminars, workshops and all the physical resources needed to put learning at the centre of company life.

Because this is one of the most obvious avenues to the Learning Company there are many examples of companies pursuing a policy of 'self-development opportunities for all'. Organizations from all sectors of the social economy are realizing both the potential and the necessity of harnessing the self-development approach for all their people. Some have taken the step of equalizing development opportunities for all staff irrespective of rank, recognizing that the usual skewing of resources towards managers and away from front line people is not in the best interests of the business.

This stems from a realistic look at what is needed to stay up to the mark. We saw in the last chapter how Motorola was so alarmed at the prospect of doing business with people whose skills were not adequate that they established their own in-house 'university' offering programmes ranging from basic numeracy to MBA (Glimpse 68); and also how Rover offered all its staff Personal Development Plans and Budgets (Glimpse 57). This sort of thinking is used on a National Health Service development programme to encourage self-management and self-development.

PERSONAL DEVELOPMENT BUDGETS IN THE NHS

Glimpse 71

A National Health Service development programme for general managers includes £300 for each individual to spend as they wish. They can use it to buy books, to make visits, to buy in expertise, to go on a seminar. This is a very concrete way to empower learners and can produce self-management pay-offs out of all proportion to the smallish sums of cash involved.

The idea of personal development budgets is spreading in companies who want to step up their learning. There is nothing that demonstrates commitment to self-development more than giving a small but no-strings-attached cash budget to individuals. One company has divided its whole training budget by the number of staff and given complete responsibility for spending to individuals.

Most people are parsimonious with their budgets, finding very economical ways to support their learning and often pooling with others to put on special events. The budgets tend to lead people to look for value for money and also to break the habit of thinking, 'If it's learning it must be a course'. They can stimulate much careful thought about learning and development needs – by the individual *and* by their manager.

Some companies have systems that require submission of plans for approval to managers or committees before the budget can be spent, but it is very easy to kill interest and motivation by introducing such controls. Given the right size of budget, most people spend carefully and the problem can be getting some to use the money in time. The aim is to give control and responsibility for managing themselves to each person and then create opportunities to review learning and development on occasions such as annual appraisals.

Having Personal Development Budgets usually means that you have to have some sort of Personal Development Planning in place. Personal Development Plans (PDPs) are part of the new 'social technology' of the Learning Company and can have very helpful effects in terms of creating equal opportunities for learning. However, there is a danger that they can be 'captured' by the inexorable urge to systematize things and become too rigid, formal and lifeless.

PERSONAL DEVELOPMENT PLANS IN HALLAM CITY COUNCIL

Glimpse 72

Personal development plans (PDPs) are part of the 'software' of the Learning Company – everyone should have one. In Hallam City Council PDP's are part of the natural order of things. Here, unlike some other big organizations that have attached management control mechanisms such as performance reviews and produced rather too much paperwork, the city's plans are agreements between individuals with no central recording.

The idea is simple. Hallam believes that each individual is in a process of development – as a person and as a manual, clerical, professional or managerial worker. We can become aware of this process and, to some extent, direct ourselves towards desired ends – towards becoming the professional and the person we want to be.

Here is an outline of Hallam City Council's PDP. This particular form is just one of many possible variations of a written PDP format – if you like the idea, you need to develop a form that suits your company.

Learning contract

This learning contract represents an agreed commitment to development between _____ (participant) and _____ (sponsor) of Hallam City Council.

Date:

Part 1: preparation (A set of questions to help the person think through their needs and ambitions)

- Current job
  What are your key skills and areas of strength?
  Which tasks do you find the most difficult?
  What talents are not being used in your current job?
  What skills/knowledge do you think you lack?
  ... and so on.
- Career interests
  What alternative career paths are open to you?
  What work areas or tasks would lead to these?
  How is the work/home balance for you right now?
  Where could you be in five years' time?
  ... and so on.
- Development
  What education, training or development do you need?
  What's happening in your out-of-work life?
  What talents and abilities do you want to realize more?
  ... and so on.

Part 2: development plan (A list of goals with target dates, resources needed, etc.)

Development area	Objective	Method
For example: 1. Computing skills	1. Learn to operate, e.g. programming and keyboard skills on IBM PCs by 30 September	1. Coaching and hands-on practice
2.		
3. ... and so on.		

What kind of experience, special assignments, personal improvements, education and training would be helpful in the next 12 months? (It helps here if all the resources available in the company are listed, e.g. projects, attachments, libraries, open learning materials, people willing to coach on certain skills, sources of information, seminars and courses – internal and external, career counselling and so on.)

1. Computing: attachment to Geoff Dean's office (needs negotiating; can Celeste help?)
2.

. . . and so on.

Part 3: action plan (What can I do? Who can help? Would it be helpful to contact others? Who and when?)

Actions at work	Actions outside work
1. Computing: talk to Celeste, then to Geoff and fix, say, a regular half-day per week.	1.
2.	2.
. . . and so on.	

Review dates	Others involved

The PDP is an important building block not only because it ensures that attention is paid to each person's learning needs but also in creating the right sort of learning climate in the company. It is probably not a lot of use providing self-development opportunities for everyone if the organization has an unhealthy learning climate. For this reason, these last two of the 11 Characteristics of the Learning Company – Learning Climate and Self-development Opportunities for All – are often inseparable in practice.

However, it is important to create the right sort of PDP for each individual organization. The approach used by Hallam City Council fits with their culture – people are accustomed to formal procedures and to being publicly accountable for the use of funds and resources. However, at Keatings, a specialist printing company in North Wales, things are very different. We met Keatings earlier (in Glimpse 35) – in this company the only things that most people write down are job cards and telephone messages.

Glimpse 73

MULTI-SKILLING: LEARNING WITH AND FROM WORKMATES

At Keatings, a photogravure printing company, as in many firms, there is a technical logic in the order in which tasks must be completed that influences the work flow. One of the critical points in this flow is the Ohio – a computer-controlled engraving machine that can be left to cut away all night. Only a few people know how to use it, and they went to America to learn, but others would like to learn. There it sits in its glass room, separated from the dirt and noise of the plant, always on display, central to the work process. Because of this centrality, hi-tech nature and restricted access, the Ohio has a somewhat magical aura.

Company policy is to encourage all staff to develop themselves and to take personal responsibility for managing the firm, so it was decided to embark on a multi-skilling process. This included the creation of opportunities to learn how to use the Ohio, but would also give flexibility and strength in depth across the company. A list of all the jobs in the plant was drawn up – film making, engraving, proofing, plating, as well as accounting, sales and customer relations. Each person was asked to rate themselves regarding these jobs in four categories:

- learner
- competent worker
- craftsperson
- coach

Those who were the acknowledged masters at the job in question were invited to become coaches and given tuition in coaching skills. Those who wanted to learn a given job were encouraged to find a coach and set up agreed times for learning. These can be short full-time attachments, but are more usually small amounts of time each day or on a regular weekly basis.

Overall there has been a considerable development of new skills. Other benefits include a greater width of experience giving people more of a sense of the work process as a whole. However, the scheme worked better for some people than for others. The nature of relationships at Keatings is informal and they lacked that certain critical level of bureaucracy needed to maintain it. When the consultant who managed the scheme was not there, application was patchy.

Even so, at Keatings, everyone who wants to be can be a learner and a coach.

Multi-skilling increases the organization's capability to flex and adapt quickly. Combining the push towards multi-skilling with harnessing people's capacities to be both teachers or coaches and learners with each other is another hallmark of the Learning Company.

Career planning is often a key human resources management function in larger organizations. This provides yet another structure and opportunity for personal development planning.

COLLABORATIVE CAREER PLANNING

Schein (1978) has described careers as the result of a series of deals struck between individuals and the organizations they work for. It follows that the productivity of careers – for people and their companies – depends on how well informed each party is about the other's needs and intentions and also on the quality of the negotiating process. Many personnel problems are the result of bad deals between individuals and companies.

Collaborative career planning creates good deals for both parties. While the specifics of these vary with culture and circumstances, the general features of this process are that:

- individuals regularly take stock of themselves in terms of
  - what they're good at
  - what they have the potential to be good at
  - what abilities they are using and not using now
  - what they want to do and fulfil in the future
  - what is their image of their career
  - their view of the company's future and of particular developments to which they could contribute
  - avenues for personal development that might serve the company's interest as well as their own
- people have the opportunity to talk through their thoughts with those responsible for negotiating their careers on behalf of the company so that they have knowledge of and are involved in
  - company policy issues, options and likely areas of change and development
  - the implications of these for structures, roles, needed competencies and abilities in the future
  - a view of the opportunities and constraints that this will create in terms of career possibilities
- these discussions provide for an exchange of information allowing for mutual adjustment of views and, as part of a regular process of taking stock and discussing possibilities, they create a better informed background for making decisions, both at the personal and corporate levels.

Collaborative career planning can be more or less formal or systematized. It can be integrated with other processes such as appraisal, performance review and business planning. Information from career discussion can be fed into central databases to create a view of the collective competence and aspirations of staff who, in turn, are better informed about what they should choose and negotiate for themselves.

FOLLOW UP
Schein, E. (1978) *Career Dynamics*, Addison-Wesley, Reading, MA.
Germaine, C. and Burgoyne, J.G. (1984) 'Self-development and career planning: an exercise in mutual benefit', *Personnel Management*, April.

A good way of offering various learning opportunities within the company is to attach them to this career planning process. This was done at Express Foods which is very concerned, along with other organizations, to attract the very best talent into the company in the future. Once you have attracted able people you have to keep them. To keep them you have to offer them the opportunities to develop their abilities and add to their experience.

Glimpse 75

A LEARNING LADDER AT EXPRESS FOODS

Worries about future managerial talent led Express Foods in the UK to set up a learning ladder that offers a variety of programmes, starting with adult literacy and culminating in an MBA degree. The reasoning behind the scheme is that future job seekers will be in a 'buyer's market' and will choose employers who offer development opportunities as well as decent pay and conditions.

The personnel director spent a year thinking about the idea before he started to talk to his fellow directors. He attended seminars and read books about likely future demographic changes and the emergence of more flexible, adaptable organizations. He took time to talk personally to all his colleagues before tabling the idea. He felt it was crucially important not only to allow it to 'ferment' properly but also to arrive at the form most appropriate to the business.

Express Foods' learning ladder took five or six years to assemble. This amount of time was necessary to create the infrastructure to support it. For example, an underlying principle is that line managers are responsible for the training and development of their people, therefore, to enable the scheme to work well, all managers are offered the opportunity to practise their skills as coaches, counsellors and mentors.

The personnel director chose a local business school to be the company's collaborating partner. The teaching and academic assessment are carried out by the business school, but it is the managers who bear the crucial responsibility for ensuring that what individuals learn is welcomed and brought back into the business. One of the scheme's selling points is that not only will it attract young people and encourage all staff to develop further, but that once people have a foot on a rung, they will want to climb higher.

Express Foods hopes that the learning ladder will not only bring people in, it will keep them in.

There are very many ways of producing good learning opportunities for people. As we have seen in the Glimpses offered so far in this chapter, often the best place to start at is the job and the career structure. In its ideal form, work is a developmental experience and the Learning Company aims to make this true for all its people. However, because this is often difficult to practise for all people all the time, any organization that takes learning seriously will offer access to a wide range of opportunities.

The training and development profession, mindful of the managerial appetite for anything new and good, is prolific in terms of producing new designs for training and new methods for learning. One of the areas most under development over the last twenty years or so has been the use of the small group to assist people with the challenging task of their own self-development.

Many of these group designs, whether they be project teams, task forces, quality circles, productivity improvement teams, and so on, also put the task at the centre of the learning process. Action learning, developed by Reg Revans over many years, is arguably the archetype underlying more specific variations. In action learning there are three key elements – a person who is open to learning, with a problem that requires action, supported and challenged by a small group or set of colleagues.

ACTION LEARNING

Action learning is the philosophy of Professor Reg Revans, one of the architects of the Learning Company idea. It is an approach to personal and organizational development, involving small sets of people, each of whom takes a difficult task or problem in the company and acts to change it, bringing the results back to the set for review and learning. In Revans' words: 'There is no learning without action and no (sober and deliberate) action without learning.'

To start an action learning set:

- recruit six people who wish to develop themselves through tackling a live, company problem, for example, increasing quality, cutting waste, improving a service
- ask each person to write a brief description of the problem to be tackled and a picture of how things will be when it is resolved – what benefits will result?
- find a sponsor or mentor for each person who can act as a company 'aunt' or 'uncle', smoothing the path, giving advice and so on
- agree a programme of meetings, say half a day every two weeks or a day every month, for the group to meet, perhaps with a set adviser to manage the process and encourage members to give and take with and from each other
- at each meeting members share the time and report in turn on their efforts since the last meeting; other members help each person learn from their actions by questions and feedback, support and challenge and finally each person ends by summarizing what they have learned and by setting goals for action by the next meeting.

This seemingly simple process, is harder to enact than it may appear. Only people prepared to give it a go and to take a risk will be able to act and learn in this way. Only companies open to learning will allow members this sort of freedom. Like other forms of learning, action learning is vulnerable to the toxins prevalent in organizational life.

FOLLOW UP
Pedler, M.J. (1997) *Action Learning for Managers*, Lemos-Crane, London.
Revans, R.W. (1983) *The ABC of Action Learning*, 2nd edn. Chartwell-Bratt, Bromley.
Weinstein, K. (1995) *Action Learning*, HarperCollins, London.

Action learning is one of the most powerful methods of development to emerge from the 1970s and 1980s. You can make it part of a longer course, or you can have free-standing sets. These days it is getting hard to find a well-designed development programme without at least an action learning component.

Self-development groups differ from action learning sets in that they are not restricted to work issues – they can deal with anything that is important to their members. They are more likely to be managed and facilitated by the members themselves. This means that members have the freedom to choose who joins, where, when and for how long the group meets, how long the group continues and so on. Although they include work as an important part of life, self-development groups are person-centred often considering longer-term biographical questions and that of next steps – what do I do now?

Glimpse 77

A WOMEN'S SELF-DEVELOPMENT GROUP

Eda set up a self-development group for herself and seven other women that she knew. Like her, three of them worked for Loxley Travel, two were friends of some standing and the other two were neighbours. Eda wanted help to sort out her life. She was interested in her career and committed to the company, but her husband Duncan and their three growing children complained that she neglected them. It didn't help that she earned more than Duncan and had better career prospects.

Eda approached eight people in all to join her, only choosing women and asking each if she had an important question or concern that she wanted to consider in such a group. She had suggested meetings of three hours or so at two-weekly intervals, meeting in the evenings or at the weekends.

One of those she approached felt she did not have the time, while another said that 'it didn't feel right for her'. Those who joined had very different concerns. Jean's husband was out of work and she had a struggle to make ends meet; Val was considering becoming a Quaker; Sylvie was trying to make up her mind whether she should leave her secure job to go freelance.

After two meetings, Eda could not imagine being without the group. She had found using her 30 minutes of 'air time' difficult at first, but afterwards found that she had moved in her thinking quite considerably. The response of the others, their own stories and even jokes at her expense, had been very revealing to her.

The group continued to meet for almost three years and, after two members left, the others held a party and celebrated the end. Although one member felt 'it hadn't done much for her, although she had enjoyed the company', everyone else felt that the group had been very significant in helping them make decisions and, more importantly, in giving them a sense that they could, to some extent, take responsibility for themselves and their lives.

FOLLOW UP
Kemp, N. (1989) 'Self-development: practical issues for facilitators', *Journal of European Industrial Training*, **13**(5).
Pedler, M.J., Burgoyne, J.G., Boydell, T.H. and Welshman, G. (eds) (1990) *Self-development in Organizations*, McGraw-Hill, Maidenhead.

Action learning and self-development groups are just two of the many possibilities for helping people with their self-development. Although there are likely to be plenty of courses available to people in the Learning Company it is important that these are not too programmed or determined for people.

The first principle of self-development is that each of us must take the primary responsibility for deciding what it is we want or need to learn. If, having decided this, *and after looking at alternative ways of learning*, a particular course fits the bill, then all well and good. However, it constantly amazes us that people are prepared to go away for several days to courses with titles like 'Finance for non-financial managers' without ever having had a conversation with their own finance people – many of whom would probably be delighted to answer their questions, allow them to work shadow, give them a project and so on.

Learning resources centres are one of the ways in which many organizations are now seeking to support the self-development efforts of their people.

LEARNING RESOURCES AT FORWARD TRUST

Glimpse 78

In the financial services industry, there is a constant need for staff to update their skills and knowledge in response to changes in legislation, markets, new products and to new ways of selling and delivering services. At Forward Trust, part of the HSBC banking group, what spurred them into action was the Consumer Credit Act which required major changes to their financial services compliance regulations.

Having invested heavily in computer-based training programmes they were faced with the question: 'How do we deliver this training?' Their solution was to create learning centres – quiet study areas in which all staff could learn at their own pace and in their own time, away from the demands and distractions of telephones and colleagues. Their TALENT scheme (Total Approach to Learning Employing New Technologies) includes four learning centres for regional office staff and three for head office staff in London, operational staff in Birmingham, and factoring staff in Worthing. Additionally a mail order system has been developed based on Texaco's ASSET model, which offers:

- a central library of learning resources including training videos, audio cassettes, computer-based training programmes, books and other text-based resources
- a catalogue of these learning resources, each with a short synopsis and a symbol to identify it as a book, film, audio tape, video or computer package, etc. to make it easier for staff to make choices
- a computerized method for logging resources in and out, showing stock levels and availability.

Forward Trust have learned a great deal from their experiments with learning resource centres. Some were underused, and others used for the wrong purposes, such as holding meetings. However, the mail order system is popular and future ideas include a 'help line' for suggestions and advice and the incorporation of interactive video.

FOLLOW UP

This Glimpse is based on Dorrell, J. (1990) 'Learning resource centres' in Pedler, M.J. Burgoyne, J.G., Boydell, T.H. and Welshman, G. (eds) (1990) *Self-development in Organizations*, McGraw-Hill, Maidenhead, pp.106–113.

Cooper, S. (1988) 'Self-development in Texaco' in Pedler, M.J., Burgoyne, J.G. and Boydell, T.H. (eds), *Applying Self-development in Organizations*, Prentice-Hall, London, pp.211–219.

Sometimes, learning on the job or very close to the job, does not fit the bill. There are times when it is appropriate and highly developmental to take time out. This is not the one or two day 'time out' so beloved of many management teams, but an extended period away from work to study or to simply take a break. There are various reasons why this sort of development opportunity may be necessary or useful, but it is often to do with a person reaching a certain threshold in work or in life where a fairly fundamental reappraisal or retraining is indicated.

For example, in a fast-changing environment, it will be necessary from time to time to invest in developing new skills or knowledge; or at mid- or late-career points it is useful to take stock and think about past, present and future directions. For the pressurized professional it helps to take a break from time to time perhaps to study new methods or ideas.

Glimpse 79

SABBATICALS

Tired, anxious, depressed, worried about your health? You may be suffering from 'burnout' or overwork. Jobs are less secure, work is more pressurized and something has to give. With the fashion for long hours now so firmly entrenched in many places even for junior managers, the idea of sabbaticals is gaining ground as a way of combating fatigue and refreshing skills.

Traditionally, sabbaticals are the preserve of academe, where every seven years, university teachers take one year to carry out research, devote themselves to writing and update their knowledge. In the UK companies such as the BBC and John Lewis are interested in flexible working patterns that include career breaks and sabbaticals. These can range from a month to a year and the longer ones tend to take the form of unpaid leave. Another form of sabbatical is the secondment to another organization, perhaps to a charity or to a company overseas.

Each of these forms may meet the objective of helping people to simply take a break, or to achieve an aim of updating their skills, or finding a better home/work balance. However, there are obvious downsides to accepting sabbaticals. Older staff in particular might fear that they will not be missed or that their skills may fall off outside the specific work environment. Sabbaticals seem to work best with staff who see them clearly as personal development opportunities or who simply use them to extend a holiday to take a special trip.

Perhaps it is senior managers who might most fear to take a sabbatical – and yet it can be argued that it is they who need it most. The final Glimpse in this chapter offers an interesting cultural slant on development opportunities for these people who may sometimes be seen as prescribing 'self-development opportunities for others'.

DEVELOPING SENIOR MANAGERS

Charles Handy tells an interesting story of a cultural contrast between British and Japanese managers. It concerns the different attitudes taken to spending time on development with increasing seniority and is graphically illustrated in Figure G80.1.

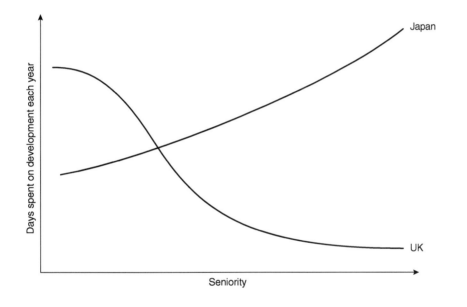

Figure G80.1 British and Japanese policies on development and seniority

If further explanation is needed, the suggestion is that as UK managers become more senior, they see themselves, and are seen to be, less in need of development. In Japan, we are told, senior managers have the contrary view: the more senior, the more need there is for development.

19. The BICC Story

The 11 Characteristics of the Learning Company are brought to life in the case of a company-wide organization development effort at a division of BICC. This chapter is a story of BICC seeking to survive and develop in difficult and changing times and while the 11 Characteristics do not provide a blueprint of how to work towards the Learning Company, the action and learning achieved here address the critical dimensions of the model.

Context

BICC is a large UK-based engineering company. Its cables' business has several product-based divisions including power transmission, fibre optics and copper-based telephone cables. This is the story of an organization development project based on Learning Company principles at BICC Telephone Cables, Manchester, UK. Manufacturing copper-based telephone cables, this plant, with a workforce of 400 people, is on a 100-years-old site in Blackley, a fairly depressed area of the city. Despite this the manufacturing plant is reasonably modern and in good working order.

For many years BICC and two other manufacturers had enjoyed a 'cosy' relationship with British Telecom (BT) – the sole UK customer for such cables. BT was a state-owned monopoly, not much concerned with value for money or profitability, so that BICC and the other companies split the market between them, more or less setting their own prices and standards of quality and delivery.

All this changed when BT was privatized and lost its monopoly. Suddenly and aggressively interested in cost, price, quality and delivery, BT reallocated the market shares between the existing suppliers, stating its intention to deal only with three in the first instance, then with two and probably later only with one.

This presented a considerable challenge for BICC. Its market share was cut to 17 per cent – turning a healthy profit into a major loss. To remain in this business it would have to make major improvements in quality and delivery, while reducing prices significantly. Additionally, due to increased use of fibre optics, the total UK market for copper-based telephone cable was shrinking.

An organization development project

BICC Telephone Cables, Manchester, decided to respond positively to this threat. This took the form of a development project led by Tom Boydell and Malcolm Leary, which fell into four main phases:

1. Setting the scene (March–August 1992)
2. Removing the barriers and creating the right environment (September 1992–June 1993)
3. Introducing teamworking in manufacturing (April 1993–April 1994)
4. Creating a learning environment (November 1993 onwards)

Phase 1: Setting the scene

- obtaining senior management commitment
- agreeing strategy and carrying out basic planning
- initial communications with employees and union representatives.

This phase involved deciding whether or not to attempt to keep the plant open, and, if so, to agree a strategy for so doing. After much consideration senior group management support was gained and a broad *Business Strategy* for the copper-cables division was formulated (short-term survival and return to profit; long-term growth, increased market share and exporting), with a related *People Strategy* (obtain a competitive edge by reorganizing and fully utilizing employees and secure continuous improvement by moving towards becoming a learning organization). The learning organization strategy was chosen because it was seen being as particularly appropriate for:

- being an integrative approach – working holistically on all systems
- 'learning through' to BICC's own solution in a situation with no standard blueprint
- providing the basis for self-sustaining, long-term transformation
- integrating organizational and individual development
- empowering individuals and enabling them to use their considerable insight and skills, hitherto largely ignored.

Phase 2: Removing the barriers and creating the right environment

- establishing a new site management team
- integrating all functions on to the one site
- reducing staff and contracting out of services
- creating a single status environment
- establishing a 'people contract'
- improving the working environment
- improving management/employee communications
- changing the manufacturing management structure to facilitate the introduction of teamworking.

BICC's relaxed relationship with BT prior to privatization was mirrored in the management–union relationship within the plant. Management tended to go along with any requests made by the union, who, in many ways, ran the plant. The new situation called for a very different set-up and, after initial communication of the new strategies, great effort has gone into creating new management–workforce relationships, with a significant change in the role of the trade unions.

It was decided to replace the existing site management team. It was also clear that redundancies were inevitable, and with the contracting out of certain services (sometimes to people who were currently employees, such as in the works canteen), employees decreased to 300. At the same time some production functions carried out elsewhere were brought to Manchester.

Cable manufacturing involves seven sequential processes, each with its own employees, skills and machinery and carried out in its own 'area'. Much greater flexibility was needed both within and across these areas. A major hindrance to any form of job flexibility was the cumbersome set of over 30 wage scales The move to a single, unified wage scale covered all production employees across all processes and areas constituted a major change. This single-status environment took six months to negotiate, made more difficult by the redundancies taking place at the same time. Part of this negotiation led to a 'people contract':

Employer's undertakings

- stating expectations and setting standards
- complying with legislation
- encouraging employees to take the initiative
- providing reasonable facilities
- listening to employees' views and opinions and providing feedback
- increasing job-related skills and knowledge and providing further education opportunities
- working with the trade unions for the good of the business.

Employees' commitments   Accepting responsibility for:

- operating the required quality system and standards
- attending regularly and punctually
- keeping their own work area clean and tidy
- participating in problem solving
- providing training to colleagues
- operating flexibly
- recognizing the need to improve productivity continually.

A joint commitment

- to improve quality, increase productivity, review practices regularly and to respond positively and rapidly to uncertainty.

Considerable cleaning up and refurbishment of the plant was also carried out, including the provision of a team room in each of the manufacturing areas for breaks, meetings, information display, and the new IT production control equipment.

Phase 3: Introducing teamworking in manufacturing

- recruitment and selection of shift managers and team leaders
- off-job training and at-job development of team leaders and their teams
- inter-company learning
- improved information system

Another major change was to the manufacturing structure that in the past had no real vertical linkage. For example, day-time production managers worked quite different hours from the shift supervisors, who rotated on a weekly basis. Perhaps even worse, there was no horizontal integration below the level of the manufacturing manager, except at night. In addition, stores, despatch and engineering maintenance were on day-times only.

Three new shift managers were recruited, two of whom were external appointments, new to the industry. Employees throughout the plant were encouraged to apply for the 23 team leader posts (7 areas, 3 shifts; plus stores and despatch). Applicants, who included existing surpervisors and chargehands and also some direct production workers, were assessed by a combination of tests, groupwork and individual interviews. The training of the appointed team leaders emphasized their real concerns, issues and opportunities such as:

- how 'teamworking' is at the plant now
- how we would like it to be in the future
- hopes and fears about the outcomes of the change to teamworking
- what we want senior management to know

and included a dialogue with the works and manufacturing managers. This coincided with a difficult period of negotiations, which delayed the actual start of the teamworking. The consultants spent time with the team leaders helping to handle feelings of disillusionment creeping in as a result of the delay.

After three months, the teamworking system got under way with each production area coming on stream at approximately two-weekly intervals. Teams were given more authority and autonomy and were encouraged, indeed required, to sort out their own working processes. For the first time, they were given their own budgets, and considerable technical and commercial information on output, financial performance and upcoming orders that had always been withheld in the past.

On the Friday and Saturday before an area formally switched to teamworking, the three shift managers and team leaders, together with most of the teamworkers (anything from 25 to 75) went away for training. While all were encouraged to attend, both verbally and practically (e.g. by arranging transportation or for other individual needs to be met), it was not compulsory and around 10 per cent were unwilling or unable to attend. Again the training focused on real concerns:

- issues in our area, within our own shift team
- issues in our area, between shift teams
- issues between our area and other areas
- issues with senior management.

Dialogue and role negotiation were used to deal with issues within teams, between shift teams in the same area, and with senior management – as the works and manufacturing managers attended part of each workshop.

After the workshops, the consultants provided support on the shifts, working with teams and team leaders, facilitating the resolution of issues and the using of opportunities as well as giving further direct training (see Table 19.1 for some of the issues, teamworking competencies and outcomes). During this time leaders and some team members were also encouraged to visit other companies where teamworking had been established. There were also various spin offs from the workshops; they had provided opportunities for the shift managers to meet together for the first time (thereafter they continued to meet fortnightly) and a process of regular meetings with the works manager were instituted.

Phase 4: Creating a learning environment

After the basic team training and ongoing support was well under way, a number of further initiatives were taken aimed particularly at individual learning and development, including:

- establishing a personal development programme (for more basic personal skills, including some literacy/numeracy training, foreign languages, and so on)
- creating an open-learning facility on site
- further developments of team leader and team member training, based on a process of self-assessment
- integration of production and maintenance skills training (i.e. 'technical') with nationally recognized occupational qualifications, e.g. National Vocational Qualifications (NVQs)
- establishment of a training and development programme in service/support functions
- launch of a process improvement initiative
- commitment to gain a National Award ('Investors in People').

The changes in BICC and the 11 Characteristics of the Learning Company

Some of the measurable outcomes of this work are as follows:

- employee productivity up 113 per cent
- scrap down 50 per cent
- absenteeism reduced by 58 per cent

Table 19.1 Issues, teamworking competencies and visible changes at BICC

Stages	Issues	Teamworking competencies	Visible Changes in BICC
Stage 0 Getting ready	Preparation for new teamworking initiative, taking into account previous experiences, attitudes and opinions of actual and potential team members.	Briefing, listening, questioning, allaying fears. Obtaining resources. Networking. Recruiting.	Focusing on the business imperative (in this case survival of the plant). New salary system – single status agreement. Team leaders selected and appointed.
Stage 1 Getting started	Launching the team; dealing with basic issues, getting down to what is essential and necessary to start working together; identifying areas of concern that are to be dealt with at Stage 2.	Listening, questioning, discussing. Instructing making specifications, setting targets, clarifying operational definitions. Running meetings – team meetings, briefings.	Concerns and fears as well as hopes and expectations about teamworking freely expressed. Open discussion and building a picture of what teamworking will be like (no standard blue print); then an enthusiastic lunch.
Stage 2 Getting going	Sorting out issues, roles and relationships sufficiently to be able to get the task completed.	Using investigative procedures, causal analysis. Team decision making processes. Assertiveness, raising issues, making presentations, presenting cases, handling disagreements.	Basic procedure established for operational arrangements, e.g. shift handovers. Ground rules drawn up for teamworking. Information supplied to teams on scheduling, targets, etc. Team left to make own arrangements for machine allocation, etc. Increased flexibility of working. Team meetings held on a regular basis – action taken on points raised.
Stage 3 Getting results	Becoming effective and efficient, working well as a task oriented, business-like unit. Becoming ambitious enough to look for areas of improvements. Formulating and implementing improvement plans.	Performance improvement methods. Running special project meetings, e.g. Quality Improvement Teams. Setting and working to performance targets.	Priority areas for improvement identified by team members. Quality Improvement Projects initiated. Outcomes measured and results recorded and disseminated.
Stage 4 Getting together	Learning to cooperate and collaborate – requiring that any residual relationship issues be addressed and difficulties worked through.	Giving and receiving feedback (positive and negative). Influencing skills. Supporting, challenging. Handling people with different temperaments.	Team members assisting each other, standing in, cooperating – without being directed. Decisions made more quickly. Better decisions made (emphasis on implementation). Team leaders and members take up issue directly with senior management.

Table 19.1, cont'd.

Stages	Issues	Teamworking competencies	Visible Changes in BICC
Stage 5 Getting through	The team is working creatively, generating new solutions, trying new methods. Team members help each other to become more imaginative and creative.	Delegation, mandating procedures for team decision making. Positivity. Leaning to learn, reviewing, monitoring, evaluating.	Suggestions for new ways of working, new roles and moves towards 'self-managed' teamworking structure. Teams run their meetings, take action, keep records and supply information.
Stage X Getting on with others	Developing better working relationships with customers, suppliers and other teams, internally and externally. Cross-functional working.	Customer mapping. Role negotiation. Bargaining.	Inter-shift and production meetings held; actions followed through. Customer mapping/supplier mapping leads to improved relationships.

- UK market share up from 17 per cent to 40 per cent (BICC is now one of the two remaining suppliers to BT)
- new export contracts
- on-time deliveries highest ever (98 per cent)
- move from loss of over a £1 million to profit of over £1 million
- at least 300 jobs saved.

These outputs were the result of the totality of changes made throughout the period of the project. Each of the 11 Characteristics of the Learning Company was addressed, although not necessarily in 'sequence'. By working on all the characteristics simultaneously, a vessel was created within which people could apply their existing knowledge and acquire new knowledge, not only about how to make cable but also about how to work together.

The changes in BICC can be summarized against the Learning Company Project's 11 Characteristics of the Learning Company (see Table 19.2).

FURTHER READING

Learning Company Project (1993) *The 11 Characteristics Questionnaire*, Learning Company Project, Sheffield.

Table 19.2 The 11 Characteristics – Progress towards becoming a Learning Company at BICC Blackley

Learning Company Characteristics	Intervention at BICC Blackley	Visible and reported effects	Bottom Line effects
		Combined effects of all the interventions include:	*Overall effects after 9 months of team working*
■ Learning Approach to Strategy	● Feedback to top team from shift managers, team leaders and teams	◆ Better communications within the team	★ Productivity per employee up 113%
	● Business and development strategies constantly revised in light of national and international changes	◆ Discussing things, leading to more viable decisions	★ Scrap costs down 50%
■ Participative Policy Making	● System of briefing and 'business meetings', with two-way flow of information and ideas	◆ Talking together, solving 'problems'	★ Lead times reduced
	● Team leaders' meetings with senior managers	◆ 'Job gets done more quickly'	★ On-time deliveries 98% (best ever)
■ Informating	● Computerized production information made available to team leaders and members	◆ Making suggestions for improvements	★ Market share up from 17% to 40%
	● Regular 'business meetings' with shifts managers, team leaders and team members – sharing technical and hitherto secret commercial information – team members taking responsibility for writing and circulating meeting reports	◆ Giving opinions ◆ Volunteering to take on extra tasks and responsibilities ◆ Using 'spare' time to good effect; picking up on work that needs to be done in the section	★ New export contracts won ★ Moved back into profitability ★ Absenteeism down by 58%
	● Briefing groups, providing information, with full background and underlying reasons	◆ Giving each other assistance as and when required, without being restricted by payment issues	★ 300 jobs saved
	● Written back up of verbal communications	◆ More variety of work	
	● Notice boards with continuous display of updated production and commercial information	◆ When appropriate team members move away from their machines to see what is going on in the section overall and to discuss points with the team leader or other members	
	● New plant newspaper – *Livewire* – published regularly		

Table 19.2 cont'd.

Learning Company Characteristics	Intervention at BICC Blackley	Visible and reported effects	Bottom Line effects
■ Formative Accounting and Control	● Shift managers and team leaders given responsibility for, and authority over, their own budgets	◆ 'More awareness and responsibility for the whole process, not just one part'	

■ Internal Exchange	● Team working system
	● Facilitated dialogue and agreements
	  – within teams
	  – between shifts
	  – between areas
	  – with other functions
		◆ Team members working on trials and experiments
		◆ Using more appropriate documentation	

■ Reward Flexibility	● Single status system	◆ Regular training, which 'once planned is adhered to'	
■ Enabling Structures	● Team working system ● Single status package ● Negotiating clear statements of rights and responsibilities – management, team leaders, team members	◆ Meetings well organized ◆ Thinking about the next shift, i.e. what can be done to make things easier	
■ Boundary Workers as Environmental Scanners	● Dialogue with existing and new customers	◆ Generally much cleaner site ◆ Gathering information	
■ Inter-company Learning	● Visits to other companies, by managers and team leaders ● Visits from other companies ● Networking ● Obtaining and giving information through journals, conferences, etc.	◆ Being constantly on the look out for areas where improvements might be made ◆ Using tools and techniques to carry out quality improvements and measure the effects of these	

■ Learning Climate	● Development of team leaders and members in taking initiatives, assertiveness, asking questions, giving information
	● Coaching team leaders in learning through active reflection
	● Coaching team leaders in how to run meetings
		◆ Being assertive, e.g.
		  – saying no
		  – asking why
		◆ Flexible machine allocations
		◆ 'Looking at the consequences and implications of proposed actions'	

Table 19.2 cont'd.

Learning Company Characteristics	Intervention at BICC Blackley	Visible and reported effects	Bottom Line effects
	● Regular briefing group sessions, giving information and raising questions	◆ Liaising with others, i.e. other – shifts – areas – functions	
	● Regular 'business meetings' with shift managers, team leaders, team members, sharing experiences and raising issues	◆ Providing clear information	
	● Quality project groups; team members training in mandating, thus involved in taking a mandate/responsibility, reporting back, making presentations, as well as training in systematic problem solving and quality improvements	◆ 'Recognizing that other people have the same problems' ◆ Making the most of learning opportunities	
	● Regular meetings between manufacturing manager and shift managers	◆ When something has been learned, reporting it back to the team	
	● Senior managers' encouragement and 'permissiveness', allowing team leaders and members to voice opinions, try out new ideas	◆ Understanding the need for information ◆ Enjoying each others' company	
	● Physical changes, e.g. team rooms, general clean up		
	● New suggestion scheme		
■ Self-development Opportunities for All	● Selection of team leaders based on aptitude and potential, not on seniority		
	● Multi-skill training and flexibility		
	● Systematic identification of 'hard' and 'soft' skills required for team leaders' roles		
	● Training and development in these skills		
	● Opportunities for other personal effectiveness development		

PART 4 REFLECTIONS
– FURTHER THOUGHTS AND DIRECTIONS

Part 4 surveys some of the emerging directions in organizational learning and the Learning Company. This work has developed in the five years since the publication of the first edition of this book and these chapters are more speculative and exploratory than in the earlier parts. They offer the opportunity for further reflection and exploration; a return from action back to thinking.

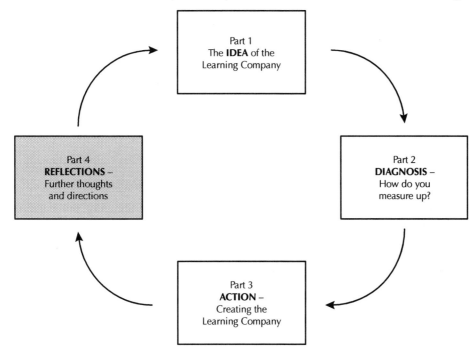

Figure P4.1 The Learning Cycle

The themes in this last part of the book include:

- a move to *Stage 3 working* on organizational learning and the Learning Company. This represents a recognition that success in interpreting these ideas at Stage 2 *does* lead to adaptive, responsive successful organizations, but that their 'success' may be bought at great cost to people in terms of their jobs, quality of life, their communities and the environment. Stage 3 working emphasizes the need to work at a higher level that the individual company in order to achieve healthy and sustainable development. Chapter 21 explores the idea of levels or *Modes* in more detail.

Stage 3 functioning is encouraged by the organization ecology perspective (Chapter 25) – the unit of development is not just the single unit – what use are learning organizations unless they also enrich their economic, social and biological environments? – but the 'company-in-its-context' From this follows ...

- a concern with *whole system* – whether this be the company as a whole system, the company and its trading set, or the locality, or the industry – the larger set of which the company is a part. Chapter 23 – 'Whole Systems Development' – specifically addresses this, but echoes are found throughout the other chapters in Part 4. One way of thinking about this approach to organizational learning is that it is concerned with ...
- ... a focus upon *dialogue* between the different parts and 'voices' in a system. The idea of dialogue can be interpreted in a number of ways as discussed in Chapter 22, and crops up frequently in writings on the learning organization. Dialogue emerges as an essential aspect of what we mean by organizational learning. For example, the two main models in this book– The 11 Characteristics of the Learning Company and the E-Flow – can be read largely in terms of seeking to increase flows of information, energy and learning between parts, across functions, through boundaries. This is a form of dialogue, but a very different one from what we may usually think of – a face-to-face meeting in a group or community. However, as Chapter 24 shows, computer networks have an important role to play in creating opportunities for non-face-to-face (or f2f in the argot of the computer conferencers) and non-'real time' communication and dialogue.

Chapter 20 opens this part of the book with a survey of some of the important writers on organizational learning and the Learning Company. Such is the richness and volume of the relevant literature that there are inevitably many omissions. However, here you will find some of the people who have made important contributions to our understanding so far.

20. Writers on the Learning Company

In a relatively short time, the literature on the Learning Company, learning organization and organizational learning has achieved massive proportions and continues to outpour. In such circumstances, a literature review is a book length project on its own, and we hope someone is working on it. Yet it seems incomplete to present just our ideas without acknowledgement to those who have shaped and are shaping the field.

Here is a brief flavour of seven authors or pairs of authors who are influential. Many others, including many who have influenced one or other of us, are missing. This includes Gregory Bateson, perhaps the most widespread influence of all in this field because of his pioneering work on levels of learning in 'The Logical Categories of Learning and Communication' (*Steps to an Ecology of Mind* (1973) London: Paladin, pp.250–279).

The authors discussed are:

> Tom Peters and Robert Waterman
> W. Edwards Deming
> Reg Revans
> Chris Argyris and Donald Schon
> Roger Harrison
> Peter Senge
> Nancy Dixon

Tom Peters and Robert Waterman

Tom Peters and Robert Waterman's *In Search of Excellence* was perhaps the most influential management text of the 1980s. In responding to the idea of not just becoming excellent but also staying that way, the Learning Company goes beyond excellence to make learning the central process. However, Peters and Waterman were centrally concerned with adaptability, responsiveness and learning, even noting, 'The excellent companies are learning organizations'. (p.110)

What they mean by this is that the excellent companies 'experiment more, encourage more tries and permit small failures; they keep things small; they interact with customers – especially sophisticated customers'. They also 'encourage internal competition and allow resultant duplication and overlap; and they maintain a rich informal environment, heavily laden with information, which spurs diffusion of ideas that work'. Interestingly these companies couldn't articulate what they were up to – they just knew it worked. (p.111)

Peters and Waterman's view is very much a Stage 2 view of the learning organization. Their focus is upon the survival of the single unit and the societal perspective is entirely lacking:

> ... we believe that the truly adaptive organization evolves in a very Darwinian way. The company is trying lots of things, experimenting, making the right sorts of mistakes; that is to say, it is fostering its own mutations. The adaptive corporation has learned quickly to kill off the dumb mutations and invest heavily in the ones that work. You can't go it alone; you do it with customers. (p.114)

Peters and Waterman's position on the learning organization is still that of many people in organizations. Yet the reliance on the simple Darwinian analogy, the emphasis upon customers to the exclusion of other stakeholders, and above all the heroic elevation of a handful of USA corporations, seriously limit the relevance of their model for our fragmented times.

REFERENCE

Peters, T.J. and Waterman, R.H. (1982) *In Search of Excellence: Lessons from America's Best-Run Companies*, Harper & Row, New York.

W. Edwards Deming

The most radical of the TQM gurus, and certainly more so than Peters and Waterman, Deming recognizes not only the basic principles, such as negotiating customer–supplier needs, measurement, continuous improvement and so on, but also emphasizes that total quality requires fundamental shifts in the way we manage and organize.

This is clear from his famous 14 points, which fit well with the Learning Company:

- create constancy of purpose for improvement of product and service, with the aim of becoming competitive, staying in business and providing jobs
- adopt the new philosophy: we are in a new economic age, created by Japan; Western management must awaken to the challenge, must learn their responsibilities, and take on leadership for a change
- cease dependence on inspection to achieve quality, eliminate the need for inspection on a mass basis by building quality into the products in the first place
- improve constantly and forever every activity in the company to build quality and productivity and to drive down costs
- remove barriers ...

- that rob hourly workers of their right to pride of workmanship – the responsibility of supervisors must be changed from sheer numbers to quality
- that rob people in engineering and in management of their right to pride of workmanship, which means, *inter alia*, abolition of the annual merit rating and of management by objectives
- break down barriers between departments – people in research, design, sales and production must work as a team to foresee problems that may be encountered with the product or service
- eliminate slogans, exhortations and targets for the workforce asking for zero defects and new levels of productivity – such exhortations only create adversarial relationships; the bulk of the causes of low quality and productivity belong in the system and thus lie beyond the power of the workforce to rectify
- eliminate work standards (in the sense of numerical quotas), management by objectives, any management by numbers – substitute leadership
- institute leadership – the aim of leadership being to help people, machines and gadgets to do a better job
- institute training on the job, including (but not exclusively for) management
- institute a vigorous programme of training and self-improvement
- end the practice of awarding business on the basis of the price tag: purchasing must be combined with the design of the product; manufacturing and sales must work with chosen suppliers – the aim is to minimize total cost, not merely initial cost – move towards a single supplier for any one item on a long-term relationship of loyalty and trust
- put everyone in the company to work to accomplish the transformation; the transformation is everyone's job.

RERERENCES

Deming, W.E. (1986) *Out of the Crisis*, Cambridge University Press, Cambridge.
Sherkenbach, W.W. (1986) *The Deming Route to Quality and Productivity*, Ceepress Books, New York.

Reg Revans

Revans has much in common with Deming, starting as a mathematician and operational researcher and moving later to focus on organizations and learning. Although best known for his theory and practice of action learning, Revans has always worked with a vision of the learning organization and is a major though often unsung contributor, especially in the USA. His concern has been to empower the manager struggling with intractable problems, and the highest expression of action learning is in the concept of the learning community or learning system.

Action learning is an educational *idea* or philosophy, aimed at healing the split that Revans saw as having developed historically between thinking and doing, between ideas and action. In presenting action and learning as parts of each other, he aimed to contribute to more effective action on the many urgent and pressing problems facing society. In particular he is concerned about those not able to help themselves and has recently described the essence of action learning as 'helping each other help the helpless'. The ultimate purpose of action and organizational learning goes far beyond any single organizational purpose.

Revans is a radical and his writings contains a clear moral philosophy involving:

- *Honesty about self* – the most valuable question learned by the top managers on his Belgian programme was 'What is an honest man, and what do I need to do to become one?' (1971, p.132)
- *Seeing action, not thought, as the defining characteristic of human beings* – Revans quotes both St James: 'be ye doers of the word, and not only hearers of it' and Shaw's echo: 'It is not enough to know what is good; you must be able to do it' in *Back to Methuselah*. (1983, p.6)
- *For the purpose of doing some good in the world* – Revans quotes both the Bhudda 'To do a little good is better than to write difficult books' and John Macmurray in *The Self as Agent* 'All meaningful knowledge is for the sake of action, and all meaningful action for the sake of friendship'. (1983, p.6)

Revans is always on the side of the individual seeking to act and learn, but is also concerned to specify the conditions that organizations should establish to promote learning. His 'upward communication of doubt' is perhaps the briefest description for the Learning Company, but in his 1969 paper 'The Enterprise as a Learning System' (in Revans, 1982) he outlines the conditions for this to be achieved and lays out a prescient conception of the symbiosis of work and learning under the sub-heading of 'The qualities of autonomous learning systems':

> 'We observe that all expert systems here referred to must now be imposed upon the enterprise from above or from outside. But action learning must seek the means of improvement from within, indeed from the common task.... The daily round offers constant learning opportunities (and) the quality of such learning is largely determined by the morale of the organization ...
>
> ... the conditions for success seem to include the following:
>
> (i) ... that its chief executive places high among his own responsibilities that of developing the enterprise as a learning system: this he will achieve through his personal relations with his immediate subordinates
>
> (ii) ... maximum authority for subordinates to act within the field of its own known policies that become known by interrogation from below
>
> (iii) ... codes of practice ... and other such regulations are to be seen as norms around which variations are deliberately encouraged as learning opportunities
>
> (iv) ... any reference to what appears an intractable problem to a superior level should be accompanied both by an explanation of why it cannot be treated where it seems to have arisen and a proposal to change the system so that similar problems arising in future could be suitably contained and treated
>
> (v) ... persons at all levels should be encouraged, with their immediate colleagues

to make regular proposals for the study and reorganization of their own systems of work.'

The distrust of experts and the commitment to the learning of the individual-within-the-company as the route to salvation, marks out Revans as one of the most perspicacious of commentators on organizational learning.

REFERENCES

Revans, R.W. (1982) 'The enterprise as a learning system' in *The Origins and Growth of Action Learning*, Chartwell-Bratt, Bromley, re-printed in M. Pedler (1991) *Action Learning in Practice*, 2nd edn, Gower, Aldershot.
Revans, R.W. (1971) *Developing Effective Managers*, Praeger, New York.
Revans, R.W. (1983) *The ABC of Action Learning*, Chartwell-Bratt, Bromley.

Chris Argyris and Donald Schon

Argyris and Schon made one of the most valuable contributions to the literature in their book *Organizational Learning: A Theory in Action Perspective*. The first chapter is entitled, 'What is an organization that it may learn?' and this usefully problematizes both the ideas of organization and learning. How are we to organize in order to learn? And, what do we mean by learning?

Argyris and Schon have introduced the idea of single- and double-loop learning as a way of translating Gregory Bateson's levels of learning into an organizational setting. They suggest that most organization learning is single-loop [O–I], which they describe as 'error-detection and correction'. Double-loop learning [O–II] is found only rarely, because this is learning that challenges current operating assumptions and changes existing norms and practices. Double-loop learning involves deeper enquiry and questioning and implies conflict and power struggles. Because of this they say:

> We have yet to establish, in a full and sustained example, the feasibility of an O–II organization, nor are we aware of anyone else having done so. (1978, p.312)

A third variety – *deutero-learning* (literally second order) – is to do with learning about learning. For Argyris and Schon, organizations only learn through the agency of individual members, and it is through deutero-learning that the capacity of the whole to learn is brought about:

> When an organization engages in deutero-learning, its members learn, too, about previous contexts for learning. They reflect on and enquire into previous episodes of organizational learning or failure to learn. They discover what they did that facilitated or inhibited learning, they invent new strategies for learning, and they evaluate and generalise what they have produced. The results become encoded in individual maps and images and are reflected in organizational learning practice. (1978, p.27)

Argyris and Schon also recognized the importance of metaphor in the way organizations frame their understanding of the situations they are in, and generate diagnoses and actions. The way problems are understood and the way learning takes place is also governed by these metaphors:

> We suspect that organizations tend to develop characteristics modes of knowing; that organizations tend to differ from one another, in important ways, in their characteristic cognitive modes; and that individual members of organizations can learn to reflect on these cognitive modes, to extend their capacity for multiple viewing of organizational phenomena, and to develop the capacity for richer, more coordinated, and more adequate ways of representing organizational phenomena. (1978, p.318)

This was a key insight, which was later put to good use by Morgan (1986). Argyris and Schon's aim is to help organizations become better at double-loop learning and to learn how to carry out the kinds of enquiry, including the ability to tolerate and deal with the inevitable conflict, to achieve this. They propose a model of expert-facilitated intervention, combining:

> (a) the mapping of an organization's O–I learning system, (b) helping members of the organization make the transition from model I to model II theories-in-use, (c) guiding and facilitating members' collaborative reflection on and restructuring of, their own learning system, (d) modelling and helping members to model good organizational dialectic in their efforts to detect and correct error in the organization's instrumental theory-in-use. (1978, p.313)

Learning or just changing?

However, in a later book, Argyris (1990) seems less sure about the value of expert intervention. Commenting on a study by Beer, Eisenstat and Spector (1988) of large-scale change programmes that all failed, either wholly or partly, he notes that the companies embarked on the change programmes because of the many poor practices they had developed that were damaging to their competitiveness. Argyris asks why it is that managers produced these practices in the first place and why the change programmes then failed. One conclusion is that most of the change programmes were pre-packaged, off-the-shelf products not intimately connected with what was going on in the organization, and were chosen because companies copied what others used because these were easiest to 'sell' to senior people. Argyris reflects:

> Human beings … show remarkable ingenuity for self-protection. They can create individual and organizational defences that are powerful and in which that power is largely in the service of the poor to mediocre performance as well as of antilearning. (Argyris, 1990, p.157)

The gradual building of these polluting 'defensive routines' creates a 'boiled frog'* problem that is not amenable to the expert-facilitated intervention on which Argyris (with Schon) had earlier pinned his hopes. The route now lies more in encouraging reflective thinking in organization members:

> The result of these countless everyday actions is to deaden individuals' awareness to the ethical pollution they are generating. My generation never realized that we

---

*A metaphor that suggests that a frog in a slowly heated pan of water goes to sleep rather than jumps out (see page 197).

were contributing to the pollution with the gas guzzlers we drove. Once we saw and understood it, we cooperated to change our actions.... It makes little sense to enact laws and rules against organizational defensive routines.... The equivalents of such laws are already in place and they do not work. The answer, as in the case of prohibition, lies in each one of us becoming self-managing and helping to create organizations that reward such self-responsible action. (Argyris, 1990, p.161)

REFERENCES

Argyris, C. and Schon, D.A. (1978) *Organizational Learning: A Theory in Action Perspective*, Addison-Wesley, Reading, MA.

Argyris, C. (1990) *Overcoming Organizational Defences: Facilitating Organizational Learning: A Theory in Action Perspective*, Allyn & Bacon, Needham Heights, MA.

Morgan, G. (1986) *Images of Organizations*, Sage, London.

Roger Harrison

In his classic paper 'Defences and the need to know' written almost 30 years before Argyris' *Overcoming Organizational Defences*, Harrison shows that our defence mechanisms are part of who we are. 'Defensive behaviours' help us adapt to a changing world and seeking to destroy them does not make us more effective:

> To put it strongly, the destruction of defenses does not serve learning; instead it increases our anxiety that we will lose the more or less effective conceptual systems with which we understand and relate to the world and we then drop back to an even more desperate and perhaps unrealistic defense than the one destroyed. Though it may seem paradoxical, we cannot increase learning by destroying the defenses that block it. (1995a, p.290)

Harrison has written a great deal on learning and organizational learning in the last 30 years. Of particular interest is the importance he gives to the place of powerful emotions that frustrate leaders' attempts to change organizations. He holds that leaders usually underestimate the prevalence of fear and anxiety in their organizations, and that anger and resentment are rising due to a widespread sense of betrayal of trust. Leaders' underestimation of the power of negative emotions contributes to what Harrison calls the bias and 'addiction to action' found in so many companies. (1995a, pp.389–410)

The strength of feelings is such that organizations are primarily in need of healing before they can learn, change and adapt. Organizational healing is a major theme for Harrison (1995b, pp.152–170). In noting the levels of exhaustion and burn out among people in public sector organizations suffering from 'mandated change' he says:

> Their organizations were in retreat, their clients and colleagues were in shock, and they were feeling inadequate as they tried to drum up enthusiasm for upbeat, forward looking programmes in organizations reeling from one imposed change after another. My discussions with the participants convinced me that it was time to reframe the work of organizational development, making a shift from the idea

> that organizations needed *agents of change* to the idea that they needed *facilitators of healing.* (1995a, p.166)

Harrison has also questioned the purposes of organizations and suggested that, given the dominating and powerful institutions they are today, they should be attuned to planetary purposes:

> Seen from the planetary point of view, the organization exists only as a part of a larger reality, supported and nurtured by the larger system on which it depends. Its purposes are not solely determined or decided by itself, but are 'given' by its place in the larger system. Organizational purpose is not simply decided by its members but is rather to be *discovered....* Viewed in this way, a primary task of an organization is the discovery of its place and purpose in the larger system. (1995a, pp.174–175)

REFERENCES

Harrison, R. (1995a) *The Collected Papers of Roger Harrison*, McGraw-Hill, Maidenhead.
Harrison, R. (1995b) *Consultant's Journey*, McGraw-Hill, Maidenhead.

Peter Senge

Senge's bestselling *The Fifth Discipline* has been largely responsible for bringing the learning organization idea into the mainstream of business thinking. Building upon Argyris and Schon, Senge takes a systems perspective on the learning organization and requires us to practise five disciplines – the fifth of which is fundamental, underpinning all the others:

Personal mastery which involves self-development, of 'continually clarifying and deepening our personal vision, of focusing our energies, of developing patience and of seeing reality objectively'.

Sharing mental models Everyone has their own view of the world, their own pre-conceptions and assumptions. If the organization is an organism, then to some extent we have to think as a collective not least to create....

Shared vision A shared picture of the future 'to foster genuine commitment and enrolment rather than compliance'. This can lead people to 'excel and learn, not because they are told to but because they want to'.

Team learning Teams are 'the fundamental learning units in modern organizations'. 'The discipline of Team Learning starts with *Dialogue*' which is the capacity to 'think together' in a 'free-flowing of meaning through a group'.

Systems thinking The Fifth Discipline that integrates the others – the discipline for seeing wholes rather than parts; for working with the patterns and relationships in the subtle interconnectedness of living systems.

Systems thinking is a methodology for seeing in wholes and for recognizing the patterns and the interrelatedness of parts in wholes. Senge has memorably stated that, 'We are literally killing ourselves through being unable to think in wholes' (1991, p.42) and suggested that organizations suffer from seven 'learning disabilities' because of their inability to do this 'joined-up-thinking':

> Learning disabilities are tragic in children, especially when they go undetected. They are no less tragic in organizations, where they also go largely undetected. (1990, p.18)

1. *I am my position*   A narrow focus on *my* job rather than on the purpose of the whole.
2. *The enemy is out there*   We blame others when things go wrong, yet 'in here' and 'out there' are part of the same system.
3. *The illusion of taking charge*   'Taking charge' is often a reaction to outside events; true proactiveness comes from seeing how we contribute to our own problems.
4. *The fixation upon events*   A focus on short-term events means that we don't notice the slow gradual processes, such as ...
5. *The parable of the boiled frog* ... where subtle changes in the environment are not detected until it is too late.
6. *The delusion of learning from experience*   We learn best from experience, but because we act in isolation, our actions have unintended consequences of which we know nothing and therefore do not learn.
7. *The myth of the management team*   'Teams' may appear cohesive, and function well on routines, but they are full of internal 'turf' conflicts and can fall apart under pressure.

More fundamentally, Senge also offers *Three Levels of Explanation in a System* (1990, p.52) which parallel our three levels of the Learning Company:

Level 1:	Events	(Reactive)
Level 2:	Patterns of behaviour	(Responsive)
Level 3:	Systemic structure	(Generative)

Understanding things in terms of patterns of behaviour (level 2) enables us to get out of the reactiveness trap and to become responsive to trends. The third and deepest level of explanation – systemic structure – focuses on what causes these patterns of behaviour. This is important in order to escape from seeing events as caused by individual actors or firms and thence leading to individual corrective actions or blaming behaviour. A systemic understanding of the patterns reveals that no one unit or person is to blame for what are the joint productions of many individual actions.

This level of explanation is *generative* because it is provides the deeper insights that enable people to reflect upon their patterns of behaviour and begin to think about how they might change them. Where 'event thinking' is the norm in organizations, this generative learning cannot occur.

REFERENCES

Senge, P. (1990) *The Fifth Discipline: The Art and Practice of the Learning Organization*, Doubleday Currency, New York.

Senge, P. (1991) 'The Learning Organization made Plain', *Training and Development*, October, pp. 37–44.

Nancy Dixon

Nancy Dixon is a student of both Reg Revans and Chris Argyris. She represents the latest phase of development of the learning organization idea, which is concerned with trying to put ideas of organizational learning into practice. Dixon defines organizational learning as:

> the intentional use of learning processes at the individual, group and system level to continuously transform the organization in a direction that is increasingly satisfying to its stakeholders. (1994, p.5)

Dixon emphasizes the new construction of meaning in her definition. Organizational learning occurs when there is a shift in collective meaning making structures. On the basis of empirical evidence, she suggests that organizations learn cyclically in much the same way as individuals but, because this is a collective process, the cycle is more complex involving multiple stakeholders and necessitating intra- and inter-company dialogue to collectively interpret organization information and decide on action.

Dixon's model of the organizational learning cycle (1994, p.70) has four elements (see Figure 20.1 opposite).

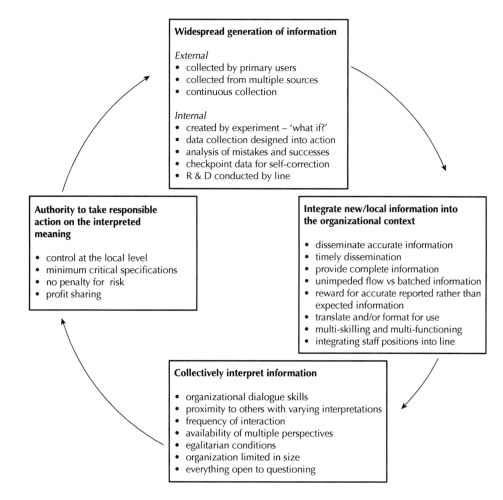

Figure 20.1 Dixon's organizational learning cycle

Nancy Dixon's work demonstrates how individual and collective learning can be integrated and shows the importance of processes of dialogue among diverse perspectives in making sense of information for organizational learning.

REFERENCE

Dixon, N. (1994) *The Organizational Learning Cycle*, McGraw-Hill, Maidenhead.

21. Modes of being and learning

Introduction

The framework described in this chapter is in the first instance a model of individual learning. However, as will be seen, it can also be used in the context of organizational learning.

The modes originated at the NPI in the Netherlands, and were then taken further in the UK by Transform (Leary et al., 1986), through a programme of in-depth research in organizations from a range of sectors. Subsequently a number of instruments have been developed to measure modes profiles of individuals, as well as overall organizational learning cultures.

As presented here, the modes, like a number of other frameworks in this book, is a stage model of development. It might be useful therefore to have a brief look at the nature of such models.

Stage models of development

For illustrative purposes it is helpful to take a stage model that we have all experienced – that of a baby's development of mobility (see also Boydell 1992; Morris 1995; Palus and Drath 1995).

Figure 21.1 depicts four stages in such a development beyond static: rolling, crawling, walking and running. Each stage is qualitatively different from those either side of it. For example, crawling is different from rolling. Learning to roll faster will not enable you to crawl. Indeed it may prevent you from doing the latter; if you can get all you want by rolling, why bother with developing further? There is a sequence, an order in which the stages – or modes of mobility – appear: 'You can't run before you can walk.'

In this case, and indeed with the modes of being and learning, the stages are additive. That is, once you have developed the ability to walk, you can still roll and crawl should you so wish. However, your relationship to rolling and crawling is very different. Whereas they used to be your sole means of getting around, now that you have added walking to your repertoire you will only crawl

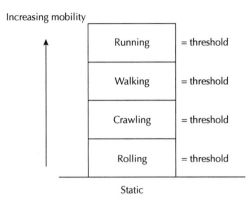

Increasing mobility

Running	= threshold
Walking	= threshold
Crawling	= threshold
Rolling	= threshold

Static

Figure 21.1 Four stages of development (1)

or roll in certain circumstances, for example to play with a young child, or to go through a narrow space.

Some stage models, however, are totally irreversible, such as caterpillar – chrysalis – butterfly. The butterfly can never choose to be a caterpillar again. Nor, for that matter, may a 50-year-old human become a teenager, although some appear desperately to try to do so!

Each stage is separated by a threshold. Crossing such a threshold is often referred to as 'development', while gaining further abilities within a stage is called 'learning'.

So in sum we have:

- development is about crossing a threshold into a new qualitative state or stage
- the new state/stage is added to our repertoire of those that went before
- we can gain extra expertise within a state/stage through a process of learning.

Some people object to stage models on the grounds that since they are hierarchical, they are necessarily élitist. This view, however, seems to confuse development with the way that development is used.

Thus, a child who has developed the ability to roll, crawl, walk and run is better equipped – has a greater repertoire – than one who can only roll and crawl. This isn't élitism. What would make it élitism or worse is that if all those who were able to run had the power to treat as slaves or in some other way dominate and abuse those who could not yet do so. Élitism and autocracy come from the way people or organizations use the power they have developed, not from the process of development itself.

Nonetheless, to overcome the hierarchical connotations of ladder-like presentations such as Figure 21.1 alternatives are sometimes useful. One

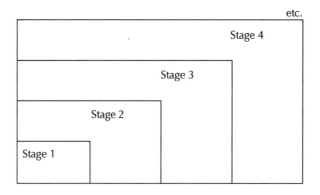

Figure 21.2 Four stages of development (2)

example, from Rooke (1996) shows successive stages as nested within a larger whole (Figure 21.2).

In this form, stage 2 includes stage 1, stage 3 includes stages 1 and 2, stage 4 includes stages 1, 2 and 3. This representation is often referred to as a 'holarchy', rather than a hierarchy; each 'stage' being called a 'holon', after Koestler (1976), a holon being an entity that is itself a whole while simultaneously being a part of a larger whole. (See Wilber, 1996, for an excellent description of the significance of seeing things – everything in fact – as holons.)

The seven modes of being and learning

The Transform research (Leary et al. 1986) elaborated the NPI's original picture of seven modes, as in Table 21.1. In general terms, as a person develops through the modes they become more self-directed, more conscious. Increasingly they make their own meaning or sense of the world around them.

Mode 4 may be seen as a turning point. In modes 1 to 3, what I do is largely determined by external factors – rules, procedures, norms; the outside world is acting on my self. Then in mode 4 for the first time comes the ability to be myself, to make my own meaning. From then on we might say that my self is working on the outer world, exploring it, making sense of it, changing, transforming and creating it (modes 5, 6 and 7 respectively).

Although a model of individual development, other people are always present. As I develop, the role of others changes. In early modes they are the source of threat or help; of punishment or reward; of deprivation or gratification.

Table 21.1 The seven modes of being and learning

Mode	Orientation	Characteristics of mode	Positive aspects	Negative aspects
1. Adhering	Situation is dangerous or threatening. Therefore I seek protection or safety	• Memorizing information by rote • Working to set standards laid down by others • Using rules, checklists, procedures, recipes, routines, 'to the letter'	Useful in highly prescribed situations, or those that are new (for me) and where I seek the established correct procedure or answer	In the long term I will become stuck, rigid, dependent on someone else's 'correct' procedure or answer
2. Adapting	Situation is still dangerous or threatening. I now seek to conquer or tame it	• Responding to variations from 'normal' or routine by modifying what I do • Making procedures 'work better' by making *ad hoc* adaptations (no sense of preplanning or generalizing form specific effect of such adaptation) • Noticing what seems to work better but not thinking or caring about 'why' or wider implications	Seen as useful for short term, 'improvements' and quick-fixes	In the long term isolated quick-fixes and tampering lead to bigger problems elsewhere in larger system
3. Relating	Situation is attractive. I seek acceptance, belonging, membership	• Understanding (i.e. relating to) what is going on, in terms of currently accepted ideas, theories, explanations • Explaining other people's ideas in my own words • Tuning in to what's expected/accepted, in terms of predominant norms, values, standards. Identifying with these norms, with what is appropriate behaviour	Good for solving 'puzzles', i.e. questions to which there already exists a solution, using existing knowledge [*The difference between puzzles and problems is attributed to Revans*]	Danger of shallow, manipulative skills being seen as wisdom. Will not move us on to new ideas or methods. May become brilliantly competent at yesterday's skills
4. Experiencing	A pivotal point. Situation is exciting and interesting. I seek experiences and my own understanding	• Learning, i.e. making my own meaning, from what happens by noticing, reflecting, making sense of it • Working things out, thinking things through, for myself	The essential prerequisite for moving forward (modes 5 to 7) and creating new knowledge, developing new processes	May become stuck here – an experience junkie

Table 21.1 cont'd.

Mode	Orientation	Characteristics of mode	Positive aspects	Negative aspects
5. Experimenting	The situation is intriguing. I seek personal insight – deepening my own understanding	• Wanting, needing to deepen my knowledge and understanding • Experimenting, in a systematic way, to discover my own new meaning • Planning the experiments – thinking about thinking • Finding out new ways of doing things, for myself and others	Need for solving 'problems', where no solution currently exists, by pushing out the frontiers of existing knowledge	May become narrow-minded, arrogant, competitive, out of touch with alternative viewpoints
6. Connecting	Situation is a whole, interconnected, magical, awesome. I seek connections, wholeness	• Realizing that things (i.e. people; groups; functions; departments; units; countries; genders; races; ideas; time) are inter-connected, part of a whole, interdependent • Acknowledging difference and diversity within an overall sense of unity • Looking at consequences and implications for others, over a range of timespans • Being able to work across a whole field of activity • Consciously seeing the broader picture, different mind sets, other perspectives	Transforms the situation into something new – new ideas, relationships, ways of working	Can become overwhelmed by complexity, apparently indecisive due to multiple viewpoints
7. Dedicating	Situation is living, in need of my help. I seek my contribution, my purpose, with and through others	• A sense of the task ahead – the task of the times, of my and our part in it • Having a sense of purpose, of conviction • Finding fulfilling meaning in what I am doing, or what we are doing together • Working purposefully with others in a community of practice	Enables the purposeful co-creation of something new	Danger of self-delusion, self-aggrandizement. One person's or group's dream is another's nightmare

Later on this changes. In mode 5, although there is still a strong individual emphasis, others become increasingly involved as co-workers in experimentation. Then in mode 6 there is the strong recognition that we are all human beings together, each of us unique and yet members of one vast system or community. Finally in mode 7, we can use this shared sense of community – of diversity with unity – to create something new together.

Learning in each mode

Just as with our earlier analogy of stages of mobility, each mode, stage or holon of consciousness is qualitatively different from its predecessor (and its successor, too). Therefore it is not surprising that learning and development methods will be very different for each mode.

A brief summary of these, including help by others, is given in Table 21.2 adapted from Boydell and Leary (1996).

Table 21.2 Learning in the seven modes

Mode		Description	Learning processes	Help by others
Mode 1	Adhering	Learning to do things 'correctly', sticking to rules, procedures and laid down ways of doing things	Instruction, drill, rote learning, memory games, practice with feedback of results	Tell people what to do Give feedback of results Allow time for practice Act as role model for adhering to rules and procedures
Mode 2	Adapting	Learning to modify rules, procedures and methods, discovering short cuts and modifications to make them work better	Observation of effects of *ad hoc*, trial and error adjustments	Support *ad hoc* changes Act as role model for adaptation
Mode 3	Relating	Learning to understand established 'correct' explanations of why things are as they are, why they work as they do, and internalizing the ways things 'ought' to be done	Expository teaching; from known to unknown, concrete to abstract, particular to general, simple to complex; summarizing, testing understanding	Explain why and how things work, are done Encourage questions Ask questions to elicit level of understanding Act as role model for relating to established ways and norms
Mode 4	Experiencing	Learning to make one's own meaning from experiences, from things that happen; creating or discovering one's own understanding	Having experiences, reflecting, forming new ideas, trying out	Providing variety of experiences Encourage reflection Ask questions to cause them to think through their own ideas Act as role model for learning from own experiences
Mode 5	Experimenting	Learning to find out, in a systematic way, more about something, by hypothesizing, carrying out carefully planned experiments or pilot projects, analysing and reviewing the results of these	Systematically structuring experiences – Shewhart's cycle – Plan-Do-Check-Act; continuous improvement tools such as flow-charts, brainstorming, fishbones, Pareto, nominal group technique, correlation analysis, control charts	Champion and support initiatives Provide opportunities for systematic experimentation Support training in systematic improvement techniques Be receptive to new ideas Act as coach, mentor, facilitator Act as role model for continuous improvement

Table 21.2 cont'd.

Mode		Description	Learning processes	Help by others
Mode 6	Connecting	Learning to see systemically – wholes, connections, patterns, interdependencies; hence to empathizes, identify with others, acknowledge and value diversity	Reflecting, seeking patterns, themes, assumptions; dialogue, relationship mapping, role negotiation, speak out, fishbowl, talking stick, Quaker meeting; continuous improvement tools, also affinity diagrams, cluster analysis; repertory grid; meditation	Support training in dialogue, assumption checking and other holistic techniques Encourage and support establishment of autonomous teams Support autonomous teams by making clear they are indeed autonomous Act as coach, mentor, facilitator Act as role model for holistic approach
Mode 7	Dedicating	Learning to recognize and commit to one's purpose in life, in the sense of doing something in and for the external world	Biography work Whole Systems Development future search	Support individual, team and organization biography work Act as role model for sense of purpose

Links with the three levels

Throughout this book we have used various forms of a three-level (three stage, three holon) model. We often find it convenient to condense the seven modes into such a framework too, as shown in Table 21.3.

Table 21.3 Three types of learning

Type	Modes	Description	Best form	Danger
I_1	1–3	Learning to **implement**, through being taught the correct *content*. Doing things well	Constant reliability achieving best current practice through instruction	Stagnation; being left behind; dependency
I_2	4–5	Learning to **improve**, through a *process* of initiative taking and systematic experimentation. Doing things better	Continuous improvement through systematic feedback and reflection	Tampering; instability; limited improvements within existing boundaries
I_3	6–7	Learning to **integrate**, through changing the *context* or relationships within which the other types of learning are occurring. A holistic approach – doing better things by seeing and creating new possibilities	Creative through dialogue	Confusion over identity. Soggy compromise rather than true synthesis

From this it's a short step to postulating three types of learning company (Table 21.4).

Table 21.4 Three types of Learning Company

	Type	Description	Danger/double
I_1	**Implementing**	Does things well. Matches best current practice, consistently, reliably. Does not respond to changes in the environment	Gets left behind. Becomes rigid, inward looking, unresponsive to change. Standards fall due to lack of systematic improvement procedure. Privileging routine and obedience leads to high costs
I_2	**Improving**	Does things better. Continuous improvement through systematic feedback and reflection. Responds to changes by adapting	Tampering, instability. Limited improvements within existing boundaries. Privileging economic efficiency leads to high costs elsewhere (e.g. social, environmental)
I_3	**Integrating**	Does better things. Creativity through holistic, systematic problem solving and dialogue. Co-creates its environment	Confusion over identity. Soggy compromise rather than true synthesis

We can also see how customers and suppliers are treated in each – with the addition of a pre-I_1 stage, Table 21.5.

Table 21.5 External relations in different types of Learning Company

Customers, clients and suppliers are ...

I_0	**Non-implementing**	Betrayed	Ignoring, defusing complaints; defensive litigation
I_1	**Implementing**	Satisfied	Responding positively to complaints, rectifying mistakes quickly, without question
I_2	**Improving**	Delighted	Actively seeking feedback suggestions and consultation with customers and suppliers. When things do go wrong, proactively providing redress
I_3	**Integrating**	Delighted, involved and committed	As improving, but consultation becomes dialogue, and extends systemically to avoid negative side effects

In fact, as we move through the three levels, different groups of stakeholders become more important, Table 21.6.

Table 21.6 Stakeholder levels

I_0	**Non-Implementing**	Owners	(ruthless entrepreneurism)
		Employees	(inefficient bureaucracy)
I_1	**Implementing**	Owners	
		Customers	
I_2	**Improving**	Owners	
		Customers	
		Suppliers	
		Employees	
I_3	**Integrating**	Owners	
		Customers	
		Suppliers	
		Employees	
		Society	
		Environment	

We can also link these three levels with views of leadership, as in Table 21.7. It will be seen that this table also refers to our Energy-Flow model. (For an exciting exploration of Leadership as meaning-making see Drath and Palus, 1995).

Perhaps we should comment on the words 'democratic' and 'empowerment', which are included in Table 21.7 in quotation marks. This is because although these terms are often used in the literature, they still refer to ways of getting others to do what I, the leader, want them to do, albeit in a friendly rather than unfriendly way.

Table 21.7 Leadership types and the Learning Company

Leadership type	Ends	Means	Leadership processes	Related theories	E-Flow
L_1	Decided by leader	Decided by leader; implemented by followers	Coercion 'Democratic' influence	Great Man Group Trait Behaviour	
L_2	Decided by leader	Decided and implemented by followers	'Democratic' influence 'Empowerment'	Great Man Group Trait Behaviour Contingency Effective habit Excellence Pseudo-transformational	
L_3	Jointly decided by all stakeholders	Decided by mandated sub-groups; Implemented variously	Dialogue Mandating	Transformational Meaning making	

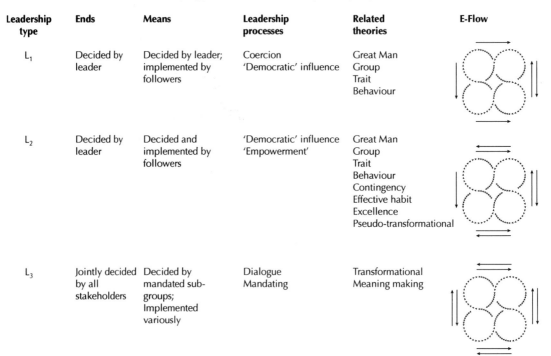

Organizational modes

Coming back to the three levels, expressed now in term of modes, we can say that

In the *implementing* organization, people ...

1. ● do things correctly, sticking to rules, procedures, established methods and ways of doing things
2. ● make small-scale, *ad hoc*, modifications to rules, procedures, methods, discovering short cuts to make things work better
3. ● understand established explanations and reasons why things are as they are, why they work as they do
   ● identify with the way things ought to be done.

In the *improving* organization, people also ...

4. ● reflect on their experiences and make their own meaning from them, creating their own understanding

5. ● find out, in a systematic way, more about what they do and how to improve it, by carrying out structured experiments and pilot projects.

In the *integrating* organization, people also ...

6. ● see systemically – wholes, connections, interdependencies – hence working across boundaries and functions, avoiding negative side-effects of limited-scale experiments and co-creating new processes and products
7. ● have a sense of purpose and meaning through working together.

This formulation provides a useful basis for diagnosis. For example, an instrument that asks people their perception of ...

● how important each mode is for the organization right now

or

● how good the organization is at supporting people working in that way

... provides a measure of importance and performance of each mode that can be plotted as in Figure 21.3, which uses data from a transportation company. This can then be used as the basis for further exploration and developmental change.

Importance	Urgent	Good... but...
	Mode 6	Mode 3
Above average importance	Mode 7	Mode 5
	High importance Low performance	MAY STILL BE A PRIORITY FOR IMPROVEMENT
	OK – for now	Good enough (too good?)
	Mode 1	
Below average importance	Mode 2	
	Mode 4	
	Low importance Low performance	Low importance Low performance

Figure 21.3 Modes – Importance and performance in a transportation company

REFERENCES

Boydell, T. (1992) *Modes of Managing*, Transform, Sheffield.
Boydell, T. and Leary, M. (1996) *Identifying Training Needs*, Institute of Personnel and Development, London.
Drath, W.H. and Palus, C.J. (1995) *Making Common Sense: Leadership as Meaning-*

making in a Community of Practice, Center for Creative Leadership, Greensboro.

Koestler, A. (1976) *The Ghost in the Machine*, Random House, New York.

Leary, M., Boydell, T., van Boeschoten, M. and Carlisle, J. (1986) *The Qualities of Managing*, Training Agency, Sheffield.

Morris, L. (1995) 'Developmental strategies for the knowledge era' In Chawla and Renesch (eds) *Learning Organizations*, Productivity Press, Portland.

Palus, C.J. and Drath, H. (1995) *Evolving Leaders: A Model for Promoting Leadership Development in Programs*, Center for Creative Leadership, Greensboro.

Rooke, D. (1996) 'Organizational transformation requires leaders who are strategists and magicians', paper presented at *Learning Company Project Annual Conference.*

Wilber, K. (1996) *A Brief History of Everything*, Shambhala, Boston and London.

22. Dialogue and organizational learning
Adapted from an original paper by
Chris Blantern

Introduction

There has been much recent interest in the theory and practice of dialogue within the field of organizational learning. Senge makes its practice central to his *team learning* (1990, pp.238–249). Based on the ideas of physicist David Bohm, dialogue is contrasted with discussion (a 'ping-pong' contest in which each side seeks to prevail). Bohm suggests that the original meaning of dialogue was of 'meaning passing through ... (of) a free flow of meaning between people':

> 'Dialogue' comes from the Greek *dialogos. Logos* means 'the word', or 'the meaning of the word', and *dia* means 'through' (not two – a dialogue can be among any number of people; even one person can have a sense of dialogue within him- or herself if the spirit of dialogue is present). (Bohm, 1991, p.10)

The purpose of dialogue is to go beyond individual understanding and to 'become open to the flow of a larger intelligence'; through dialogue a group accesses a larger ' "pool of common meaning" which cannot be accessed individually' (Senge, 1990, pp.240–241).

The value of dialogue is in dealing with intractable situations that are not amenable to normal strategies. For example, Hampden-Turner (1990, pp.7–15) has suggested that many organizational decision situations are best seen as *dilemmas* – not as good or bad choices, but as choices between good and good. Harrison (1995, pp.152–170) has criticized the 'bias to action' in organizations, linking learning with a need for healing and dialogue in 'appreciating dilemmas that don't go away'.

In the 'knowledge era' it is becoming more and more necessary for organizations to develop ways of managing that address diversity, difference, multiplicity and dilemma while achieving some commonality of purpose and direction. It is a mistake to view dialogue as yet another technique. Because it aims at making collective sense in a particular group, organization or community, dialogue is a much more political activity than many writers allow.

Dialogue as a way of making sense

Although organizations run on words, dialogue must mean more than just talking to each other. The notion of dialogue can take on a somewhat mystical air because it is based on a deep intuition that the world and our changing times cannot be fully understood through our existing ways of knowing. However, dialogue is not magic or complex, but is both profound and practical.

The model of knowing implicit in the Western world is a scientific one. We assume that the world exists independently of how we look at it (objective knowledge) and that it awaits our discovery in ever more detail. From this point of view knowledge is hierarchical, handed down by experts who have found it out. It is also more or less universal, true everywhere except for some local and superficial variations. This way of knowing serves us well where we need universal and enduring truths.

However, in many aspects of life, such truths are not available. This is partly because, in Whitehead's words, 'knowledge keeps no better than wet fish' – experts disagree in almost every field from butter versus margerine, to how to manage the economy. This leads to a second issue; if universal knowledge is no longer up to the task, then whose knowledge do we take to be true? In our organizations is it the view of the:

... chief executive?
... shareholders?
... front-line staff?
... consultants?
... shop-floor workers?
... regulators?
... suppliers?
... finance department?
... human resources?
... trade unions?
... customer?
... or even the knowledge of the community at large?

In organizations there are many kinds of knowledge, how can we make sense of them all? Knowledge is verified by particular social processes. If we assume that all knowledge is made of the same stuff we can ask 'Is it true?' using certain rules to establish pedigree. However, once we question the existence of single, universal truths we can see better what constitutes these legitimizing processes. For example, here are some rules, in descending order of legitimacy, that reflect Oliver Wendel Holmes junior's dictum 'Truth is what I can't help believing and what I believe is what the highest authorities tell me':

1. From how high has it descended? (the higher up the better)
2. How expert is its source? (the more expert the better)
3. Does the source have social status? (the more socially acceptable the better)

4. Does the source have practical or contextual status? (did it work – is it mainstream or esoteric?)
5. What is my previous experience of knowledge from this source? (is it a reliable source?)
6. Does it fit with my current experience? (I generalize from my experience)
7. Is it backed up by anyone else? (the subjective knowledge of others is even less believable than my own experience)

When someone disagrees publicly with their boss or if two or more different accounts are given of the same event, we usually want one version of 'what really happened?'. The versions abandoned first are those of the less powerful voices. For many organizations even participation or consultation is a sophisticated process for achieving a legitimized and sanitized unitary view.

This is why organizations often do not know what all their individual members know. Most people instinctively recognize the way power is used to fix meaning, and may decide to collude rather than be identified as disloyal, resistant, inarticulate, stupid, or even crazy.

What we are beginning to see then is that knowledge is created through social processes characterized by relationships of power. Language and its rules enable us to act together in particular ways to achieve particular ends. In 'conversation', an exchange of power takes place and meanings are arrived at by what it is that conversation enables us to do. In this view, knowledge is not universal truth (or 'monologue') but a set of cultural rules that enables us to do things together. For example, 'science' enables us to do scientific things just as the rules of 'hockey' enable us to play hockey together. Where it is important to find ways of doing things together, as in organizations and communities, we would be better off dropping the idea that the rules of science help us to fulfil all human aspirations and focus on our relationships and on our future together.

The emerging need for dialogue – some indicators

Before going on to what dialogue might do, let us consider some of the practical issues facing organizations who know only how to monologue – who perpetuate a public system of knowing, either through 'command and control' or more subtly through 'mission–vision–empowerment' approaches, which reduce the complexity and multiplicity of voices to a unitary whole.

1. In the knowledge era organizations need to increase their knowledge stocks. It makes progressively less sense to censor what the individual or component parts (stakeholders) of the organization know – that is to render them inaudible or unknowable by the organization as a whole. Technological change and information proliferation means that it is no longer possible for any small group of people to take an overview. Faced with information overload organizations will need to find ways of making sense of data from many sources. Everyone is effectively doing research on behalf of the organization.

2. It follows that organizations are better off when they have access to the tacit knowledge within its system that reflects the diversity outside. The rate of social and economic change requires organizations to incorporate learning processes that enable self-managed continuous change at the whole organization level. Collaboration across functional and hierarchical boundaries is becoming increasingly important and the defensiveness that marks out organizational territories is a block to learning at the whole organization level.

3. The trend towards increased specialization, fragmentation and disintegration in organizations weakens the idea that organizations are coherent machines driven by a single power source.

4. The cost of policing difference is increasing. Energy put into getting people to fit our view of them, either through sanctions or by trying to 'develop' them, seriously undermines the added value created by the business process. There are important considerations here for the 'management of change' as a growing activity and major cost for organizations.

5. As Murphy bears out (Murphy, 1995):

> Internal and external partnerships are a means of achieving projects that cannot be undertaken alone – adding know-how, increasing efficiency, defending territory or opening information channels to influence markets. Research shows that where partners see their partnership very differently, such difference is usually viewed as problematic and yet it is this very difference that makes the partnership attractive in the first place! Partnership failure is both costly and likely where that difference cannot be valued or even accommodated.

No doubt there are many more examples in world affairs or from your own community or organization that come to mind. The argument here is that the conditions of our times point to the increasing redundancy of universal ideologies as the primary means for enabling organizational and social cohesion. Unilateral approaches to organizing are increasingly unworkable and yet there are many who would remedy this sense of dissatisfaction with a call for strong leadership. However, strong leadership may be met by strong resistance. There are many more voices in the world today (perhaps there always were!). So how can we do things together and still be different? How can we have unity in diversity?

Ironically, at a time of prolific globalization and yet because of it, what is becoming increasingly visible is that knowledge is a local and a social phenomenon. It comes out of the way people do things, work out what is the next step, how they go on together in given communities – whether those communities are separated by time, geography, function or purpose.

Doing dialogue

Dialogue is relevant to all contexts where we need to act together to get things done and where difference is manifest or latent. From a traditional point of view difference is posited as problematic – that is it must be overcome, smoothed out or denied in order to move on. From that perspective a great deal of social energy is taken up in dealing with difference. From the dialogical perspective it is acknowledged as a simple reality and that we would be better of getting on and doing things together rather than becoming preoccupied by our differences. It is important to stress that this does not mean ignoring difference but rather seeing it as an everyday characteristic of our relationships which, if honoured, allows us to be mutually productive.

Here are some principles that can guide practice (see also Chapter 23, 'Whole Systems Development' which is based on similar principles):

- *Emphasize the task rather than the process*   What is compelling? What is the next important thing to do which affects us here?
- *Get the whole system in the room or conversational space*   'The issue defines the system' – that is, involve all the diverse perspectives or voices or stakeholders affected by the issue. This diversity helps to define the issue and its sharing can lead to the possibility of different action. Reducing diversity or sticking with what we are comfortable with tends to confirm or maintain things as they are.
- *Keep things public*   Make available the conversations we have with ourselves and others as we do things. This enables the emergence of collective meaning as we act, that is, as we create a community of practice, together.
- *Privilege relationship over ideology*   Keep the task up-front, acknowledge different stories as equally real but don't get bogged down on processing difference (proving ideology).
- *Focus on what we can and want to do together in the immediate future*   whatever remains different (past).
- *Don't try to change or steer people*   Avoid the temptation to know what is best for others. Trust that the dialogical structure (or container) for getting on with the task will allow participants to make the connections and meanings they need to get things done.
- *Tell people what you are trying to achieve by what you say*   Ask people what they are trying to achieve by what they say to each other.
- *Avoid process facilitation which claims a neutral or unstructured view*   This usually creates the mystique of expertise and can generate dependency. Be explicit about the rules of the dialogical structure and make the principles available.

Finally, here is an introduction to three activities based on the principles of dialogue which are used by and are available from the Learning Company Project (for address see p.239):

- Dialogue Cards (for use with individuals in one to one or small group relationships)
- The Dialogue Circle (for groups up to 20)
- Future Search (for large groups 25–100 people)

Dialogue Cards   (developed by Chris Blantern)

Dialogue cards acts as prompters of dialogical behaviour – where both (all) parties mutually construct the meaning that leads to possibilities for action – in situations where difference is preventing people from doing things together. The purpose is to help people to do things together even though there may be differences. People have used the cards in situations as diverse as establishing a sense of direction for a work group and in a stormy personal relationship.

Participants are asked to share their notion of the common task and to keep it in mind. In the ensuing conversation about what they want to do next participants can either draw upon the cards to assist their own turn in the conversation or alternatively, and possibly more adventurously, they may offer to play a card on behalf of the other.

Figure 22.1 shows a sample of the dialogue cards. You might like to consider which of these might have been helpful to you in a recent situation where differences were writ large.

The Dialogue Circle   (developed by Anne Murphy and Chris Blantern)

The Dialogue Circle was devised to help groups of people, through a real task, to reveal the common ground for action in pursuit of a desired future. Groups can devote a great deal of energy to smoothing out or attempting to eradicate differences on the assumption that this is necessary before we can act together. Explorations in participation often reverberate between the calls for involving people on the one hand and quick and decisive action on the other. The Dialogue Circle can help to uncover the common ground within small groups while honouring differences.

We have used the Dialogue Circle to trawl for joint action following individual or small group visioning exercises. In the usual creative surge that accompanies such activities, ideas begin to flow of how people will reach their desired futures – next steps, possible actions and so on. Each participant is then invited to write their suggestions for action on a card (one suggestion per card). Commonly we suggest up to three suggestions per person but this can vary depending upon the size of the group and the time available. The bigger the group – the fewer the suggestions.

The circle is formed with participants seated and facing inwards. People are invited to read out a suggestion in turn and then to place the card in the centre of the circle. Any member of the group may remove any card placed in the centre if they personally feel unable to take this step. An important rule here is that no one else is allowed to speak other than to read out their suggestion. The rationale is that in traditional debate such speech is used to attack or defend and in an attempt to expose this we ask participants to write down what they would like to say so that it can be said later.

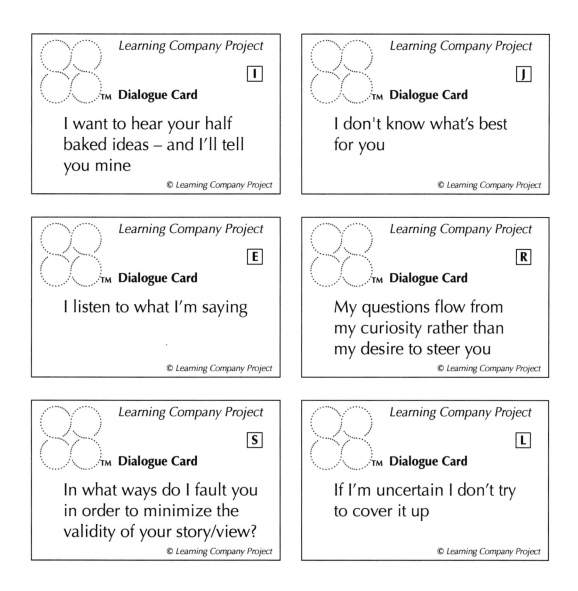

Figure 22.1 Some Dialogue Cards (© Learning Company Project)

The turn taking and removal of cards continues until only the cards that everyone wants in the circle remain. Participants are then invited to speak if they want to – on one condition – that they also reveal the function of what they intend to say. This makes public the conversations we are having with ourselves enabling others to avoid speculation about the intention. It seems to enable a quality of honesty and trust that increases commitment to different action.

Finally participants are invited to revisit the cards they have removed to establish whether they are (a) common ground, (b) possible future or (c) intractable difference. Common ground suggestions can be acted upon right now and this can lead to the repositioning of other differences.

Future Search   (developed by Marvin Weisbord and Sandra Janoff)

The Future Search methodology developed by Weisbord and recently his colleague Janoff (Weisbord and Janoff, 1995) has many similarities with Whole Systems Development and shares the same historical roots (see Chapter 23). Here is an extract from a brief description of the method by Weisbord:

> A Future Search Conference is an intensive method for planning the collaborative action steps we can do now in order to bring about our joint futures. It involves five small group tasks requiring about 16 hours of actual work. These tasks honour diversity, the exploration of common ground, complexity and confusion, and our ability to learn from experience. The work is undertaken mostly in small groups of 8 people. In between these tasks the conference convenes as a whole so that everyone gets to find out how the pieces come to make up the whole. There is no pressure to shift positions (views) and everyone hears all the perspectives. A Future Search Conference is not:
>
> - 'empowerment', 'involvement' or 'participation' towards a preconceived result (getting the many to buy into the vision of the few)
> - expert or top team driven
> - a talk-in for people who see themselves as 'from the same mould'
> - a discussion forum without action
> - a problem-solving or conflict management meeting (we do not attempt to resolve differences)
> - a team building workshop
> - a seminar, training or diagnostic exercise
>
> A Future Search Conference differs from typical participative meetings in that:
>
> The WHOLE SYSTEM participates – a cross section of as many interested parties as practical. That means more diversity and less hierarchy than usual and a chance for each person to be heard and to see other ways of going about the task in hand.
>
> FUTURE SCENARIOS are put into a HISTORICAL and GLOBAL perspective. That means thinking globally, together, before acting locally. This enhances shared understanding and greater commitment to act as well as increasing the range of possible actions.

People SELF-MANAGE their work and use DIALOGUE (openness and commitment to listening) – not problem-solving as the main tool. That means helping each other to do the tasks and taking responsibility for our perceptions and actions.

COMMON GROUND rather than 'conflict management' is the frame of reference. That means honouring our differences rather than feeling the need to reconcile them. The common ground and public commitment to action emerge from the whole group so PLANNING and IMPLEMENTATION are in the hands of the same people.

Conclusion

The practice of dialogue is still in its infancy and many experiments are taking place. As we move around organizations it does seem that more and more people have stories of dissatisfaction with traditional, unitary approaches to organizing and management. It is certainly easier to talk about. We are not suggesting that these dialogical methods will sweep away all that we have hitherto known but in the right conditions they are an important addition to the managerial repertoire.

REFERENCES

Blantern, C. (1996) *The Action Orientation of Dialogue and Organizational Learning*, Learning Company Project, Sheffield.

Bohm, D. (1991) 'For truth try dialogue', *Resurgence*, no. 156, pp.10–13.

Hampden-Turner, C. (1990) *Charting the Corporate Mind*, Blackwell, London.

Harrison, R. (1995) *Consultant's Journey*, McGraw-Hill, Maidenhead.

Murphy, A. (1995) 'Building on difference for successful partnering', *Research report to ATKearney Ltd*, ATKearney Ltd, London.

Senge, P. (1990) *The Fifth Discipline: The Art and Practice of the Learning Organization*, Doubleday, New York.

Weisbord, M. and Janoff, S. (1995) *Future Search*, Berrett-Koehler, San Francisco.

23. Whole Systems Development

Whole Systems Development is one of the names given to a whole organization change process that is exciting attention because it seems to address some of the causes of failures experienced in previous designs for organization-wide change. Arguably, it offers a way of avoiding the twin obstacles of senior people being unwilling or unable to share their power and less senior people 'resisting' or subverting major change programmes. Weisbord and Janoff's *Future Search* (1992) is one formulation of this process and is the culmination of a stream of work going back for at least 40 years.

Whole Systems Development can be traced back to socio–technical systems thinking (Emery and Trist, 1965). In the late 1940s and 1950s UK researchers were concerned with understanding technological change in industry. Trist and Bamforth (1951) studied the introduction of long-wall methods in coal mining and noted how mechanization caused severe difficulties with the informal social relationships amongst the miners. They concluded that every technical system has a matching human system and that successful change has to deal with both.

From these early studies, systems thinking was developed on both sides of the atlantic in the 1950s and 1960s. Researchers in the UK and the USA applied the idea to group behaviour (Bion, 1959; Bales, 1950). Menzies (1960) produced a classic study that demonstrated that rigid nursing hierarchies can be understood as a defence against the endemic anxiety found in hospitals. About the same time, von Bertalanffy (1968) elaborated the biologically-based concept of organizations as 'open systems' and created the basis for the organic metaphor of organization.

The ideas of systems theory are very rich and include the notion of wholism and the interrelatedness of events in the parts of the whole. Systems are goal seeking and self-regulating seeking equilibrium via adjustment, control and learning. Other key ideas include 'minimum critical specification' – which reverses the bureaucratic impulse and suggests that a minimum enabling structure is most useful for self-organization and learning; 'Equifinality' and the 'redundancy of parts' allows for multiple paths to be found to goals. Ashby's 'Law of Requisite Variety' suggests that there must be a matching variety in a system to absorb the variety inherent in any given problem. The Law of Requisite Variety can be managerially counter-intuitive because:

> ... it argues in favour of a pro-active embracing of the environment in all its diversity. Very often managers do the reverse, reducing variety in order to achieve greater internal consensus. For example, corporate planning teams are often built around people who think along the same lines, rather than around a diverse set of stakeholders who could actually represent the complexity of the problems with which the team ultimately has to deal. (Morgan, 1986, p.101)

Maturana and Varela coined the word 'autopoieisis' to describe systems as self-designing, becoming more complex as they try to absorb more variety. Organism and environment are seen not as separate, as previously assumed, but as part of the same whole (Morgan, 1986, pp.235–240). This is highly relevant to organizational learning because it suggests that we shape our own environments as well as being shaped by them.

There are other antecedents to Whole Systems Development ideas and methods. Action research involves data collection, feedback to the system and joint action planning. Revans's (1983) Action Learning posits action on problems as the means of learning and emphasizes as primary the pursuit of 'questioning insight' and the re-ordering of knowledge. Argyris and Schon (1978) and recently, Senge (1990) have been responsible for a revival of interest in systems thinking as applied to learning organizations – a notion which involves putting many of these principles into practice.

However, the recent upsurge of interest in Whole Systems Development stems most directly from the idea of Search Conferencing (or Future Search: Weisbord, 1992; Weisbord and Janoff, 1995). From initial developments by Emery at Bristol Siddeley Engines in the UK in 1960, it has been pursued ever since, particularly in Australia and Norway. Involving whole communities, occupational or residential, in collective analysis, planning and action, this process 'gets everybody into improving the whole' (Weisbord 1992), Weisbord explains the sudden prominence of Future Search as the culmination of an historical learning curve of social action:

1900   Experts solve problems
1950   Everybody solves problems
1965   Experts improve whole systems
2000   Everybody improves whole systems

What is the Whole Systems Development process?

Whole Systems Development is a way of involving large numbers of people in face-to-face dialogue with each other and with the leaders of the organization. The purpose is to ensure that everybody has a hand in painting the big picture and to start to align their own actions, along with those of colleagues, to bring this into being. These events create temporary organizations in which people, who are normally part of a hierarchical order, can experience different relationships with one another. However, the design only works where leaders are prepared to be open and experimental, and claims that such events alter power relationships in the host organization must be treated with scepticism.

One account of the Whole Systems Development in action in a UK local authority (Wilkinson and Pedler, 1996) specifies five 'keys' to the process:

Key 1 'Getting the whole organization into the room together'

The first principle is that anyone who will be affected by a change should also be an architect of it. An important part of the process are the 'Big Events' which can involve anything from 30 or 40 people to several hundred grouped around dozens of tables. 'Getting everyone in the room together' happens in two ways:

- as part of a diagnostic process, data is collected from all parts of the organization including the views of users, customers and other stakeholders
- decisions are made in meetings of representatives of *all* organization members and stakeholders. (In a small organization this might mean literally everybody; in a larger one representation is necessary.)

Key 2   Public learning

Whole Systems Development derives its power from *public* evidence of learning and commitment from 'everyone in the room'. People hear colleagues from other departments make action plans to change relationships; everyone sees the senior management team being questioned on their policies and receiving feedback which often leads to changed direction. This needs effective preparation by a number of teams including a *leadership team* of the chief executives and senior officers to give overall leadership and direction to the change; a *design team* of representative members to develop the design of the change process and also a *consultants team* to guide the change process itself.

Key 3   Diversity

The full diversity and complexity of the system should be represented and be present in the room together. The full range of departments, professional groupings, grades and status, gender, ethnic composition, age and any other relevant criteria and also a full array of stakeholders and service users are included.

Key 4   Effective small group working

So that the diversity of the complex whole is present in all the parts of the change process, participants work in 'max–mix' (maximum mix) groups in order to have the chance to speak and to listen to the views and ideas of others; and also in organizationally-based groups to agree actions to deliver the joint agenda. This can include:

- posting the deliberations and proposals of all groups around the room with the full membership giving their responses via various polling methods

- tables formulating questions and signalling responses on issues through the use of roving microphones and sound systems
- inputs, viewpoints and responses being made from the podium
- question and answer session workshops and other meetings of departmental and other functional groups.

Key 5   Follow through

Well prepared and sequenced large scale events produce potentially transforming outcomes. However, a common cause of failure is the raising of heady expectations during 'Big Events' followed by gathering disillusion and cynicism when nothing changes thereafter. Failure to provide frameworks for further development and support – in effect treating the Big Event as a stand-alone activity – not only throws away such exciting gains, but may lead to greater levels of inertia than previously existed. This only serves to strengthen the position of those in the organization, in particular those who want to maintain the status quo and existing ways of working.

The importance of 'follow through' can scarcely be overemphasized. The creation of 'exit strategies' must precede any Big Event and the resources for continuing support for action and learning must be secured. These will enable the new ways of doing business and delivering services generated by the process to be brought to life.

Conclusion

Whole Systems Development holds out the promise of Participative Policy Making and more, showing what can be achieved when the intelligence, creativity and skill of a critical mass of the whole staff, supported by users, customers, suppliers and other stakeholders, conspires to achieve a common strategic purpose. In such a process, people are drawn towards an offer they find difficult to refuse. They are involved, feel valued and are listened to – factors missing in many workplaces – despite the rhetoric of 'empowerment'. It makes legitimate to ask of oneself, and of others, 'What's in this for me ... and ... for you?' In this is a deeper question: 'What is my responsibility to engage with others in making these changes happen?'

However, all this makes great demands upon leaders – which most may not be willing or able to meet. First, they must be able to change policies and practices; in public service especially, there are often clear limits on this requirement. Second, they must be prepared to act in good faith if they are to undertake such radical participation in their organizations. Unless there is a true desire to transform the governance of the company in this way, then it is far better not to start. Third, they must accept their part in the 'public learning' for they will be the most visible of learners and actors, playing a large part in setting the tone and determining, by their subsequent actions, whether there is real development taking place or not.

Whole Systems Development offers a promising way forward for organizations faced with complexity and uncertainty. It is perhaps particularly relevant for public service where the desire to improve service and quality must be achieved in the face of finite and often declining resources together with competing demands from service users. It is a process that can take account of some of the critical dimensions of managing in the public service environment including the issues of accountability, managing with professionals and the conflicting demands of multiple stakeholders. (Pedler and Aspinwall, 1995, ch. 6)

Because of its ability to include a diverse range of stakeholders, Whole Systems Development offers one way of working towards the Learning Company, which is enabled in developing and transforming itself by harnessing the intelligence and variety of all its members. Through not only taking data from members but also involving them in making meaning and taking action in a process of collaborative enquiry, Whole Systems Development represents an important piece of the social technology to move towards this attractive, if elusive, goal.

REFERENCES

Argyris, C. and Schon, D.A. (1978) *Organizational Learning: A Theory of Action Perspective*, Addison Wesley, Cambridge, MA.

Bales, R.F. (1950) *Interaction Process Analysis*, Addison Wesley, Cambridge, MA.

Bion, W.F. (1959) *Experiences in Groups*, Basic Books, New York.

Emery, F.E. and Trist, E.L. (1965) 'The causal texture of organizational environments', *Human Relations*, 18, 21–32

Menzies, I. (1960) 'A Case Study in the Functioning of Social Systems as a Defence Against Anxiety', *Human Relations*, 13, 95–121

Morgan, G. (1986) *Images of Organisation*, Sage, London.

Pedler, M.J. and Aspinwall, K.A. (1996) *'Perfect plc?': The Purpose and Practice of Organizational Learning*, McGraw-Hill, Maidenhead.

Revans, R.W. (1983) *The ABC of Action Learning*, Chartwell-Bratt, Bromley.

Senge, P. (1990) *The Fifth Discipline: The Art and Practice of the Learning Organization*, Doubleday Currency, New York.

Trist, E.L. and Bamforth, K.W. (1951) 'Some social and psychological consequences of the Longwall method of coal getting', *Human Relations*, 4, 3–38.

von Bertanlanffy, L. (1968) *General Systems Theory: Foundations, Development, Applications*, Braziller, New York.

Weisbord, M.R. (1992) *Discovering Common Ground*, Berrett-Koehler, San Francisco.

Weisbord, M.R. and Janoff, S. (1995) *Future Search: An Action Guide to Finding Common Ground in Organizations and Communities*, Berrett-Koehler, San Francisco.

Wilkinson, D. and Pedler, M.J. (1996) 'Whole Systems Development in public service' *Journal of Management Development*, **15**(2), 38–53.

24. The contribution of computer networks to organizational learning
Adapted from an original paper by
Chris Blantern

Introduction

Rapid change, fragmentation and uncertainty require the individual to be self-sufficient and to become aware of and be able to manage their own learning processes. Yet how can these individual learnings resonate with the rhythm of the collective? How can they be jointly and severally valued, integrated and implemented by something we might call 'the organization'? How can learning be organized for mutual productivity rather than being organized for control? How can we manage the organization of learning?

We are all still learning about how to put the attractive idea of the learning company into practice and our traditional notions of learning and organization are being challenged. Thanks to information technology, a quiet revolution has been taking place – exchange via computer networks is growing apace and is beginning to make a powerful contribution to the organization of learning.

Over the last few years desktop computers and networks have proliferated. More and more people use them as part of their everyday activity which, in turn, transforms that activity. As they have spread beyond the control of technical specialists, so, too, have their uses moved beyond the technical designs of 'automating' and 'informating'. As computer networks become more popular they are used for more popular purposes. They can now enrich the more human aspects of group working and increase the possibilities for unleashing the potential and learning of individuals, groups and, indeed, the whole organization.

However, many organizations have invested heavily in IT and computer networks without much return. In terms of what concerns us here they may not yet be aware of how such systems can be used to enhance and share individual and collective learning, enthusiasm and ideas. This chapter focuses on how computer networks can be used in this way, prefaced with some thoughts on:

- the revision of learning theory in accordance with current social and economic reality
- the central importance of the integration of individual and collective learning in organizations – relationships of participation.

Revision of learning theory

We are changing the way we think about learning. Some themes emerge:

- In a rapidly changing world universal knowledge 'keeps no better than wet fish' and individuals and organizations are better served by developing and practising their learning and critical enquiry skills rather than relying on 'off the shelf' or 'quick fix' solutions. As Revans put it, 'learning inside must be equal to or greater than change outside or the organization is in decline'.
- Knowledge of local conditions and sensitivity to context are necessary for effective learning. Knowledge grows out of action in particular communities or cultures – there is no universally 'true' way that transcends context.
- Different and various views and ways of doing things are a source of richness rather than a problem.
- Our beliefs (mental models) about the world determine the meaning of our individual and collective interactions. The more we are willing to be open to new or modified beliefs, in ourselves and others, the greater the possibilities for individual and corporate learning.
- Learning is a social phenomenon – our ability to learn and what we can know is determined by the quality and openness of our relationships. Our mental models of the world and our 'selves' grow out of our relationships with others. Dialogue with others, which involves continuous critical reappraisal of our views, increases the possibilities for learning. Dialogue is incompatible with self-sufficiency.

Integrating individual and collective learning

There are two aspects to understanding how individual and collective learning may be related.

First, the rapid increase in the rate of change in the social and economic world in the latter half of this century has weakened the possibilities for command and control in organizations.

Holding on to universal approaches to managing organizations as right and true, in a world characterized by change, ephemeralism, fragmentation and difference, no longer fits with social and economic reality. Organizations waste energy trying to impose universal regimes in response to change ('initiative fatigue') and they become less flexible by trying to impose flexibility. They will be more creative and productive by valuing and including, not excluding, difference. Accordingly, greater attention is being focused upon local exchange, meaning and learning and how this can be incorporated into the whole. Organizing, seen this way, is less about organizing and managing to 'control' and more about organizing and managing to 'learn'. Technologies of participation, facilitating individual and local learning and integrating it with the whole, are now important managerial tools.

A promising approach is to ask how these different views and purposes, accommodate and inform each other (their 'fit'). What seems to be particularly important is how the deep, often hidden, assumptions in our particular views influence our experience and learning and our relationships with others.

This 'informal' and largely subconscious process in organizations has tended to be suppressed and important learning has been ignored or denied. As such an organization may change without being able to take advantage of much of the collective learning of its members. Managing organizational learning invites the opening up of this process and the development of a climate to enable and support the explicit sharing of our different views and their attendant assumptions.

Second, all individuals in the organization learn – but whether this learning is grasped as significant by the individual learner, valued by the organization and incorporated into the organization's new ways depends not only on the 'fit' mentioned above but also on the ability to share the learning in a pragmatic and accessible way. As organizations become physically and geographically more extensive, more specialized and decentralized, organizational memory and learning becomes fragmented and the corporate benefits are lost.

There is little point in empowering individuals if participation in the 'whole' is not also to be developed so that situational learning can be incorporated. There must be a framework for sharing learning and making collective sense. New and more radical ways of sharing, which access the tacit organizational processes are needed. 'Participation' then, is not only a matter of ethics but also a necessary pragmatic ingredient in organizational learning.

The rapid development of computer networking technology

Zuboff (1988) noticed that organizations used computers in two distinct ways – to automate and to informate.

The first use is in automating existing, time consuming and tedious procedures – like running the payroll or production machinery. The automation of business processes generated new pools of information. For example, supermarket scanners automate the checkout process and simultaneously generate data useful for stock control, delivery logistics and market analysis. These processes can be used to 'create a vast overview of and organization's operations and to see into the workings of the organization in a more transparent and sharable way. This second approach to using computer technology – 'Informating' – has moved beyond the traditional logic of automating. The development of 'Informating' creates a new dimension of reflexivity – of seeing into the processes of the organization in a sharable way.

It provides a deeper level of transparency to activities which had been partially or completely opaque. (Zuboff, 1988)

Until about six years ago most computers were specialist mainframe or mini-systems and, although offering vast Informating capacity, they tended to be used by a minority of trained specialists and on the whole were consigned to particular compartments of organizational life. To the rest of us these text-based systems were unattractive and awkward to use. Furthermore, quite what information we needed, and for what purposes, was still largely determined by a pre-IT concept of organizing.

Now there is a third dimension. The advent of the PC and friendlier graphical displays (e.g. Windows) has made computers more popular. 'Cheap' personal computers have proliferated in the home and the workplace. More and more people use one as part of their everyday work, including working from home ('Teleworking'). Notebook computers have even become a fashion accessory.

The advantages of linking computers together were soon apparent and networks, too, have begun to grow rapidly. It is estimated that there are at least 900 public worldwide networks not counting the 10 000 or so local/national networks that are linked by the Internet. The Internet alone has approaching 20 million users and the population has been growing at over 15 per cent per month for the last few years. Electronic networks, for work, social and educational purposes are growing apace. Not only do people share files and databases nationally and internationally but more qualitative exchange and participation through e-mail and computer conferencing is rapidly increasing. Mass computer-mediated networking is upon us.

Telemating

Rheingold sees this shift as radical, just as Zuboff saw the informating stage as a radical departure:

Most people who have not yet used these new media remain unaware of how profoundly the social, political and scientific experiments under way today, via computer networks, could change all our lives in the near future. History has shown us that a new means of mass communication usually leads to new ways of organizing our relationships – our societies, institutions and companies. The printing press was accredited with the dawn of the 'modern' era of democratic nations. Ivan Illich predicted the decline of the Soviet Empire when access to telephones achieved critical mass. News of Tienanmen Square emerged from China via computer networks. (Rheingold, 1993)

We call this form of collaborative enquiry via computer networks 'telemating', which goes well beyond Zuboff's informating, because it uses the medium for creating shared new understanding and meaning. There are increasing signs that people are becoming aware of the possibilities here. Research by the Learning Company Project reveals the following insights and questions from discussions with organizations:

> We know networked IT and 'groupware' are going to be very important but how can we use them to build learning companies?

> We've got the technology but we're not making the best use of it for our collective learning – I'm sure there's more we could be doing.

> We simply need to increase the flow of information exchange around the organization which shouldn't be constrained by the structure of our existing systems.

These companies are sensing the possibilities for learning becoming available through network technology:

> We want an arena where we can readily share our individual and collective learning in a 'no-fuss' way.

> It would be really good to get managers working in an everyday way with Learning Company ideas without having to set up special events or use special labels – to which there is often resistance. We could do that with some easy to use software on a network.

> We need instant and continuous feedback about how as well as what our company is learning.

> I want everyone to be thinking about how our organization learns – not just the senior strategists.

Organizations are making the link between individual and collective learning and their existing IT investment:

> We need to open up the organization and to make use of the potential of our people through increased participation. I think electronic networking can really help.

> I want to find a way of getting people to contribute who are currently not doing so.

> We heard about an experimental project which we are thinking of repeating in our organization. If we could 'informate' that, that is make it available to everyone in the organization and get them to participate in some way, it would be a real breakthrough.

Towards the networked Learning Company

There are a number of important areas where Learning Organization ideas and practice are realizable through computer networking. We have observed the following:

- As work becomes more computer oriented the informating needs of different organizational specialisms become more available across functional boundaries. Networked IT can enable specialist and fragmented information to be reinterpreted and readily exchanged internally.
- Computer networking enables feedback of opinions and individual learning into the collective organization where previously it had been hidden in filing cabinets, in people's heads, discussed covertly by the coffee machine or,

indeed, forgotten. Computer conferencing is a powerful medium for encouraging and remembering this sharing.

- The endorsement of more open networking systems helps people to feel more involved as they see their contribution to the organization's legitimate view of itself. What we take our organization to be, its story-line, is not solely the creation of senior management.

As the whole of the organization becomes visible and available to our collective awareness, this greatly increases the potential for enhanced learning relationships among the members of the company. For example:

- Networking expands time and compresses space. There is no need for people to be in the same place at the same time in order to have a sense of live exchange. Individuals can contribute when it suits them and build relationships across different work sites or even continents.
- There is no competition for 'air time' or 'floor space' with networking. Everyone can contribute if they wish. There is more time, too, to contemplate one's contribution.
- The tendency for people to keep their views to themselves when 'powerful' people are present can be reversed with the sensitive use of networking.
- Networking can be used to promote collaborative learning as a focus for more flexible ways of organizing. It tends to loosen the rigidifying structures inherent in models of organizing based solely on the principle of control.

Some specific software applications, designed to promote learning, can be established on the network:

- Learning/problem solving data bases can be established to capture individual learning or inform 'task force' or project team selection.
- Electronic learning sets can be established and facilitated to develop teams and individuals and to promote learning as the spirit of coordination.
- Software systems designed to support individual and collective learning can be networked, for example – self-development systems, open learning catalogues and live resources, career development systems, diagnostic instruments, decision-making aids, opinion surveys and even means of achieving instant and continuous feedback about the learning of the team, department or organization. These software systems are integrated with other software tools, such as 'project managers', spreadsheets, databases and word processors and become part of day-to-day activity, language and know-how.

However, as Table 24.1 shows, the readiness of an organization to use information technology in this way depends upon many contextual factors. Chief among these are the company's approach to organizational learning – are they aiming to be type 1, 2 or 3? Informating cannot be used in a company that keeps a tight, centralized control of information and telemating will only work where there is a genuine desire to encourage and participate in company-wide learning and sense making. The learning models and methods used in the company are also likely to reflect the overall level of aspiration and development – as is the overall managerial ethos.

Table 24.1 IT use in context

Organization learning type	Mode of IT use	Model of learning	Key learning method	Ethos
1. Memory	**Automating**	Teaching	Courses, demonstrations, etc.	One right answer or way
2. Asserting/improving	**Informating**	Critical review, experimenting	Quality circles, action learning, experiential programmes	What works – norms established by most powerful
3. Mutuality	**Telemating**	Reflexivity	dialogue, collaborative enquiry	Multiple views, make up the system

Conclusion

Who now, can afford to ignore the advantages of information technology? As Informating has become attractive for its ability to make the opaque production processes of organizations more transparent so telemating is beginning to transform corporate learning processes. Telemating via computer networking is becoming established as a powerful means of exchange within organizations.

This helps to release the vast learning potential of organizations. As the new logics of informating, learning relationships, electronic networking and telemating become available the processes of organizational learning become more accessible and manageable. The learning organization can now be consciously re-viewed as the organization of learning.

However, the transforming effects of these computer network-assisted processes do not happen in isolation. Unless there is a shift in other processes, including those of participation, management style and perhaps governance, then only local learning is likely to occur.

REFERENCES

Blantern, C. (1994) *The learning organization (organization of learning) and the emerging contribution of computer networks*, Learning Project Company, Sheffield.
Rheingold, H. (1993) *The Virtual Community: Homesteading On The Electronic Frontier Reading*, Addison-Wesley, MA.
Zuboff, S. (1988) *In The Age Of The Smart Machine: The Future of Work and Power*, Heinemann, London.

25. Organization ecology

> ... companies collectively constitute a sentient, intelligent, non-human species at a relatively early stage in its evolution. (Lloyd, 1990, p.xii)

As a branch of organizational theory the organization ecology perspective raises some interesting questions about organisational learning and the Learning Company (see for example Hannan and Freeman, 1977). To put this view in context, we have suggested that organizations are formed from three forces; from *Ideas* – the visions that founders seek to realize and which must be renewed or transformed from time to time; *Phase* – the life stages and life cycle of the company; and *Era* – the economic, social, political and cultural context.

Approaches to the study of organizations can be seen to favour one or other of these forces. For example, *organizational development* focuses on the *idea* of a particular organization and what it can become next; as a sub-set of this *organizational biography* (see Chapter 6) also takes a single organization perspective, paying particular attention to the *phases* in the life of the individual company over time. *Organizational ecology* eschews the study of single units for studies of population survival rates in particular environments. The agentic assumptions of organizational development and organizational biography – that organizations control their own destinies and can plot their future course – are confronted here by more deterministic ones that give primacy to environments, contextual forces and *era*. For the latter, the actions of individual companies are inconsequential and of little interest.

The organizational ecologists have brought to our attention the traumas of organizational conception, gestation, birth and death (Kimberly and Miles, 1980). Death does not figure greatly in the theories of organizational development, which may account in part for their tendency to 'look on the bright side', but contemporary evidence suggests that the ecologists' assumption is now the likely fate, sooner or later, of all companies. The infant mortality rates of new companies are as high as 40 per cent in the first year, in some samples. But established companies, even the largest and most powerful, are not immune. Pascale (1991, pp.11–17) notes that, 'Of the corporations in the Fortune 500 rankings five years ago, 143 are missing today. (By comparison, in the twenty-five years, 1955 to 1980, only 238 dropped out.)' This appears to be an accelerating trend. Commenting on Peters and Waterman's 1982 sample of 'excellent' companies, he further notes that, 'Only five years after the book's publication, two-thirds of the companies studied had slipped from the pinnacle'.

Organization ecology is basically an analogy of classical Darwinian theory as applied to organizations. A focus on the evolution and survival of organizations as species raises some interesting and potentially disturbing questions from an organizational learning point of view. For example, it suggests that individual companies and firms may not learn or adapt very much, but that industries (by analogy equivalent to species) do. The 'random' mutation of new business ideas leads to new organizations, which are then ruthlessly called by natural selection (the survival of the fittest) leaving an industry full of 'survivors' that will, however, only survive as long as their core business idea remains viable, and that will ultimately be replaced by the next generation of naturally selected 'winners'.

This perspective can be taken, whether we find it attractive or not, as a 'scientific' proposition about what is going on, but it can also be taken as an ideological perspective clearly associated with a view of the virtues of the competitive free market, enterprising individualism sharpening its performances in continuous competition with fellow 'players'.

The challenge to organizational learning

A number of observations about company and organizational life can be made to support the organizational ecology interpretation. Supporting Pascale's points about corporate mortality, Senge (1991) observes that the life expectancy of established firms seems to be about half the human life cycle (40 years or so). Other observation of cases suggests that established firms do get going with a single or closely related cluster of business ideas, and survive and perish with the overall product life cycle of the class of business activity they get into. In other words, they 'single loop learn' to vary products and services around their core idea, but they rarely 'double loop learn' to adapt that idea itself.

This image of the organization with limited adaptive capacity playing out its part of the larger game of the survival and adaptation of its industry by natural selection is also reminiscent of Charles Handy's (1989) image of the company as a 'boiling frog'. We also find it hard to imagine Charles checking this out on his cooker, but apparently a frog slowly heated goes to sleep and perishes rather than jumping out of the pot. The metaphor does seem to fit the behaviour of many organizations as they gradually get into trouble.

One response to this at least partially convincing perspective, from a Learning Company point of view is to say:

> Precisely that is how it is now, and that is why we need more Learning Companies, so that industries can develop by a less wasteful, destructive and painful process

– a species of learners is going to do better than a species of non-learners – that is why, by conventional criteria, human beings come out on top of the evolutionary heap in the animal kingdom.

The stage 3 Learning Company

Another is to say, in the 3 stage model of Learning Companies from Chapter 1:

Stage 1   **Surviving**   Companies that develop basic habits and processes and deal with problems as they arise on a 'fire fighting' basis.

Stage 2   **Adapting**   Companies that continuously adapt their habits in the light of accurate readings and forecasts of environmental changes.

Stage 3   **Sustaining**   Companies that create their contexts as much as they are created by them, who achieve a sustainable, though adaptive, position in a symbiotic relationship with their environments.

'This is all very stage 2 stuff – the competitive, adaptive firm, What about stage 3? Does this not work by different rules?' The theoretical argument that we find attractive is from one of our favourite thinkers, Gregory Bateson, who mounts a critique and a development of the classical Darwinian idea, both as a literal theory of species and as broader metaphor for the change process:

> It is now empirically clear that Darwinian evolutionary theory contained a very real error in its identification of the unit of survival under natural selection. The unit which was believed to be crucial and around which the theory was set up was either the breeding individual or the family line or sub-species or some similar homogeneous set of conspecifics. Now I suggest that the last hundred years have demonstrated empirically that if an organism or aggregate of organisms sets to work with a focus on its own survival and thinks that this is the way to select its adaptive moves, its 'progress' ends up with a destroyed environment. If the organism ends up by destroying its environment, it has in fact destroyed itself.... The unit of survival is a flexible organism-in-its-environment. (1968, pp.425–426)

This gives us a choice in how we see the 'unit of survival' – is that which lives or perishes just the individual in the species, or is it the species (which happens to be made up of disposable individuals) or is it the holistic entity that can be thought of as *individual-in-species* emphasizing the joined up and wholeness of the system? (This can be taken still further to involve species-in-society, world or cosmos as in the Gaia hypothesis of the earth as a self-sustained and self-producing unity (Large, 1981, p.14).) From Bateson's perspective, the stage 3 Learning Company, seeing itself as a 'flexible organism-in-its-environment', emphasizes the connectedness of the learning process inside and outside.

This choice makes a profound difference to the policy, operations and action we might decide to take. A stage 3 policy might work in quite a different direction from a stage 2 one. Should schools, for example, be encouraged to see themselves as autonomous, independent organizations competing for resources, star teachers and bright students? Or, given a national curriculum of some sort, should they see themselves as part of a wider system where they not only need to be aware of their internal learning processes but also of the importance of sharing and collaborating with other schools and with related organizations such as university researchers, as part of improving the quality and effectiveness of their service?

Looked at this way, the Darwinian metaphor suffers from the classical artificial problems of reductionist splitting of the things that are better seen as wholes. In case such ideas seem fanciful, it is worth pointing out, for example, that some contemporary theories of industrial marketing have moved from seeing organizations as players in an open competitive free market to being organizations that position themselves in industrial networks collaboratively, or by negotiation with other organizational players.

Organizational death

However, the ideas of birth and death, as applied to organizational life offer some interesting possibilities. There is a complexity in the concepts of the beginnings and endings of the companies that might repay further study. What are the multiple rather than unitary processes of 'beginning' a company? Are the finality of 'death' and 'birth' eroded, given the continuity and carryovers of identity, ideas, spirit and resources that are possible in organizational life?

This leads to the 'immortality vs good death' debate. Some organizations, seeing organizational learning as a lifeline and as a possible route to corporate immortality, may seek to perpetuate themselves long beyond their useful life, their purpose spent while continuing to consume useful resources for useless or even anti-social ends. Should 'organizational death' be seen as more desirable? Applying an ecological 'nothing is wasted in nature' perspective might be very productive. If some of the insights of 'EcoManagement' (Callenbach et al., 1993) were added to the traditional organization ecology approach, then questions of recycling and of a better understanding the 'metabolic' flows into and out of organizations, might lead to interesting policy suggestions on 'good organizational death'.

Conclusion

The organization ecology perspective offers a valuable corrective to the 'headiness' of the Learning Company vision and illustrates some of the limitations of the single learning company approach to organizational learning, especially those of the unquestioning assumption of 'agency' in the single company. It also offers various interesting avenues for research and further development – perhaps especially when extended via organizational learning or 'EcoManagement' ideas.

Against this the environmental determinism of organizational ecology, developed partly in reaction to the single case study tradition of organizational research, also has severe limitations. A survey of the organization ecology perspective concludes:

... the premises of ecology are too restrictive to accommodate recent developments in theory ... we must have an evolutionary perspective on organizations, one that focuses on change within organizations as well as on turnover of organizational populations. (Meyer, 1990, p.298)

REFERENCES

Bateson, G. (1968) *Steps to an Ecology of Mind*, Paladin, London, pp.425–426.

Callenbach, E., Capra, F., Goldman L., Lutz R. and Marburg S. (1993) *EcoManagement: The Elmwood Guide to Ecological Auditing and Sustainable Business*, Berrett-Koehler, San Francisco.

Handy, C. (1989) *The Age of Unreason*, Business Books, London.

Hannan, M.T. and Freeman, J. (1977) 'The population ecology of organizations', *American Journal of Sociology*, **82**(5), 929–964.

Kimberly, J.R. and Miles, R.H. (1980) *The Organizational Life Cycle*, Jossey Bass, San Francisco.

Large, M. (1981) *Social Ecology: Exploring Post-industrial Society*, Martin Large, Gloucester.

Lloyd, T. (1990) *The 'Nice' Company*, Bloomsbury, London.

Meyer M.W. (1990) 'Notes of a skeptic: From organizational ecology to organizational evolution' in Singh, J.V. (ed.) *Organisational Evolution: New Directions*, Sage, Los Angeles, pp.298–314.

Pascale, R. (1991) *Managing on the Edge*, Penguin, Harmondsworth.

Senge, P. (1991) 'The learning organisation made plain' *Training and Development*, October, p.43.

The Learning Company Project – a footnote

The Learning Company Project runs Learning Programmes, Conferences and a Consortium for organizations wishing to realize the corporate learning potential of their computer networks by working in a learning community. The Consortium involves workshops, telemating via the LCP's computer conferencing network and on-site consultancy, including a number of days from the Partners – Tom Boydell, Mike Pedler and John Burgoyne.

Current members include British Airways, ICL, British Gas PGS, Mid-Essex Hospitals Trust, Humberside TEC, The Post Office, Rolls-Royce & Associates, Cable & Wireless College and Anglian Water. Further information about this Consortium can be had from LCP:

Learning Company Project
28 Woodholm Road
Sheffield S11 9HT UK   Tel and fax: 0114 2 621832

Index